sa   ͻR

n

"By the time we reach adulthood, most of us have learned to operate through such deeply engrained patterns of language and behavior that virtually all of our communication involves projection, assumption, and bias. No wonder we often feel so cut off and all alone! Mr. Sofer deftly weaves together his mindfulness practice and principles of Nonviolent Communication to help us learn how to find one another again. This is a powerful guidebook to thinking, speaking, and listening with authenticity and care. Bravo!"
—Sharon Salzberg, author of *Real Happiness* and *Real Love*

"This tremendous book addresses one of the biggest challenges in any relationship: how to combine heart with strength, compassion with assertiveness. Written with great warmth and clarity, it brings together well-researched principles, effective tools and suggestions, powerful experiential practices, and many examples. It is down-to-earth and completely accessible while also being so deep, even profound. If I had just one book to recommend about interpersonal communication, it would be this one."
—Rick Hanson, PhD, author of *Resilient: How to Grow an Unshakable Core of Calm, Strength, and Happiness*

"Oren Jay Sofer's eloquent book *Say What You Mean* could just as well be titled *Living What You Mean*. Going beyond the surface level of communication, he describes our relational journey together in its inherent connections with how we behave, how we express, perceive, and meet the needs of ourselves and others, how we engage with difference and even conflict, how we negotiate love and anger—in sum, how to fully live this complex life. Sofer gives essential frameworks, perspectives, and skills for our shared humanity."
—Larry Yang, Buddhist teacher and author of *Awakening Together: The Spiritual Practice of Inclusivity and Community*

"Words have tremendous power—both to harm, and to heal. In *Say What You Mean*, Oren shares a three-part process for communicating with mindfulness, clarity, and compassion and creating more connection and understanding in our relationships. In these times of turbulence and conflict, we need this more than ever before."

—Chris Kresser, MS, LAc, *New York Times* best-selling author of *The Paleo Cure* and *Unconventional Medicine*

"Meeting the enormous challenges of living in these times calls for an integration of inner practices of mindfulness with outer practices of communicating with honesty, vulnerability, strength, care, and empathy. Oren shows us a way to do just that."

—Miki Kashtan, Certified Nonviolent Communication Trainer and author of *Spinning Threads of Radical Aliveness*

say what you mean

a mindful approach to
nonviolent communication

Oren Jay Sofer

foreword by Joseph Goldstein

SHAMBHALA
Boulder
2018

Shambhala Publications, Inc.
2129 13th Street
Boulder, Colorado 80302
www.shambhala.com

14 13 12 11 10 9 8

Printed in Canada

♾ This edition is printed on acid-free paper that meets the
American National Standards Institute Z39.48 Standard.
♻ This book is printed on 100% postconsumer recycled paper.
For more information please visit www.shambhala.com.

Shambhala Publications is distributed worldwide by Penguin
Random House, Inc., and its subsidiaries.

Designed by Greta D. Sibley

Library of Congress Cataloging-in-Publication Data
Names: Sofer, Oren Jay, author.
Title: Say what you mean: a mindful approach to nonviolent
communication / Oren Jay Sofer.
Description: First edition. | Boulder, Colorado: Shambhala Publications,
Inc., [2018] | Includes bibliographical references and index.
Identifiers: LCCN 2018009367 | ISBN 9781611805833
(pbk.: acid-free paper)
Subjects: LCSH: Interpersonal communication. | Nonviolence.
Classification: LCC HM1166 .S64 2018 | DDC 302.2—dc23
LC record available at https://lccn.loc.gov/2018009367

For the teachers and friends
who showed me the way.

And for my mother, my first teacher,
who gave me a solid foundation
and taught me to write.

The fish trap exists because of the fish;
once you've gotten the fish you can forget the trap.
The rabbit snare exists because of the rabbit;
once you've gotten the rabbit, you can forget the snare.
Words exist because of meaning.
Once you've gotten the meaning you can forget the words.
Where can I find a man who has forgotten words,
so I can have a word with him?
—CHUANG TZU

Returning hate for hate multiplies hate,
adding deeper darkness to a night already devoid of stars.
Darkness cannot drive out darkness; only light can do that.
Hate cannot drive out hate; only love can do that.
—DR. MARTIN LUTHER KING JR.

contents

part four
  bringing it all together

foreword

IN ONE WAY or another, we spend our lives communicating. For most of us, the predominant mode of communication is speech, the words we use and the emotional tone underlying our words. Interaction forms the bedrock of all our relationships, and the patterns through which we engage in conversation determine, to a large extent, the quality of our lives. What's more, our habits in communication establish a template for our relationship with ourselves, and with our society at large.

In this wonderful book, Oren Jay Sofer explores the many nuances of the way we speak, illuminating the patterns that foster well-being and harmony, and those that simply lead to greater frustration and distress. The perspectives and methods in this book also hold an essential key to the healing and radical transformation that is so desperately needed—not only in our lives as individuals but collectively in our communities and on our planet. Drawing from his extensive training in mindfulness practices, somatic healing, and Nonviolent Communication, Oren provides both the insight and the skill necessary for us to transform communication into a vehicle for greater intimacy, honesty, and compassion, and to point our social lives toward greater equity and peace.

Through clear theoretical frameworks and a wealth of stories and examples, *Say What You Mean* offers an array of useful tools for strengthening awareness of our habitual patterns, as well as many specific suggestions for how to communicate with greater care and effectiveness. Oren discusses the essential role of empathy in listening to others and proposes, in very precise ways, how to cultivate it. As he writes, "Communication practice is not about what we say. It's about where we're coming from and how we say it."

He also clearly describes practices for recognizing and understanding our thoughts, perceptions, and emotions, and how they influence, often unconsciously, the words we use and the motivations behind them. Without this understanding, we often find ourselves caught in the many tangles of our conditioning, not seeing our way to greater connectedness and inner freedom.

Besides being a detailed and comprehensive roadmap for cultivating wise communication, there are also many little gems in this work that can act as reminders through the day. One of my favorites is the simple understanding that "we have more clarity and power when we use fewer words with more sincerity."

One of the foundations of this book is that communication, like any other art, takes practice. Once we have the basic skills, we can begin to expand the ways we think, speak, and interact, making our speech a pathway to greater harmony and insight in our lives.

I've known Oren for many years, since the early days of his meditation practice. It brings me great joy to see him integrate the deep awareness of his meditative insights with his profound understanding of communication in an accessible method of training. This book, with his characteristic warmth and lucidity, is a great gift to anyone seeking more connection, clarity, and compassion in their life.

—*Joseph Goldstein*

acknowledgments

SKILLFUL COMMUNICATION RESTS upon a profound recognition of our interdependence. Like so much in life, this book is the work of many hands and the result of countless interactions.

For the insight that I hope graces these pages, I am deeply indebted to my teachers. Acarya Anagarika Munindra and Godwin Samararatne opened my eyes and revealed what was possible in this life. Robert Pryor's humble and steady work shepherded so many of us to the Dharma. Venerable Ajahn Sucitto, Joseph Goldstein, and Michelle McDonald: your wisdom, generosity, and skillful guidance has helped me to mature and understand what it is to be human. Sarah Doering believed in me and offered support during a difficult time.

I am equally indebted to my Nonviolent Communication teachers for guiding me to translate the beauty of the Dharma into action, and for teaching me how to say what I mean. Marshall B. Rosenberg's vision, clarity, and warmth touched me deeply. I learned a great deal from Inbal Kashtan, who died too early of cancer. (I miss you, Inbal.) I especially want to express my sincere appreciation to my friend and colleague Miki Kashtan, whose uncompromising commitment to the values and vision of NVC continues to push me beyond my edges, and who offered penetrating comments on key portions of the text. Kathy Simon gave essential input on short notice. I'm also grateful to Penny Wassman, whose care and enthusiastic endorsement welcomed me into the Certified Trainer community, and to my colleagues at BayNVC, whose authenticity has taught me something valuable about how to embody these skills.

Steve Hoskinson and Anthony "Twig" Wheeler provided gentle support in service of my well-being and wholeness. David O'Neal, senior editor at Shambhala, saw potential in my writing and reached out. Editor

Matt Zepelin's intelligence has enhanced the manuscript. Joe Kelly offered to help and edited several chapters after a serendipitous walk.

I am fortunate to be part of a thriving community of spiritual friends, who continue to challenge me lovingly and show me what kindness really means. Several colleagues also offered useful feedback on various chapters: Matthew Brensilver, Donna Carter, Derek Haswell, Sumi London, Ali Miller, Donald Rothberg, Ben Rubin, and Aaron Soffin. My mother, father, and brother humored and loved me through many awkward moments as I learned NVC. Evan A. Wong offered steady, tender encouragement through many long days and late nights at the computer.

I also want to thank the many folks on my email list and social media accounts, who followed along and cheered me on through the process. This book also would not be possible without the students who have attended my workshops, classes, and retreats, whose genuine feedback inspired me to write and whose fortitude and courage inspire me daily.

Any errors are my own. Thankfully, life is a process of learning.

say what you mean

introduction

WHAT WE SAY matters. We've each felt the power that words have to heal, soothe, or uplift us. Even one caring remark can make the difference between giving up and finding the strength to face life's challenges.

We each also know something of the great harm that can be inflicted through speech. Sharp words laced with anger or cruelty can break a relationship and burn for years. Language can be used to manipulate and coerce on a mass scale, to fuel fear, war, and oppression, and to advance political agendas of genocide or terror. Few things so powerful are also so commonplace.

Words are woven into the fabric of our lives. Your first love. Your first job. Your last goodbye to someone you love. Our beginnings and endings and the countless moments in between are punctuated by a play of words as we share our thoughts, feelings, and desires.

My parents tell me that I was a gregarious child. "E-A-T, O-R-E-N," they would spell out at meals, trying to redirect the stream of questions that bubbled from my small body as they reminded me to eat. My fascination with words began at an early age. I still recall the thrill of discovering the meaning of simple compound words such as *seaweed* or *sunset*—that moment of realization when abstract sounds were suddenly transformed into their more familiar parts.

Words are a kind of magic. To be alive and self-aware on this remarkable planet with its forests and lakes, its oceans and mountains, in this vast universe with billions of galaxies, is mysterious enough. What a marvel to be able to look into each other's eyes for an instant and form words that tell something of our lives.

The creation myths of many cultures and religions through time—East, West, and Indigenous—recognize the generative power of words, giving the potency of speech a key role in the beginning of the cosmos. Indeed, words have the power to shape our reality. As we think, so we perceive; as we perceive, so we act. Moreover, the teachings of all world religions reflect a universal understanding about the ethical implications of language—its potential for good or harm—and include moral guidelines around the appropriate use of speech.

My childhood fascination with language crystallized into a firm commitment to understand how to use words wisely when I attended a meditation retreat with the Vietnamese Zen master, poet, and peace activist Thich Nhat Hanh. His modern rendering of the Buddha's guidelines on "Right Speech" struck a chord deep within, motivating me to learn as much as I could about communication. It still inspires me today:

> Aware of the suffering caused by unmindful speech and the inability to listen to others, I am committed to cultivating loving speech and deep listening in order to bring joy and happiness to others and relieve others of suffering. Knowing that words can create happiness or suffering, I am determined to learn to speak truthfully, with words that inspire self-confidence, joy, and hope. I will not spread news that I do not know to be certain and will not criticize or condemn things of which I am not sure. I will refrain from uttering words that can cause division or discord, or words that can cause the family or the community to break. I am determined to make all efforts to reconcile and resolve all conflicts, however small.[1]

What we say matters—perhaps now more than ever.

We live in times of great change, in which much is being asked of us. We live at a time when we are less and less able to listen and really hear one another in society, at a time when those with different views, beliefs, or backgrounds are (once again) so easily cast as the "other." At this time when great forces of political, social, economic, and environmental change are sweeping the globe and intensifying our separation from self, others, and life, we need to learn how to speak and listen in a new way. We need to learn how to reperceive our world with fresh eyes, beyond inherited historical and economic structures of competition and separation that can so easily determine our relationships. True dialogue is more than the mere exchange of ideas. It is a transformative process based on trust and mutual respect, in which we come to see another in new and more accurate ways. As theologian David Lochhead explains, "it is a way of knowing truth that neither party possesses prior to the dialogue."[2]

It is heartbreaking to know the good of which we are capable yet to see so much destruction and violence. In Japan, there is a saying: the cherry blossoms are beautiful because they are fleeting. We each have an opportunity to use the time and energy we are given with integrity. My hope is that this book might, in some small way, help us begin to realize our potential for good as humans by learning to bring more compassion, wisdom, and kindness to how we navigate the relationships that make up our everyday lives. I hope that it might help us to transform the mechanisms of thought and perception that make violence seem like a viable strategy, that it be one step in creating a world that works for all.

A Confluence of Waters

In my mid-twenties, toward the end of a ten-day retreat with Marshall B. Rosenberg, the founder of Nonviolent Communication, I had breakfast with Dr. Rosenberg and his wife. I had met Rosenberg a few years prior and was eager to share my gratitude for the profound changes I was experiencing in my life due to his system of communication. Being a longtime meditator, I was also keen to offer my perspective on how meditation could support the NVC process.*

This was in the early 2000s, before mindfulness exploded into the public sphere. I explained how mindfulness practice developed inner awareness, a prerequisite for being able to identify and stay conscious of feelings and needs—the core of Nonviolent Communication—and therefore a key missing piece in the NVC model. I was excited and a bit stunned when he completely agreed! He shared, with a bit of dismay, that he'd been trying to figure out how to teach people to meditate for some time

---

*I often refer to Nonviolent Communication by its acronym, NVC. If you'd like information about NVC and Rosenberg's work, see the "Further Resources" section in the back of the book.

using a baby giraffe hat, a modified version of one of his signature puppets. Looking at me across the table with a wry smile, he said, "Maybe that's your work to do."

Thus began a journey of nearly two decades in which I have worked to integrate my understanding of Buddhist meditation and Nonviolent Communication. The material I share with you in these pages is a synthesis of three distinct streams of practice. The first primary stream is mindfulness, coming out of the Theravada Buddhist tradition (specifically the texts and practices of Burmese Satipaṭṭhāna and the Thai Forest tradition). The second is the system of Nonviolent Communication developed by Dr. Rosenberg, whose seminal book *Nonviolent Communication: A Language of Life* has sold over one million copies worldwide.[3] NVC has been used for international conflict resolution and nonviolent social change, interpersonal communication and mediation, as well as for personal growth and healing. The last methodology that informs this book is my training in a therapeutic technique designed by Dr. Peter A. Levine called Somatic Experiencing, which emphasizes the role of nervous system regulation in resolving trauma.

I have found that these three streams form a powerful vehicle for deepening self-understanding and transforming our habits of communication. In the early years of my practice, I discovered many synchronicities between these methods and their respective underlying theories. My passion led me through various mental contortions as I attempted to map one method onto the other, seeking a coherent master system that would encompass all that I was learning. It took time for the perspectives to settle into my body and to recognize that they were simply different ways of understanding human experience. They overlapped in some areas but didn't need to fit together perfectly to function simultaneously or be mutually supportive.

When streams in a watershed run together to form a river, you can no longer distinguish the waters of one from the other. In some sense, these three systems and their corresponding practices can live as one river, a seamless whole, each describing and supporting different facets of a holistic experience of being alive.

As such, my presentation of the material in this book is holistic. While

I don't discuss the Dharma explicitly, those familiar with Buddhist teachings will recognize clearly the presence of its wisdom in different sections. Similarly, my exposition of Somatic Experiencing is more tangential (save for one important section in chapter 13 on challenging situations). Rather than try to parse the waters from this stream or that, I have instead focused on creating what I hope is an accessible guide to the basics of interpersonal communication that can be used to create concrete shifts and changes in one's life.

Three Steps, Three Foundations

Human communication is complex. There are a myriad of factors in any interaction. Our emotions, ideas, and beliefs come into play both verbally and nonverbally. We have to negotiate patterns of relating that have been established, whether between two individuals or between the groups and communities to which we belong. Yet, in all of this, there are certain consistent foundations to skillful communication.

The overarching framework for this book is taking three steps to create effective conversation. The steps themselves are simple enough:

1. Lead with presence.
2. Come from curiosity and care.
3. Focus on what matters.

Each step is part of a much more thorough and profound training. Like three firm, solid stones placed in the middle of a fast-flowing stream, each step is only as stable and useful as the foundation upon which it rests. Thus to show up and be fully in the moment rests on training ourselves in the first foundation of mindful communication: *presence*. Coming from curiosity and care is rooted in the foundation of our *intention*. Focusing on what matters is about honing our *attention*, training our mind's capacity to discern what's essential and shift its focus in a nimble and responsive manner. The first three sections of this book correspond to our training in each of these foundations, while the fourth and final section explores how they all fit together.

How to Use This Book

Reading a book on communication is a bit like reading a manual on how to swim. No matter how clear and detailed the text, you won't learn to swim without getting in the water. This book is meant to be used in your life; consider it a field guide for conversations, a map that describes a landscape as you travel. It is likely to serve you best if you go slowly, taking time to integrate each section as you read. Every concept, analogy, or idea is meant to be tested in your life. Try it out, bash it around, and see what works.

In each chapter, you will find practical suggestions for how to implement the tools and concepts. Start small, in lightweight, low-stakes situations. To return to the swimming analogy: one doesn't learn to swim by leaping into the ocean on a stormy day. Sure, you might make it, but not without struggling and swallowing a fair amount of salt water. What's more, you're less likely to want to go swimming again! It's much easier if one begins in the shallow end of a pool, preferably on a warm day.

In the same way, I don't recommend attempting to apply these tools immediately to the most difficult conversations or relationships in your life. First learn to swim; build some capacity. Whenever possible, seek out situations where it will be easiest to practice and where you are most able to experiment and learn without too much resistance. You may want to read the book with someone else, so you have a partner with whom to practice the exercises. Or try the tools with a close friend or family member who can humor you as you stumble through the awkwardness of learning a new language.

For that's what it's like: learning communication skills is remarkably akin to learning a new language. It takes repetition. The more frequently you practice, the more quickly you will become fluent. Knowing even a few words of a new language will help you begin to say what you mean. So I encourage you to practice a little every day, whether through formal exercises or informal conversations. Even five minutes of intentional, daily practice will have an effect over time.

At the end of each chapter you will find a summary of key points and a series of questions and answers. Many of these questions are based on transcripts from students at actual workshops and retreats. They're meant to address some of the most common challenges that you may encounter along the way. (Certain names or details of stories have been changed to honor requests for privacy.) Throughout the text you'll find key terms related to mindful communication. These are italicized on first use, and their definitions can be looked up in the glossary. Notes at the end of the book offer further reflections and references that may be of interest. The "Further Resources" section contains suggestions to continue your training, including a link to companion guided meditations for select practices.

Finally, I want to point out a key distinction that runs throughout the book. In each chapter you'll find *principles*, which capture the underlying ethos or aim of a certain aspect of communication. You'll also find *practices*, which are specific tools meant to help you learn how to bring the principles into your life in concrete ways. For example, you'll encounter principles such as, "The more aware we are, the more choice we have." You'll also find correlating practices—some you can do as you read, others you can take into your practice of communication in daily life. In this instance, one practice to support this principle of awareness might be instructions for mindfulness of breathing.

The danger in any communication training is that we mistake the practice for the principle and begin to speak in rigid or robotic ways in an attempt to adhere to some kind of dogma or system. While systems are incredibly useful (and the exploration of Rosenberg's NVC comprises a major part of this book), I'm less interested in following a system than I am in learning how to understand and respond dynamically to the moment.

In other words, try not to get hung up on any one way of speaking. To offer another analogy: it's a bit like learning an instrument. Playing scales is essential, but the aim is to make music. The tools and practices here will be invaluable for retraining your communication habits, but the aim is to relax and be in the flow of conversation with ease.

What to Expect

The field of communication encompasses a wide range of areas: personal and professional relationships, higher-level skills such as group facilitation and mediation, and strategic applications such as diplomacy and nonviolent resistance. This book won't cover everything, nor is it intended to do so. Its primary focus is interpersonal communication in social and intimate relationships. If you're interested in taking your training further, the tools you learn here will provide an indispensable foundation for other applications.

This book is directly informed by my personal life experience, which means that it will also be limited by that experience in some ways. In particular, aspects of my conditioning as a heterosexual, Jewish, middle-class white male have left me ill-prepared to realize the vision that Marshall Rosenberg articulated for his work. I still get chills when I consider what he said in 2005, at a retreat in Switzerland:

> If I use Nonviolent Communication to liberate people to be less depressed, to get along better with their family, but do not teach them at the same time to use their energy to rapidly transform systems in the world, then I am part of the problem. I am essentially calming people down, making them happier to live in the systems as they are, so I am using NVC as a narcotic.[4]

Teaching is humbling; I know I have more to learn, particularly around the blind spots of my own *privilege*.[5] To the extent that I have managed to see beyond my own conditioning, the text and its ideas may support others across different social locations to learn how to liberate themselves from their own conditioning, and to step more fully into the interdependent dance of communication. Nothing would please me more. To the extent that I haven't seen beyond my own conditioning, I continue my practice of mindful communication as a lifelong path of learning and transformation.

Such an enduring commitment is the most helpful way to approach this practice. Learning to communicate skillfully is not something we complete in a weekend workshop, a six-week class, or a four-part book. It takes patience, interest, dedication, and humility. It's common to feel completely and utterly inept at various stages in the process. At times, it can even feel as if one were better off *before* trying these tools!

All of this is to be expected. Learning anything is a process of making mistakes. Expect to fall flat on your face sometimes. It doesn't matter how many times you fall down; what matters is whether or not you get back up again. Remember that each small success, every interaction in which you are able to implement one of the tools or principles, will build confidence and lay down a new pattern in your mind.

Changes to communication don't happen overnight. It took time to learn the habits we have. It will take time to unlearn them and become proficient at something new. But every minute you spend learning is worth it. It will pay off in the quality of your relationships, the amount of well-being in your life, and your ability to engage effectively in the world.

Learning to Ride a Bike

I remember well my enthusiasm and curiosity as a kid, but I also recall having a very hard time getting a word in edgewise during the fast-paced, animated dialogue of our family dinners. I have a visceral memory of sitting at that black kitchen table with a heavy sensation in my chest, a hard knot in my throat, and tears of frustration burning beneath the surface as the rest of my family plowed through the conversation, leaving little space for my voice.

Finding your voice, learning how to say what you mean and how to listen deeply—this is one of the most rewarding journeys you can take. When you have developed your capacity to speak wisely and listen well, you possess an inexhaustible resource with which to navigate and transform the world. Rather than turning your conversations into a bland, neutral wash of "being nice," the skills in this book will help you feel more alive and engaged.

When I was a kid, I owned a blue Schwinn dirt bike with a red seat and red handlebars. On many a summer evening after dinner I would ride my bike around our block in suburban New Jersey again and again, jumping curbs and racing along the sidewalk beneath old oak and sycamore trees.

Learning to communicate mindfully has a lot in common with riding a bike. It takes time. In the beginning, it's helpful to have training wheels to guide you as you find your balance. Having someone else to cheer you along tends to make the process safer and more fun. And when you take the training wheels off, you need to be prepared to take a few bruises and skin a knee or elbow. But once you learn, you never forget how to ride. It can take you great distances, and the exhilaration and joy of getting there is all the fun.

part one

the first step
lead with presence

EFFECTIVE COMMUNICATION DEPENDS on our ability to be present. Speaking openly and honestly, listening deeply, and navigating the inevitable twists and turns of a conversation all require a high degree of self-awareness. To *say* what we mean, we must first *know* what we mean. To know what we mean, we must listen inwardly and discern what's true for us.

The first step of mindful communication is to *lead with presence*, which means that we show up as fully and completely as possible. If we're not *here*, we're probably on automatic. And if we're on automatic, we're less likely to remember the tools we've learned, come from our best intentions, or access our own wisdom.

Leading with presence is a rich practice with many dimensions. In part one, we'll explore this primary foundation of skillful communication: our ability to be present. We'll look at the nature of human communication, its central role in our lives, and how we can cultivate awareness in ourselves and in conversation.

the center of our lives

Language is very powerful. Language does not just
describe reality. Language creates the reality it describes.
—DESMOND TUTU

WE ENTER THIS world vulnerable, completely dependent, and primed
for language. From the moment we're born, communication sits at the
center of our life.

A human baby is born with the innate ability to learn any of the world's
seven thousand languages. In the first weeks and months, though, we are
given just two tools to communicate our needs: crying and smiling. From
there our brains develop, neurons primed to discern the rhythm, sound,
tone, and volume of human language. And at this early age we pick it up
very quickly—whichever language circumstance (or fate) drops us into.

Along with this system of sounds, words, and grammar, we learn how
to express emotions, how to ask for what we need, and ways to try to get
what we want. Eventually, if all is functioning well, we learn how to read
and use more complex social cues; we learn metaphor, idiom, and humor.
We learn all of this through listening, inquiry, observation, and repetition.

As we enter the human family with language, we naturally pick up
whatever patterns of communication happen to come along with our
family of origin, ethnic group, class, gender, society, and the dominant
culture. Some of us learn that it's not safe to express our needs, so we try to
ensure we'll be cared for by taking care of others. Some of us learn to get
what we want by using force, so we assert ourselves and try to appear the
strongest or smartest. Some of us learn that our needs aren't valued by our
society, and so we harden inside and disconnect from our vulnerability.

And at times, we may learn that there's space to ask for what we need and still stay connected to others, working things out together.

Most of us learn some combination of these approaches to meeting our needs, yet *we've all had communication training*. Generally it's just been unconscious and unintentional. The context of our social location and cultural milieu set the frames and beliefs, and our life experiences confirm and reinforce them. That is, until something wakes up inside and says, "This just isn't working!" This realization could be sparked by a failed relationship or marital problems, a fight that results in the loss of a friendship, ongoing communication issues at work, the struggle to survive in a system that isn't designed to meet human needs, the plight of our world and breakdown of social institutions, or simply being fed up with the tyranny of the voice in our own head.

The good news about all this is that since language is learned, since our communication patterns and the emotional habits that drive them are *trained*, they can be *unlearned, retrained*. We can learn to speak and listen in a new way that's more conducive to the kind of life we want to live and the society we want to create.* We can find our voice, learn to say what we mean, and discover how to listen deeply.

Finding My Way with Words

For me, the turning point came in my early twenties. After a couple of failed romantic relationships, lost friendships, and my parents' divorce, I turned to Buddhist meditation to sort out some of the inner turmoil. After college, I ended up living and working at the Insight Meditation Society in rural Massachusetts. Buddhist teachings helped me come to terms with things and mature some. Yet I noticed that the values of clarity, kindness, and compassion I felt so strongly while meditating would often evaporate when, for example, a conflict arose with a coworker. They were even less accessible when I spoke with my family.

---

* On the collective level, since our social institutions are formed by (and simultaneously reinforce) the patterns of thought and perception that drive our communication, an essential aspect of working to transform them must be the parallel inner work of transforming our consciousness. Otherwise we run the risk of recreating the very systems we seek to change.

I remember one particularly devastating argument with my older brother, which ended with me, pushed to the limits of frustration, lifting a chair and smashing it against the floor in my grandmother's living room. Dramatic, I know—but it happened.

It wasn't until a staff communication training at the meditation center that I realized I could study and improve my habits of speech. After that first half-day workshop, I was hooked. I took an eight-week course in a small college town nearby and pretty soon found my way to Dr. Marshall B. Rosenberg.

As I explored the intersection of contemplative awareness and communication, I found that my years of mindfulness practice provided a fertile ground in which to grow new communication habits. Later contact with Dr. Peter A. Levine's Somatic Experiencing added a new dimension to my understanding of human behavior. I began to see our patterns of relating as part of our hardwiring for self-protection, survival, and *social connection*.[1] I developed a more nuanced ability to observe how these basic evolutionary mechanisms play out in dialogue and how to help people shift out of habitual patterns that no longer serve them. Through all of this, I've come to a much greater, more profound appreciation for the power and complexity of human interaction and communication.

The Universe of Communication

Communication is much broader than its rudimentary components of speaking and listening, much richer than the mere exchange of supposedly objective information. Whether one's aim is strategic (to achieve a certain end) or relational (to connect), communication involves a meaningful exchange that leads to understanding.

> **Communication** is a process of interaction or exchange creating understanding.

This isn't unique to human beings. Most (if not all) forms of life have some kind of "language," some system for transmitting information. Humans have developed this capacity to send and receive messages to an extraordinary degree. It's part of what's allowed us to cooperate and create in such astonishing ways, for good and for ill.

Yet human communication involves so much more than what we say. It includes *how* we speak—our tone of voice, volume, and pace—which transmits a wealth of information about how we're feeling, what we think of one another, how much power we do or don't have, and so on. It's also about *why* we speak. What do we want? What's our motivation? And, of course, it includes listening: how we listen, why we listen, or if we're even listening at all.

In addition to speaking and listening, awareness is another primary component at play when we communicate. Successful communication depends on our ability to pay attention. For "message sent" to equal "message received," we need *presence*, to be fully here, aware of self and other.

We can see this in the simplest of moments. Ever speak to someone who was reading or watching TV, and they don't hear you? You're speaking the same language; their ears are functioning fine—but their mind's attention isn't directed to listening. There's no awareness of you or your words so *communication doesn't occur*.

This simple truth is so obvious we often overlook it. Awareness is the primary foundation for all communication. If communication is about creating understanding, *mindful communication* is about creating understanding through awareness. We could say that the opposite is *mindless communication*—we're either running on automatic or we're consumed by an inner narrative of judgments, criticism, planning, and mind wandering. It happens more often than we'd like to admit!

Presence is one of those things that's hard to pinpoint with language, yet it makes a huge difference in the quality of our life. I define presence as the experience of being fully aware and sensing one's body in the present moment. I've found presence to be so important to communication that I begin all my trainings by pointing this out and giving participants a taste of what it's like to be present in dialogue.

Presence is embodied awareness of our direct sensory, mental, and emotional experience.

In one of the first exercises I teach, I invite participants to share a short story with one another. We begin with a few moments of quiet to feel what it's like to be fully here, aware of the body. One person listens while the other person shares their story, both aiming to maintain present-time awareness.

After a minute or so I ring a bell and ask everyone to pause—midsentence, wherever they are. I invite them to return to that sense of presence and to notice what's happening in their bodies. After a short period of silence, they continue, then trade roles so that all participants have a chance to experience pausing in the middle of things. Without fail, nearly everyone who does this exercise remarks on two things: (1) how quickly they lost touch with their body and (2) how stirred up they felt inside when they paused.

Having presence for a moment is easy and readily accessible for most people. Staying connected to presence continually is harder—frankly, it takes training. Maintaining awareness in conversation is even more challenging. The tendency to lose presence is strong: we often leave it as soon as we open our eyes. Indeed, it's amazing how difficult it is to *stay here* once we open our mouths!

Of course, there are common exceptions: the intimacy we feel in romantic relationships or moments of heightened awareness in nature. In these moments we often feel a profound sense of connection. It is precisely the combination of deep presence in relation to another or our surroundings that creates the potency of these experiences.

Bringing presence to relationship is a powerful practice. It means that we really show up for ourselves, the other person, and whatever happens between us. Yet there are several reasons why it's hard to have presence while speaking and listening:

- It's vulnerable to be face-to-face with another human being.
- Social engagement can activate the nervous system, putting us on edge.[2]
- We tend to focus our attention outward, on the other person, or inward, on our thoughts—thus losing the sense of relatedness and connection.
- We haven't practiced it.

In nature, eye contact among primates can be a sign of aggression. In spite of our large brains, when face-to-face with another human we still share that old, edgy conditioning. In an instant of contact, our biology is gauging our safety: "Is this a friend, a foe, or a mate?"

Though often below the threshold of consciousness, this conditioning is operating to some degree as we enter most interactions. Part of transforming our communication patterns is to recognize this fundamental uncertainty in our nervous system and have a means to ground and soothe ourselves. (We'll look at some methods for doing that in chapter 3).

The Human Voice, Breath, and Identity

Another reason why communication can be such a charged area has to do with how our hearing evolved. Our ears are tuned to a very specific range of sound and are particularly sensitive to one narrow frequency: the human voice. (Many animals share this attunement to a particular range of sound. The oceanic calls of whales and the deep rumblings of elephants occur at frequencies inaudible to the human ear.) Have you ever heard someone shrieking with laughter or tears and experienced an uncertain yet pressing urge to find out which it was? Or heard a pack of coyotes howling that sounded so much like humans you couldn't quite be sure?

This is tens of thousands of years of evolution at work. In order to care for our young and protect our kin, the inner architecture of our ears developed to attune precisely to the human voice and pick up immediately on sounds of human distress.[3] Remember that baby, smiling or crying? The conditioning to respond to those signals remains deep within us.

Listening uses this same architecture and therefore carries a dual potential. Hearing the human voice can activate our nervous system's fight-flight-freeze mechanisms, or it can activate the social engagement system that reassures, connects, and soothes.[4]

How we speak adds another dimension to why words can be so charged. Humans produce verbal language by controlling the flow of air over the voice box and vocal cords. Our words are carried on a wave of breath, the same breath that feeds the cells of our body with oxygen from the moment we are born until the moment we die. Pause to take this in for a moment: we use the same physiological process to speak as we do to sustain our life energy.

It goes even further. Our breath (and therefore our speech) is directly linked to our nervous system in a reciprocal relationship: a change in one affects the other. When we feel excited, anxious, afraid, or aggressive (any degree of sympathetic *activation*), our breathing quickens. When we feel relaxed, at ease, or settled (any degree of parasympathetic *deactivation*), our breathing slows and deepens.

This is partly due to the unusual position the breath occupies in our autonomic nervous system, which regulates the basic functions of our body.[5] Breathing is both voluntary and involuntary. It operates automatically, and it's also subject to our will. Speech is one of the most common ways in which we consciously and intentionally manipulate the breath.

All of this holds particular significance for our training in mindful communication. When we understand the relationship between our breath, our words, and our mental-emotional state, we gain more mastery over our experience and self-expression. At various points in our exploration, I'll offer suggestions on how you can use your awareness of the breath to hold a listener's attention, manage strong emotions, and steady yourself in tense situations.

Resting on top of this physiology is the intricate connection between the breath, the voice, and our sense of identity. Our voice is one of the most intimate and personal aspects of who we are. For most of us, it's our primary means of expression, a kind of aural signature by which we are known and recognized. Of all the things that change over the course of a life—our aging bodies; our weathered, wrinkled visage—once we enter adulthood it's our voice that changes the least and the slowest. Our sense of who we are often can become closely tied with our voice.

Beyond the unique music of our voice, consider how we identify ourselves to others. One of the most common mechanisms by which I'm known is my first name—a word representing who I am. When in conflict, challenges to our identity or self-image can be the most painful and hardest to navigate.

In addition to these root physiological and psychological components of communication, realms of emotion, class, culture, and even mystery are at play in this daily activity of speaking and listening. Considering all the layers that are present in a simple exchange, it's no wonder our communication cuts so close to the core.

A Multidimensional, Holistic Experience

As I hope you are beginning to appreciate, human communication is more than just a linguistic exchange. It's a multidimensional, embodied, lived experience that involves all of our being: feelings, thoughts, memories, and history. It is at once verbal, mental, emotional, and somatic.

Communication includes how we use our voice—the tone, volume, and pace at which we speak. It includes body language and touch. We communicate with silence: what we *don't* say, or how we use verbal space. It includes our internal dialogue: how we think and speak to ourselves. Even our social conditioning and cultural history are present in our interactions.

There is also a root somatic element to communication: the vibration of our words and the physicality of our subjective experience. Communication is dynamic, changing in real time. Skillful communication requires that we attune to our inner and outer world, continually adjusting to the moment.

Communication is also holistic; it crosses all the boundaries of our lives. We may compartmentalize our time, dividing our lives between personal, social, and professional realms, but these distinctions are only relative. We live one life. The various roles we play—parent, child, friend, teacher, student, employee—are interconnected facets of one whole person. We may speak or behave differently in different environments, but the fundamental programs running the show are the same.

We can use this holistic nature to our advantage; changes in one area can transfer to other contexts of our lives. While doing simple exercises, it's common for participants in my workshops to have powerful insights into core patterns in their lives. After practicing with the pause at a recent retreat, one woman realized how much of her speech was driven by mild social anxiety. Pausing helped her choose more carefully what she wanted to say and why.

When we learn new ways to communicate, we engage with this entire rich, multilayered realm and all the years of conditioning that we carry within it. To make lasting changes in these habits of communication, it will help to make small, incremental shifts that we can sustain over time.

> *Principle:* **Given the complexity of communication, transformation occurs most readily through small shifts sustained over time.**

Human beings are complex, living systems. When dealing with complex systems, a small change can have far-reaching effects. It's like trying to turn a cargo ship at sea. A vessel that large with that much momentum can't make sharp turns. However, a one- or two-degree course correction of the rudder, if held steady, will take that ship in a very different direction over time.

Training Our Words, Training Our Minds

Contemplating the vast extent of human communication, it can be daunting to take in the scope of the project to retrain ourselves. How are we to deal effectively with something as fundamental as the core patterning through which we relate to the world?

Fortunately we have everything we need to do this—the insights of modern neuroscience and psychology, a clear method, and a fulcrum on which to turn knowledge into practice. The method is our three-step training in presence, intention, and attention. The fulcrum is mindfulness, our ability to steady awareness and see clearly.

The need to transform these patterns is clear. If we are to live more meaningful lives, and if we are to work together to meet the radical changes occurring on our planet, in our governments, economies, and the environment, we must learn how to hear one another and communicate more effectively.

Over the course of this book I'll be encouraging you to investigate your thinking, listening, and speaking with the aim of making small shifts in your understanding and habits. If you sustain these shifts, they will lead to lasting change in your words, your relationships, and your life.

PRINCIPLES

Given the complexity of communication, transformation occurs most readily through small shifts sustained over time.

KEY POINTS

Bringing presence to communication can be challenging for many reasons:

- We haven't practiced it.
- It puts us in touch with our vulnerability.
- It can stimulate evolutionary drives for safety.
- Eye contact in primates can signal aggression.
- Hearing a human voice can be soothing or threatening.
- Verbal communication links our breath, nervous system, and sense of self.

Communication is multidimensional and holistic. It includes:

- A linguistic exchange of information
- Nonverbal communication
- Our internal dialogue (cognitive experience)
- Our emotional, affective experience
- Our somatic, embodied experience
- Personal, psychological, social, and cultural conditioning

QUESTION & ANSWER*

Q: I find it easier to stay present when I am speaking and harder to stay present while listening. Is that normal?

It's different for everyone. I find it fascinating how presence can feel more natural for some in the receptive mode and for others in the expressive mode. If you pay attention, you might even notice that it changes when talking with different people. Regard it as useful information. We want to

---

* Many of the questions found in the Question & Answer at the end of each chapter are based on transcripts from students at actual workshops and retreats.

build on our strengths and develop our capacity to be equally present with both speaking and listening.

Q: You mentioned pausing. I don't think I could do that in most conversations. I'm afraid I'd lose my turn to speak!

Having trust and confidence in our own voice, that we can take up space and speak our mind, is really important. I want any communication tools to support that kind of internal ease. Pausing in a deliberate, extended way is more of a training exercise. There may be certain conversations or relationships where it would work to take a long pause, but generally it helps to make pauses short and less conspicuous.

the power of mindfulness

There is something mysterious and sacred about being alive.
It's an awareness of something that is too important to forget.
—CHRISTINA FELDMAN

MY FATHER GREW up in the 1940s in a one-room shack in British Palestine. His mother raised chickens, goats, and rabbits while his father worked plastering walls and running a kiosk selling magazines, candy, and fresh juice. (They'd come from Belarus and Poland in their teens looking for a new life.) The oldest of three children, he was sent to a kibbutz when he turned thirteen so there would be one less mouth to feed.

He recently told me how during the first few weeks at the kibbutz, he would stand in his room each evening and watch the sun set over the fields. He told me how beautiful those sunsets were and how peaceful he felt. "A few months later, I was in my room when I looked up and realized that the sun was setting. I'd stopped noticing it." He paused and grew quiet. "It's always bothered me. Why did I stop noticing it?"

So much of the time we're not actually here; we're disconnected from our senses and the direct experience of being alive. Our attention is elsewhere, thinking of the past or the future—planning, worrying, remembering, regretting. My father's story marks a key moment that each of us faces many times in our life—when we notice that we're not living with awareness, what do we do about it?

The Ground for Connection

Mindfulness gives us back our lives. It's what allows us to enjoy the beauty of a sunset, the wonder of an old tree, or the mystery and delight of human intimacy. In such experiences, we are wholeheartedly present. The force of their intensity induces a state of natural awareness in which we are deeply here, connected with ourselves and the world around us.

This state of mindful presence is available to us at all times. It brings richness to ordinary experience, be it preparing a meal, talking to a family member, or feeling the morning air on our skin. It allows us to appreciate life and to move through the difficult parts with grace.

As I've mentioned, mindful presence also plays an essential role in communication *for the simple fact that we need to be here first to understand anything.* Have you ever tried to converse with someone who was distracted? Or had someone pull out their smartphone in the middle of a conversation? (Maybe you've done the same when a conversation lagged.) How many arguments have you had simply because one person wasn't listening? Or because someone couldn't pause and hold their tongue? We can avoid many of the difficulties we have in dialogue simply by slowing down and being more present.

> *Mindfulness* is being aware of what's happening in the present moment in a balanced and nonreactive way.

The role of awareness goes beyond being a prerequisite for understanding. Presence lays the ground for connection. We feel it when someone is engaged and listening. Presence is inviting. It gives others space, and it opens the door for them to engage with us. This kind of real-time awareness is a foundation for effective, healthy conversation. Without it, we're running on automatic at best, and we may be unintentionally sowing seeds of disconnection. (If we're not mindful, chances are we're being mindless.)

> *Principle:* Presence lays the ground for connection.

The irony is that being mindful doesn't actually require that much extra effort. In the long run, we may find being mindful actually conserves energy, compared to how we waste energy when mindless.

How often do we take the time to begin a conversation by meeting the other person with presence? Rushing through the day, we barrel into conversations and wonder why we keep crashing. What would it be like instead to start from a place of clear, grounded self-awareness? To bring composure and respect to the process of making contact with another human being?

Leading with presence is the first step to effective conversations; it is a rich and deep practice with many dimensions. Most fundamentally, it means that we enter conversations from the simplicity and strength of our own presence.

To lead with presence also means that we strive to maintain awareness throughout a conversation. It's a continual process in which we return to presence again and again, listening and speaking from awareness as much as possible. To be able to do this takes practice, especially in the heat of a difficult exchange. When we've developed this skill, our nervous system remembers how to return to presence. Like a gyroscope finding its center, we notice more quickly when we're on automatic or caught in a reaction, and we readjust accordingly.

So what is mindful presence? Put simply, mindfulness means knowing what's happening right now in a balanced and nonreactive way. It's the keen, observing eye of the naturalist who studies their subject patiently, with clarity, interest, and wonder.*

Mindfulness is not a purely mental experience. It is an intimate, embodied awareness of the richness of life: sensations, emotions, sounds, sights. To counter our tendency to associate mindfulness with a mental exercise, I use the word *presence* to refer to the experience of being mindfully aware.[1]

To give you a taste of what I'm talking about, let's try a simple experiment.

---

*Due to the lack of a gender neutral, singular personal pronoun in English, I have chosen to use *they* throughout the text to be more inclusive.

PRACTICE: Sensing the Body

Right now, as you read, can you be aware of the sensations of your body sitting? Perhaps you feel some heaviness or pressure where your body contacts the chair or the touch of your feet on the floor. Keep bringing your attention to those places of contact. Were you aware of these sensations a few moments ago, before I suggested it? How difficult was it to become aware of your direct, present-moment experience?

Mindful presence also helps us investigate our experience. Like a sturdy magnifying glass, it's an instrument we can use to refine our vision. It allows us to observe the actual process of communication: our speech, our listening, even our inner world of thoughts, perceptions, and emotions.

Mindfulness includes a certain staying power, the ability to keep being aware. It helps us *remember* the tools we've learned. We can know all manner of communication skills, but if we can't remember to use them they won't do us much good!

It's easy to be mindful for a moment, as you just experienced. What's challenging is to make that awareness continuous, sustaining it over time. Are you still aware of your body sitting? This is where practice comes in, actively strengthening presence through patient, gentle repetition.

Building on Our Strengths

Increasing our capacity for presence begins with identifying our strengths and any areas we may need to develop.

PRACTICE: Reflection on Presence

What helps you stay connected to presence? What disconnects you from presence? Take some time to think about these, making a list of each.

The longer you spend contemplating each question, the more surprised you may be at what you discover. You might find that you already know quite a bit about presence! Here are a few examples of things people commonly mention.

MAY CONNECT YOU TO PRESENCE

- Slowing down
- Breathing
- Time with a friend
- Being in nature
- Touch
- Music
- Sunshine
- Rain
- Beauty

MAY DISCONNECT YOU FROM PRESENCE

- Stress
- Feeling tired
- Being hungry
- Rushing
- Fear
- Wanting something
- Impatience
- Perceived threat
- Lack of safety

The more familiar we are with the particular conditions that connect or disconnect us from presence, the easier it becomes to spot them in our lives. For example, I tend to lose presence when I'm rushing. This means that I'm more apt to make physical or relational blunders: I might drop something in the kitchen, forget my lunch, or even say something sharp.

I learned a painful lesson about this a few years ago. I was at a farewell party for my girlfriend, Evan, who had just finished a year of service at a meditation retreat center. We had plans to drive north up the coast of California after the party, and I'd made an appointment to install a car radio for the trip. In that classic, romantic way, I wanted everything to be perfect.

As our departure time approached, I grew more and more anxious about missing the appointment. With no sign of a formal send-off, I finally spoke up and said that we needed to leave soon. To avoid any awkwardness, Evan went along with my request, but she was in tears by the time we arrived at the auto shop. She was incensed at me for cutting short a meaningful experience and at herself for not speaking up. In my fixation to create "the perfect trip," I'd missed the fact that she was already enjoying herself.

I reflected a lot on that incident, how losing presence had unintended, painful consequences.[2] In the larger scheme of things, it's a benign example. Recognizing the cost of rushing, I'm now more attuned to it. That inner pressure acts as a signal that says, "Watch out—you're losing presence!" Instead of blocking presence, it reminds me to be here.

Almost everything in our civilization points away from presence. The pressures of earning a living in modern society place extraordinary demands on our time and energy—demands that leave little space to cultivate mindful awareness.

Our instant, touchscreen culture bombards us daily with messages pointing to the future, trying to convince us that our happiness lies in the next hit of pleasure, a new gadget, or tantalizing experience. Our newsfeeds are programmed with algorithms to maximize engagement, leading to further distraction. In this blitz of information and consumption, face-to-face human interaction is becoming less a part of life. Ever notice how many people are glued to screens in public, even in parks and restaurants? Yet, no matter how long we spend meandering online or getting lost in thought, we all eventually come back to presence, here in our body.

Recognizing Presence

Our natural state of being is a relaxed, open alertness characterized by contentment and well-being. This is innate. Evolutionarily we're wired to be here in a profoundly attuned way. Even in our modern world with all its hurries and distractions, presence doesn't need to be a random occurrence. We can actively enhance our ability to rest in this balanced state, to recognize when we've left, and to return more reliably.

◀))* **PRACTICE:** Orienting

Use the following basic exercise to return to a state of natural presence.

Take a few minutes to look around where you are. Let your eyes explore with curiosity whatever you see. Is there anything new or different you notice? Let your head and neck move with your eyes as you look around.

Notice the bare experience of seeing: shapes, color, light, lines. Where are your eyes naturally drawn? If there is anything of interest, allow your gaze to linger there. Continue to explore at your own pace.

Notice how you feel after looking around. You may notice yourself taking a spontaneous, deep breath or exhaling as your body settles. Using the eyes, head, and neck in this manner activates the ventral vagus nerve and signals to our hardwired protection mechanisms that we're safe from danger in our immediate physical surroundings. Try this *orienting* practice out anytime, looking around and noticing the effect on your mind and body.

Honesty: Presence Means Being Real

Leading with presence doesn't mean feeling a specific way—if it did, it would be quite limited. Presence means being real. It's a willingness to be honest with ourselves about what's happening, just as it is.

Sometimes we feel distinctly *ungrounded*. We might be nervous, angry, or agitated. The great strength of mindfulness is that it's not about having a particular experience. Rather, it's the capacity to know and feel whatever is happening directly, without getting caught in our reactions. Bringing presence to a conversation means accepting what arises in our experience: "This is truth. This is what's happening right now."

This doesn't mean that we condone harmful actions or automatically agree with another's position. It doesn't preclude taking strong action, and it doesn't mean necessarily saying everything on our mind. ("Well, I was just being honest.") It means that we acknowledge the reality of what's happening. If we can't be honest with ourselves about what's going on,

---

* This symbol indicates a companion guided audio practice at OrenJaySofer.com /book-audio. See the index of practices on page 271.

how can we hope to hear one another, much less find resolution to a difficult situation?

This kind of honesty provides reliable information about what's happening inside and around us. We learn to access our own feelings and needs in real time and to read others' experience more accurately. This in turn helps us know what we need to say to feel heard, to move forward, or to resolve a difference.

> *Principle:* **Lead with presence; begin conversation with awareness, return to and strive to maintain that awareness, and be honest with oneself about what's happening.**

The Oil Light: Presence and Reactivity

I used to teach mindfulness to elementary school kids in the inner city of Oakland, California. I heard many stories from the children about how mindfulness helped them handle strong emotions. One boy explained he got so mad he wanted to kick his sister! "Then I remembered my mindful breathing, took a few breaths, and calmed down."

When tensions run high, presence grounds us. The more familiar we are with how it feels to be present, the more easily we detect the signs of being activated. It's like noticing the low-oil light in an automobile. If we catch that early warning signal, we can avoid a lot of trouble. What happens when you're angry, scared, or hurt? Does your breath quicken? Does your jaw clench? Do you feel hot or cold? Do you start to space out? Instead of "kicking your sister," you can use mindfulness to catch these signals and create the space inside to choose how you respond.

> *Principle:* **The more aware we are, the more choice we have.**

Feeling activated isn't "bad"—it's a healthy part of being alive. It's only problematic if we lose awareness. Yet for many of us, the pace of modern life has us running on sympathetic arousal all the time. Whether it's the stress of commuting, the volume of tasks we manage, or even the caffeine we consume, we can live in a constant state of low-grade panic, always on alert. When unchecked, this can lead to unnecessary interpersonal conflicts. As we practice mindfulness, we learn how to calm and steady the agitation of being overactivated. Even something as simple as taking a long, slow outbreath can begin to settle our nervous system.

Training in Mindful Presence

I love how portable and adaptable presence is. You can do it anytime, anyplace, without any special equipment or conditions. No one even needs to know. You can practice mindfulness—feeling your breath and body; noticing sounds, thoughts, or feelings—in the midst of ordinary life.

When it comes to conversation, it's important to have a lightweight, nimble tool such as mindfulness. I recommend taking some time every day for formal mindfulness practice. It's like having a master key that opens many doors in your heart and mind. Even a few minutes of practice can have a positive effect on your day, bringing renewed energy, clarity, and a sense of purpose.

One of the most reliable methods for cultivating presence is to anchor our attention with sensations in the body. As we move through the world and interact with others, our attention usually rushes out to sights and sounds or gets consumed by thoughts of the past or future. Anchoring attention in the body counters these tendencies by giving our awareness a place to rest. Sensations only occur here and now. Whenever you bring your attention to a sensation, you are—for that moment—present.

Here I'll share four primary methods for cultivating presence. Each of them uses a specific sensory experience—called a reference point, or an *anchor*—to ground attention in the body: weight, the *centerline*, breathing, and *touch points* such as the hands or feet.

> **An *anchor* is a reference point to which we return to strengthen mindful presence.**

The aim isn't to master all of these; it's to find one or two that help you feel more alert and grounded in the midst of your life. Experiment with the instructions below. You can do each practice individually, or as a series flowing from one to the next. As you practice, consider which is easiest for you. The best method is the one that connects you with presence.

🔊 PRACTICE: Grounding in the Body

Method 1: Finding Gravity

Sit comfortably. Start by taking a few moments to orient to your surroundings, looking around the room. Find a posture that's upright yet relaxed. Gently close your eyes and take a few deep breaths to help you settle in.

Feel any sensations of weight or heaviness in your body. You might notice your body's contact with the chair, any hardness or give in the surface you're sitting on. You might feel the sense of your whole body sitting, its mass, or warmth. Let your attention rest with these sensations of weight. Can you feel the downward force of gravity?

When you notice your attention has wandered, gently let go and bring it back to the feeling of weight or heaviness in your body. Anchor your awareness there.

Method 2: The Centerline

Next, bring your attention to your upper body. Sense how your torso rises up from your waist and pelvis. Can you feel your back, shoulders, and neck? See if you can sense the midline or centerline of your upper body. Try feeling your spine, running from your tailbone, through your back, up to the base of your head. Or try imagining a line down the middle of your torso, halfway between your front and back, in the middle of the left and right sides of your body.

Moving your torso can help reveal the centerline. Rock forward and backward slightly, until you feel the balance point in the middle. Do the same from side to side. Finally, rotate your shoulders and upper body one or two degrees to either side. Can you feel the axis around which the body is turning? That's the centerline. See if you can rest your attention here, on the centerline of your body. Can you feel how your body is upright?

Method 3: Breathing

As you sit quietly, tune in to the sensations of breathing. See if you can allow your attention to rest with the sensations of breathing in and breathing out.

You don't need to block out other sensations, sounds, or thoughts. Just tune in to the steady rhythm of breathing in and breathing out, much as you might listen to waves crashing on a beach. Let your breath come into focus naturally.

It's normal for the mind to wander to thoughts, sounds, or other experiences. Whenever you notice, gently bring your attention back to feeling your breath, appreciating that mindfulness is growing.

Method 4: Touch Points

Now explore specific areas in your body that tend to be rich in sensation. First, put all your attention in your hands. Feel any sensations there: warmth or coolness; tingling, pulsing, or heaviness; maybe moisture or dryness. Rest your attention on any sensations you can feel in your hands. You might feel the sensations of your hands touching or resting in your lap.

Now shift your attention to your feet, feeling any sensations there: temperature, weight, texture, the contact with the floor, the pressure of your shoes. Rest your attention with any sensations in your feet.

You can try this with any other part of your body that has strong sensations, such as your lips, tongue, or eyes. When your mind wanders, gently bring it back to one of these places.

Shifting Your Attention

Finally, try shifting your attention between these four areas: gravity, the centerline, breathing, and a touch point (hands, feet, lips). Which is most readily accessible? Which helps you connect most naturally with presence, that sense of being here in a relaxed and embodied way?

When you're ready, open your eyes. Look around the room, reorienting to your surroundings. Take a few moments to reflect on this exercise. Which of these four ways of training in presence would you like to practice this week?

Each method has its own strength. The downward force of gravity tends to balance the stimulating, upward movement of attention in conversations. The centerline can bring a sense of inner strength and clarity. Breathing can soothe us, while touch points can dissipate the intensity of emotions. You also can get creative and explore your own ways of strengthening presence. Some people keep a smooth stone in their pocket, using its weight and softness as a literal touchstone.

Bringing Presence to Life

You probably read the previous pages in a matter of minutes, but to incorporate these practices into your life takes time. Choose one method to start and try practicing in three distinct areas: on your own (formal meditation), during transitions (waiting in line, commuting), and in conversations (initially while listening).

When on your own, give 100 percent of your attention to the anchor. During transitions, place as much of your attention there as feels appropriate to the context. When you're interacting, put just 10 or 20 percent of your awareness there. At first it may be awkward to do during a conversation. It can feel as if your attention is flipping back and forth between what's happening and your anchor. This is completely normal. Over time, your mind will learn how to balance external sensory data with a grounded internal presence and maintain a light awareness of your body during conversation.

Initially, much of the work is simply remembering to be present. One way to support this is to take a few moments each morning to set an intention and then to reflect on how things went at the end of the day. This practice can be as brief as two minutes, or longer if you have the time.

🔊 **PRACTICE:** Beginning and Ending the Day

MORNING: Soon after rising, take a few breaths to settle your mind and feel your body. Connect your attention to the reference point with which you're working: gravity, the centerline, breathing, or a touch point. Notice how it feels to be present right now. Then, set a clear intention to return to this reference point as a support for presence as often as you can during your day. Imagine situations where you want to practice: on your commute, in a meeting, with someone specific.

EVENING: At the end of the day, take some time to reflect. Did you remember? When? What was the effect? Bring an attitude of curiosity and warmth to your reflection, being wary of any self-judgment. What would you like to do differently tomorrow? Do you have ideas for ways you can remember to lead with presence?

This structured daily practice can be incredibly useful for training your mind. As you explore the suggestions throughout this book, you can use this same process to develop any of the three foundations of mindful communication and its associated tools.

The Doorway to Resilience

At one workshop, a participant raised her hand and asked with a pained expression, "What about when it hurts to be here?" Sometimes returning to presence can feel like stepping on the wrong end of a rake: all of a sudden, you get hit in the face. We've been going ninety miles per hour; when we finally slow down to reconnect with ourselves, we can be met with a backlog of physical discomfort, stress, or emotional pain.

We often seek relief from pain and discomfort through distraction or pleasure. This can help rebalance a beleaguered nervous system. The danger is when the choice to seek relief becomes a chronic reflex to anything uncomfortable. Over time, we can become incapable of tolerating even the smallest amount of pain without immediately *doing something* to change it.

But when pain is met with genuine care and presence, something amazing can happen—healing. With patient, steady attention, emotional pain eases. Consider how it feels to be received with empathy and presence in a moment of distress.

I was nineteen when I started studying Buddhism in a monastery halfway around the world in India. I was quite homesick, and our study-abroad director encouraged me to speak to one of the meditation teachers about how I was feeling.

Godwin Samararatne was a tall Sri Lankan man with soft eyes and a playful laugh. His deep brown skin cut a sharp contrast with his traditional white garments. We sat across from one another in a sunny room, Godwin listening as I talked about missing my family and my girlfriend. After a while he tilted his head slightly and asked, "Where does it hurt?" I pointed to the center of my chest and began to feel the pain directly.

Tears welled up as the ache moved from my heart to my throat. Godwin held my gaze, nodding slowly. The hurt grew more intense for a moment, then faded and passed. I beamed and thanked him, believing he had done something miraculous. It was a long time before I understood what had actually happened: his compassion had invited me into presence, to feel the pain and let it pass.

As we delve into the patterns that drive our communication habits, we may discover difficult emotions or painful memories. Presence is an essential resource to navigate these places. It is a doorway to resilience, helping us access the innate healing and self-regulatory capacities of our mind and body. Just as our cells know how to heal a cut, our psyche possesses the intelligence to heal emotional wounds. With time, support, and caring presence, our heart can mend.

Creating a Positive Feedback Loop

As you endeavor to bring more presence to life, you may notice how hard it is. One of my first meditation teachers was fond of saying, "Mindfulness practice is simple, but not easy." We can go an entire day without remembering to be present once! When we do remember, our response is often self-critical.

We can have such unreasonable expectations of ourselves, as if we're supposed to be experts from day one. It's entirely normal to forget. Expect to forget a lot. Put another way: remembering is kind of amazing. Our communication habits have great momentum; recall the analogy of turning a ship at sea. Our job is to find ways to "hold the angle" of the rudder. Bringing even a small amount of presence to conversation will lead to profound changes over time.

Instead of berating ourselves for forgetting, *the key to success is to appreciate remembering*. Every moment of mindfulness strengthens awareness. This is cause for celebration rather than judgment. We learn more through warmhearted encouragement than bitter criticism. If you're teaching a child math and you get angry every time they make a mistake, how much will that child learn? Will they even want to study mathematics?

If you can take this understanding to heart, you'll find mindfulness grows more quickly, with more joy and ease. The secret is patient and kind persistence. Lead with presence as often as you remember, and let the rest unfold naturally.

The Power of Presence

We can be such articulate creatures, and yet words often fall short of expressing the most meaningful things in life. In moments of great love and intimacy as in moments of great loss and tragedy, our simple, enduring presence sometimes says the most.

One of the most difficult things I've ever done in my life was saying goodbye to Safta, my dad's mom. I was fourteen when her cancer metastasized; I joined my father for the trip back to Israel.

Safta and I never spoke the same language, but we had shared many loving moments over the years, playing card games or simply holding hands and laughing. She had the most amazing hands. They were small and rugged, hands that could snap a chicken's neck or caress my face. The skin on Safta's hands somehow managed to be plump and wrinkled at the same time. I can still feel the warmth and vitality of those hands.

My father and I visited her in the nursing home every day. On our last visit, all three of us spent some time together in the courtyard and then went back to her hospice room. I spoke through tears as I told her in broken Hebrew that I loved her and would miss her. Then we just held hands for a long, quiet moment. It was a wordless goodbye and the most meaningful one I could have asked for.

Sometimes it's our presence that says the most.

PRINCIPLES

Presence lays the ground for connection.

Lead with presence; begin conversation with awareness, return to and strive to maintain that awareness, and be honest with oneself about what's happening.

The more aware we are, the more choice we have.

Presence has a range of benefits:

- It gives us back our life, waking us up to the present moment.
- It helps us remember to use the communication tools we've learned.
- It gives us important information about ourselves and others.
- It gives us early warning signs if we feel activated or upset.
- It provides a container to manage reactivity.
- It helps us heal places of emotional pain or wounding.

Presence is our natural state. We can develop presence by:

- Orienting to our surroundings in an alert and balanced way
- Identifying what helps us stay connected to and what disconnects us from presence
- Practicing mindfulness of the body, grounding with an anchor: gravity, the centerline, breathing, touch points such as the hands or feet
- Beginning and ending the day with an intention
- Creating a positive feedback loop by appreciating when we remember to be present rather than judging ourselves

QUESTION & ANSWER

Q: Sometimes I feel really present with what someone is saying, but I might not be aware of my body. Is that still presence?

There are many ways to be present. We can be present cognitively, with the intellect; emotionally, with our feelings or needs; and somatically, in an embodied way. We are aiming to integrate all three of these domains. Using the body as a basis for presence lends a kind of wholeness and provides a basis for developing the other forms of presence.

Q: I tried being more present and aware when talking to a family member, and I felt so much that it made it hard to even talk or listen. It almost seemed like I got more reactive. What's going on?

It *can* be overwhelming to feel what's going on inside, especially if it's a difficult conversation. Sometimes, being more present can reveal feelings or dynamics that have been going on under the surface. Other times, we may feel more open and vulnerable. Any of this can lead to a sense of disorientation. I encourage you to keep being present. Do your best to stay balanced with whatever comes up, because the alternative is being on automatic. If things start to feel overwhelming, you can always let the other person know: "I'd like to keep talking but I notice I'm feeling a little overwhelmed. Would it be all right if we took a break for a bit?"

Q: A lot of the time I don't feel safe enough to relax and be present. How can I practice this if I don't feel safe?

I feel really touched when I hear this question. To me, it points to both our longing to connect and our vulnerability. So much about our society doesn't support the kind of familiar relaxation that our organisms long for: the ease of warm social connections and a sense of place. I want us to be able to understand our individual experience in the context of the larger structures of our society, otherwise we tend to view all our challenges personally, thinking they're somehow our fault.

When we factor in how disconnected modern culture is from a sense of community and belonging, as well as how economic pressures minimize time for healthy attachment bonding between parents and children, of course we don't feel relaxed and safe! We may have internalized a lack of safety from negative experiences based on our gender, sexual orientation, race, class, or other aspects of our social location. It's important to identify places where we may need to get support, seek resources, and work to address the structural causes of these issues.

It's also important to investigate our assumptions. Our sense of safety can become reduced to a narrow attachment to emotional comfort. Safety is illusory. We do all we can to prevent harm and stop abuse while recognizing that the world isn't safe physically or emotionally. Rather than contributing to our fear, this understanding can lead to great vitality and freedom.

The tools and perspectives I'm sharing can help us build a stable base of ease and self-connection so that our sense of safety is sourced from within rather than without. The "shallow end of a pool" training principle is essential here. Look for people or situations where you feel a little bit safer, a little more relaxed, and start to practice there—even if that's with your pet or a favorite tree. Our nervous systems long for the soothing effects of friendly, social engagement. We've been doing this for millennia, and our bodies will remember how to connect, share, and listen if we create the right conditions and give them a chance.

3

relational awareness

All real living is meeting.
—MARTIN BUBER

WHEN IT COMES to conversation, the force of our habits and the pressure of social settings can make it exceedingly difficult to maintain presence. Here, our internal practice serves as a basis. We use the arena of conversation itself as a training ground for presence, using techniques to anchor awareness within the midst of exchange and developing the capacity for relational awareness.

When I came to communication training after five years of dedicated mindfulness practice, I noticed certain changes emerging. I naturally began bringing more awareness to when I chose to speak and listen. I also began to make simple adjustments in the flow of my speech, taking pauses or making subtle shifts in my pace to modulate my nervous system. Eventually I learned to widen my awareness from my own sense of embodiment to include the other person, our connection, and the space around us.

Choice Points: Speaking or Listening

Consciously choosing when to speak and when to listen is essential for meaningful conversation. In some respects, it's the most basic communication skill. How many times have you said something only to wish you could take it back moments after the words left your mouth? Or hit "send" on an email when it might have been better to let things cool off? It's equally important to have the courage to say our piece. When we don't speak up, we can feel as if we've let ourselves or our loved ones down.

Conversation is a dynamic interplay between each person's choice to speak or listen. When those choices are conscious and respectful, conversations tend to be more productive and enjoyable. If those choices are unconscious or impulsive, conversations tend to be less productive and more stressful.

I call this juncture the "choice point" between speaking and listening. With presence, every moment offers a choice. One of my NVC colleagues uses the acronym WAIT to remind himself of this. "Why Am I Talking?" he asks, pointing to how quickly and easily we tend to open our mouths. "What Am I Thinking?" he inquires, tracking the mental process that spurs our speech.

> A *choice point* is a moment of awareness in which we decide whether to speak or listen.

Our ability to maintain presence at the choice point takes practice. Sometimes the moment of choice races by like a road sign while we are doing seventy-five miles per hour on the freeway. The impulse to speak can be so strong that it impels us to verbalize simply to release the internal pressure. If we tend toward the quieter side, it can feel as if those openings in a conversation disappear before we can muster our voice.

This is where mindfulness comes in. In meditation, we learn how to observe unpleasant sensations (knee pain, a sore back) without immediately reacting. We develop the capacity to be aware of an impulse without acting on it.

The anxiety we feel in conversation is usually rooted in deeper needs to be seen or heard, needs for safety, acceptance, belonging, and so on. The less confident we feel in meeting those needs, the more pressure we will experience to speak up or remain silent. We might fear that if we don't say something *right now* we'll never be able to do so. Or if we do say something, disaster or disconnection will surely ensue.

The more ways we find to meet those needs (and to handle them skillfully when they aren't met), the less pressure we feel to speak or remain silent; we can relax into the flow of a conversation. There's no danger in speaking our mind and no rush to say it all at once. If it's important, we'll find the right time and way to say it.

This capacity builds slowly. As we practice honoring our needs, we learn to trust ourselves. Paying attention to any small successes helps our nervous system settle and reset. With a new baseline of ease, it can stop setting off false alarms that impel or prevent us from speaking, and our ability to make more conscious choices grows. We can then discern what's going to be most helpful to move a conversation forward and how to balance all the needs on the table.

PRACTICE: Choice Points

To practice, choose someone with whom you feel relatively comfortable. This familiarity makes it easier to learn the tool. During a conversation, notice when you choose to speak. If you find yourself talking without having consciously chosen to do so, try stopping and leaving space for the other person to continue. Notice what it's like to actively choose to say something rather than doing so automatically. Pay particular attention to any urgency or reluctance to speak or any sensations of internal pressure. Use that pressure as a signal to make a more conscious choice.

Meetings

There tends to be more freedom to remain silent in meetings than during one-to-one conversations. The next time you are in a meeting, notice how the impulse to speak can rise and fall as the conversation unfolds. If there is an important point you'd like to make, choose when to do so. You can always begin, "I'd like to go back to something we were talking about a few moments ago." Notice how it feels after you speak. Is there relief? Anxiety or self-doubt?

Written Communication

Experiment with making conscious choices about when you check your inbox or social media feeds ("listening"). When you do engage, pause before replying to consider whether or not you want to "speak." Is this the right time? Would it be useful to wait or to say nothing at all?

Part of this investigation is getting to know our own patterns. Do we tend to speak easily and freely, finding it harder to leave space for others? Is it more comfortable for us to listen, finding it challenging to come forward?

Most of us tend to be stronger in one area. Circumstances and events tied to our gender, race, class, or other aspects of our social location tend to mold how we show up relationally. We've all received messages—explicitly and implicitly, personally and through media, stories, and culture—about how we are expected to behave. Through various cues of approval or disapproval, inclusion or exclusion, we learn what's safest based on our role and the expectations of others.

Our work is to uncover these patterns and develop an authentic freedom of expression. There is no ideal way to be, no one thing to do in all circumstances. The goal is dynamic flexibility through presence, choosing to speak or listen as needed.

The Power of Pace: Pausing

If I could teach people only one tool for training in presence it would be to pause. The space of one pause can make a world of difference. A colleague who teaches meditation to incarcerated youth tells a story about working with men in prison. He asks how much time they're doing; their sentences often total well over one hundred years. Then he asks, "How long did you think about it before committing the crime that landed you here?" The combined total is often less than two minutes. Facing this stark disparity, my colleague explains to the youth, "Mindfulness helps you pause between an impulse and your reaction, so that you can have more choice about what you do with your life."

The pause is pregnant with possibility. In one breath, we can notice thoughts, feelings, and impulses, and choose which ones to follow. It's like a mini-meditation, an infusion of presence to help stay clear and balanced. What happens during the space of that pause is quite open. We may ground our attention in the body or relax some inner tension, return to a specific intention, handle our emotions so they don't spill out unskillfully, or gather our thoughts about how to proceed.

Pausing is both a support for and a natural expression of mindful presence. The more aware I am of my body, the more I notice any agitation in my nervous system and corresponding changes in my pace or volume. I can ride that wave of energy (say, expressing enthusiasm or frustration) or apply the brakes. As with choice points, the aim is not to become monotone, flat, or speak calmly all the time but rather to develop skill and proficiency in a wider range of circumstances.

The pause is flexible, varying in length depending on the situation. One can take a micropause: an almost imperceptible gap in the flow of speech. It gives just enough time to ground your attention in the body or readjust your intention.

PRACTICE: Pausing

If you have a practice partner for this book, set a timer for five minutes and discuss something you did recently that you enjoyed. See if each person can pause for the space of one breath each time before speaking. Try pausing for a moment during a sentence or between thoughts. During the pause, bring your attention back to a reference point in your body or your overall sense of presence.

This should slow the pace of the conversation considerably, and it will probably feel unnatural. This is a training exercise to explore pausing and returning to presence in a deliberate way, just as one might practice a tennis stroke in slow motion.

You can also experiment with taking deliberate pauses in low-stakes conversations. Try pausing for the space of a breath before you speak or respond, as a way of gathering your attention and grounding in the body. This doesn't mean acting oddly and taking slow, deep breaths! Just slow things down a bit, pausing to consider.

Try this in dialogue in a less obvious way, pausing a few times—for a moment before you begin speaking or for a beat between ideas. What is the effect on your state of mind? On the quality of connection?

Pausing isn't always easy to do. Even when we remember, it can be hard to insert space into a conversation or to find a way to do so that's socially acceptable. We may feel concerned that we'll lose our turn to speak or appear disinterested. Here are some specific ways to create a pause or to signal that you're taking one:

- Take a deep, audible breath (especially an outbreath).
- Use a short verbal cue to indicate you are thinking, such as "Hmm . . ."
- Use a visual cue, such as looking up and to the side or furrowing your brow.
- "I'm not sure. I'd like to think about that."
- "Let me think about that for a moment."
- "Can we pause for a moment? I want to gather my thoughts."
- "This sounds important. I'd like to give it some time."
- "I'd really like to consider this more carefully. Can I get back to you on it?"

When all else fails, create a distraction. If you're out for a meal or in a meeting, excuse yourself to the restroom. I even heard of one fellow who would drop his keys or some loose change to insert a pause in conversation! Get as creative as you need to buy yourself some time and return to presence.

Sometimes we need a longer pause. If we determine that the conditions aren't right for a successful conversation, we may want to take a break for a day, a week, or longer. In these instances, *how* we pause is important. If we simply say, "I can't talk about this now," our conversation partners are left to interpret our behavior on their own. They may think we're not interested, that we don't care, or that we're avoiding them. To increase the chances that our break will be productive, we need to share the reasons behind our choice. Here are a few examples:

- "I'd really like to continue our conversation, and I'm not in the best frame of mind to do that right now. Can we take a break and come back to this . . . [tomorrow, next time]?"
- "I'd really like to hear what you have to say, and I'm feeling a little overwhelmed, so I don't think I'll be able to listen well. Let's take a break for an hour. Okay?"

- "I'm committed to figuring this out together, and I don't quite have the space to think clearly now. I'd like to put this on hold until . . . Would that be okay?"
- "I want to finish this conversation, and I don't think anything else I say right now will be useful. How about we pause here and come back later?"

Look closely at these examples. What do you notice in common?

First, they all begin with our intention to connect (the second step to effective conversation). This preempts any tendency to interpret our break as rejection or avoidance. It lets the other person know we are considering them in our desire to pause. This needs to be genuine. Find your own words to express what's true.

Second, each statement takes responsibility for our limitations or desires. We're clear that we're acting on our own need for space rather than blaming the other person.

Finally, they each end with a request to finish the conversation later, which helps reduce anxiety about what will happen. The more specific we can be about when, the better.

As we use this tool of pausing, noticing pauses (or their absence) attunes us to the pace of a conversation. This can be a very rich area to explore and a potent way to train in presence. Because speech is created with breath and because our breath is directly tied to our nervous system, the pace of our speaking is often a direct reflection of our internal state. What's fascinating is that changing our pace of speech can shift our internal state.

PRACTICE: Modulating Pace

Notice when and how your pace varies in conversation. At what pace do you feel most comfortable, confident, and relaxed? When is it slow and steady? When does it quicken or become rapid? Can you choose how quickly or slowly you speak? How does your pace affect the tone of the conversation?

Choose an easy, low-stakes conversation with which to experiment. As you speak, vary the pace of your speech. Speed up a little, speaking more rapidly. Notice the effect on your body, your thoughts, your overall energy. Slow down some. What is the effect on your state of mind and body? On the quality of connection in the relationship?

Slowing down even a little bit usually increases our ability to lead with presence. This is especially true in times of conflict, when things tend to speed up. Dialing our pace back in such situations can have a calming effect on our nervous system.[1]

Speaking at a relaxed pace can also help us claim space in a conversation and makes it easier for the listener to take in what we're saying. When we're confident and self-assured, we usually speak at a leisurely rate. There's no rush; we trust that what we have to say matters and is worth listening to. We breathe naturally and easy, taking our time. In general, our words carry more weight when we speak in this manner, which can draw and hold the attention of our listener.

It's important to note that there's no "right" pace. The ideal pace supports presence and helps create connection, and that can vary a lot depending on the circumstances or culture.

Maturing in Presence: Mutuality

Leading with presence is a rich experience that matures over time. As it develops, presence illuminates the existence of the other. The more I sense *myself*, the more aware I become of *you*. This observation is so basic we can take it for granted: relationship by definition means there are two of us! To be truly in dialogue means that we see the other person as an autonomous individual, with their own hopes, fears, dreams, desires, joys, and sorrows.

In Zulu there is a traditional greeting, *Sawubona*, "We see you." Orland Bishop, director of the ShadeTree Multicultural Foundation, explains, "The response is *Yabo sawubona*, 'Yes, we see you too.' When two humans meet in this gesture of *Sawubona* the acknowledgment is, 'We see each other.' That becomes an agreement. It's an invitation to participate in each other's life."[2] Can we bring this simple, profound recognition of another's presence to our conversations?

We've all had experiences of not being seen or of looking right through someone else. It feels as if the other person is talking "at you" rather than "to you" or like you're talking to a wall. Lack of mutuality is an absence of presence; it turns dialogue into monologue. It's that distant gaze of the checkout clerk, the flat monotone of a customer service agent.

We lose mutuality for many reasons. It happens when we're on automatic. It can occur when we are extremely impassioned or when we feel scared, upset, or angry. Tragically, we lose mutuality with the friends and family we see every day. They become so familiar that we stop seeing them.

Without the mutuality of presence there is a fundamental disconnect. "You" are reduced to an object in relation to "me." You become a mental representation from the past, a vehicle for getting what I want, or an obstacle in my way. When human beings become objects rather than persons, there is nothing we can't justify: from ordinary slights to the horrors of slavery, sex trafficking, and genocide.

Presence opens the door to mutuality. When we lead with presence, we enter a field of relationship in which both of us matter simply by virtue of our existence. We shift from seeing the other as an object, to seeing them as a subject. This is the potent, transformative shift in perspective Martin Buber famously described as the I-Thou relationship. "All real living is meeting," he wrote.[3] For Buber, respect for the innate subjectivity of life was holy.

> *Principle:* **Leading with presence includes mutuality, seeing the other person as an autonomous individual, and uncertainty, acknowledging and accepting the unknown, both of which create new possibilities in dialogue.**

To be truly alive is to enter this experience of mutuality, of sensing one another and the mystery of being here. Relational presence is a true encounter in which I see you for who you are rather than what I want or need you to be. This mutuality is the foundation of real dialogue.

Advanced Practice: Relational Awareness

In conversation we tend to focus all our attention on ourselves or on the other person. Relational awareness is the capacity to include both you and me, the external and the internal, balancing our attention in a dynamic way. It builds on the foundation of embodiment by expanding awareness to include three more reference points: the other person, our connection, and the space around us. This can increase our flexibility and give us more options to handle intensity in dialogue.

Relational awareness is an advanced practice, yet it flows quite naturally out of the exercises we've already been doing. Awareness is like a flashlight with an adjustable beam. One can vary its aperture or direct it to different locations. Try the exercises below to get a feel for shifting awareness between the internal and external.

🔊 **PRACTICE:** Expanding Awareness

Do this practice solo. Sit comfortably, close your eyes, and let your mind and body begin to settle. Ground your attention in one of the four internal reference points we've already explored: gravity, the centerline, breathing, or a touch point such as the hands or feet. Take some time here, feeling the steadiness of these tangible sensations.

Then let go of the internal reference point and open your eyes. Become aware of sights and sounds around you. Look around if you like. Notice how it feels to have your attention focused outwardly. Close your eyes, and let your awareness settle again with an internal reference point. Explore opening and closing your eyes, shifting your attention back and forth between inside and outside. Can you find a balance, some of your attention connected to your body and some connected to your surroundings?

Now, with your eyes closed, begin to widen your awareness. Bring attention to your whole body, feeling its various sensations: warmth, heaviness, pulsing, or tingling. Next, bring your attention to the surface of your skin. See if you can feel any sensations there: the touch of your clothing, the temperature of the air.

Widen your awareness further to the space immediately around your body. Can you sense the space just beyond the surface of your skin? To help notice this, imagine that you are in a crowded subway car, bodies pressed against you. Now bring your attention to the space around your body here and now. Can you notice the absence of pressure? The sense of spaciousness?

Last, expand your awareness even further to include the entire room. You can open your eyes, or notice sounds, to get a feel for this openness. Can you be aware of the space around you?

To end, bring your attention back into your body, feeling the sensations of sitting.

This series of exercises reveals the fluidity of awareness. In the next practice, we'll further explore balancing internal and external awareness.

PRACTICE: Relational Awareness

Try these suggestions individually in different settings or sequentially within one conversation. You can do this with a partner, or you can experiment silently in a relaxed social situation.

Use an internal reference point to ground your awareness in your body. Notice how it feels to keep some attention there. Next, let the awareness of your body, feelings, or thoughts be in the background and place your focus on the person before you, giving them 100 percent of your attention. Notice how this feels.

As you listen or speak, begin to shift your attention back and forth, between yourself and the other person. Can you balance your awareness between the internal and external, including both?

As the conversation unfolds, notice any sense of connection. How does it feel to be here with this person? Rather than focusing on "me" or "you," can you put your attention on "us," the sense of being here together?

Next, expand your awareness to the space between or around both of you. Can you widen your awareness to the space of the room? Noticing ambient sounds, silence, or any gaps in the conversation can help you shift your attention to this wider frame. Notice how this feels.

Finally, explore moving between these reference points: your own embodiment, balanced attention between self and other, the sense of "us" or connection, and the wider space within which the conversation is happening. What qualities do you notice in each?

These are advanced practices and require time to develop. Each lends a unique strength and can be useful at different times. Balancing attention between self and other can serve as a resting place through the shifts and changes of a conversation. The sense of "us" can be particularly useful in savoring a sweet moment or accessing compassion in a trying one. The widest frame can be helpful when things get intense, giving you a large container to hold strong emotions.

Uncertainty: Meeting the Unknown

Presence also reveals the fundamental uncertainty and mystery of being alive. Human beings are unpredictable. No matter how well I know someone, I can never be sure what they are thinking, how they are feeling, or what they will say. I can't know how a conversation will evolve. We can plan and strategize all we want, but how often do things unfold the way we imagined?

If we become fixated on a plan, we lose touch with the moment. When that happens, we lose access to wisdom. Our ability to respond appropriately to what's *actually* happening becomes clouded by preconceived ideas about what we think *should* be happening. When we plan, can we recognize our ideas for what they are: a tentative, imagined future?

There is a saying in Zen: "Not knowing is most intimate." True presence always entails a tremble of uncertainty. This is healthy; it means we are in touch with reality. When we first begin to experience the uncertainty of true presence, we may feel unsettled or vulnerable. Over time, we learn to feel more at ease with not knowing. What was initially uncomfortable gives way to a feeling of aliveness.

Here we arrive at a fuller sense of what it means to lead with presence. We are aware of what's happening within and around us in an honest way. We include the other person with mutual respect. We are alert to the inherent uncertainty of the moment, pregnant with possibility. We train ourselves to rest with this poise—flexible, honest, mutual, and uncertain.

As our skill in leading with presence grows, our embodied awareness becomes a resource that is available at any moment: helping us discern how we're feeling and what we need to say, catching the signals of reactivity and providing the space to handle that energy, and perceiving the wealth of information that's coming from our interlocutor so that we can guide the conversation toward greater connection and understanding.

The leading edge of conversation is always mindful presence. The more we see its strengths and benefits, the more we trust it as a core foundation for human relationship.

PRINCIPLES
Leading with presence includes mutuality, seeing the other person as an autonomous individual, and uncertainty, acknowledging and accepting the unknown, both of which create new possibilities in dialogue.

KEY POINTS
We can practice presence in conversation with:

- Choice Points: Notice the choice between listening and speaking.
- Pausing: Experiment with taking micropauses or longer breaks.
- Pace: Modulate our pace to bring more awareness to speaking.
- Relational Awareness: Develop a balance of inner and outer awareness.

QUESTION & ANSWER
Q: I'm confused. When I try these practices with another person, it seems as if I am less present. Am I doing something wrong?
Remember that there's a difference between using a practice and the experience of presence. The practices are tools to strengthen our capacity to stay alert and balanced in conversation. At first, they can feel unnatural and even distracting. Like learning anything, it takes time to feel comfortable.

What's most important is to choose a tool that feels relatively easeful and stick with it until it becomes second nature. It's easy to feel present when talking with a friend and all is well. But when things get heated, if we haven't trained ourselves to lead with presence, we're more likely to fall back on old habits. Developing a reliable method for cultivating presence increases our chances of remembering to use these tools when we need them the most.

Q: I get really anxious when I try bringing more presence to conversations. It feels so vulnerable, like I'm totally exposed. Do you have any suggestions?

Presence means feeling more vulnerable; that vulnerability is a sign that you are in touch with reality. Part of the anxiety may be not having enough tools. It's a little bit like a butterfly that's just come out of a chrysalis; its wings are too tender to fly.

Give the process time, like a butterfly drying its wings in the sun. Do what you can to keep from feeling overwhelmed. When we're overwhelmed, we stop learning. By contrast, if things are too comfortable, we don't grow. Aim for the middle, what NVC Trainer Miki Kashtan calls "strategic discomfort."

We can learn to inhabit that space with ease. Study the feeling of vulnerability. Investigate what's happening in your body; examine any beliefs or fears in your mind. As your capacity to tolerate the discomfort grows, you can begin to relax and find your bearings. Vulnerability is a doorway to a more fulfilling experience of being alive. It can be a gift rather than a liability.

Q: How do you actually remember to use these tools? I find myself reacting and arguing before I can do anything. Sometimes I don't remember until hours afterward!
It's humbling, isn't it? The Tibetan Buddhist teacher Chögyam Trungpa Rinpoche once said, "Spiritual practice is one insult after another." Communication practice can feel that way too! Take the long view and create a positive feedback loop. What matters most is *that* we remember, not *when* we remember. We can capitalize upon that moment by celebrating it rather than beating ourselves up.

The next part is being persistent. It's entirely possible to develop more presence in our lives; the history of human contemplative traditions is a testament to that. It takes patience, dedication, and a willingness to forget and remember again and again. Over time, the gaps get shorter. Instead of days elapsing, it's hours; then instead of hours, it's minutes; and so forth until we're able to remember in real time, in the midst of a conversation.

The wonderful thing is that most people welcome a do-over. If you realize you totally bungled a conversation, why not let the other person know? Say, "Hey, I said some things I didn't mean earlier. Would you be up for rewinding and trying that again with me?"

part two

the second step

come from curiosity and care

IF WE WANT to speak our truth and listen deeply, leading with presence gets us on the map. Once we're actually here, the next step is choosing a helpful intention to ensure that we're pointed in the right direction. This is like checking that the map is oriented correctly. We can put a lot of energy into a conversation, but if our intention is off, we might be heading in the wrong direction.

The second step of mindful communication is to come from curiosity and care. Our intention can determine the whole tone and trajectory of a dialogue. *Intention* is where we're coming from inside. It's the motivation or inner quality of heart behind our words or actions. You could say it's the vector that drives what's happening in one direction or another. Intention is about how and why we speak or listen.

A great deal of our communication is nonverbal: body language, facial expressions, gestures, tone of voice. We can say one thing and communicate the complete opposite. In other words, *how* we say something is equally important—if not more important—than *what* we say. All of this is shaped by our intention.

If we're not consciously choosing our intention, we're on automatic—relying on unconscious, habitual patterns. If that's what's happening, it's pretty hit-or-miss whether we're going toward our destination.

So where are we coming from? How are we approaching the conversation? In this section of the book we'll look at some of our habitual ways of relating to conflict, the shortcomings and limitations of that conditioning, and how we can realign our intentions to have more effective and meaningful conversations.

the blame game

Children learn to speak, though they have no learned teachers.
—UNKNOWN

I DID A lot of backpacking in my early twenties. One winter, a good friend from college and I headed out for a few days of snow camping in New York's Catskill Mountains. Aaron is a poet, musician, and composer. We'd been close in college, spending many hours together pondering religion, philosophy, and the utter mystery of being alive. Since graduating, I'd wanted to stay in touch more than he had.

On the trip I decided to try out some of my newfound Nonviolent Communication skills. I felt hurt and angry, and I expressed my desire for more connection and closeness. I asked him why he hadn't been in touch, inviting him to open up and share more. Aaron was quieter than I was, but I kept pushing. Needless to say, it didn't go well.

Looking back, I can see that I wasn't leading with presence or coming from curiosity and care. Though I genuinely wanted to connect, I was so focused on *my way* of doing so that I failed to see him for who he was or get curious about what was going on for him. I wasn't able to balance my own longing for closeness with care for his needs. I don't think I even checked if he was willing to have the conversation: "Hey man, I've missed you a lot since we graduated. I think we might have different expectations of keeping in touch. Are you up for talking about that?"

In addition, my intention was off. My approach was mixed with subtle layers of blame (I thought to myself: "*Why* hadn't he been in touch? Wasn't that what friends do?") and manipulation ("What's so hard about sharing feelings? Couldn't he just say what was on his mind?") After that trip we drifted further apart. It caused me great pain to lose him as a friend. In spite of many attempts on my part to reach out, we've never reconnected.

Intention is the motivation or inner quality of heart behind our words and actions.

This is the power of intention and the risk of not choosing it wisely. Others can feel where we're coming from inside, regardless of how polished our words are. Perhaps you've had the experience of talking to someone who's taken a communication workshop and now has fancier words to run the same old trips? We can make "I statements" and "active listen" all we want; if we're not genuine in our intention to connect, it's unlikely to bring us closer.

Our Unconscious Training

What's our default when we're on automatic? To transform our intentions in conversation, we need to examine how we are looking at things.

Let's take a fairly common situation between housemates. Have you ever lived with someone who didn't like things as tidy as you? You leave the kitchen neat while they let things pile up. When they do clean, it's not up to your standards. If this is familiar, you've probably found yourself feeling exasperated, saying, "What's wrong with you? Why are you so messy? Is it that hard to . . . ?" Maybe you even called them a slob!

Yet if you've ever been in the other role, your response probably went something like this: "Why are you such a neat freak? Can't you just relax?"

In professional situations, depending on how we relate to the details, the other person is either "disorganized and unprofessional" or "anal and micromanaging." In romantic relationships, the person who wants more closeness and affection sees their partner as "aloof" or "distant," while their partner may see them as "needy and dependent."

Do you see the underlying pattern? Whatever is happening with me, regardless of which side of the equation I'm on, becomes about *you*. If I want something different than you do, it's somehow your fault. When our needs aren't met, we play the blame game.

Step back and consider the logic here. If I want you to change your behavior, how useful is it for me to tell you what's wrong with you? What a backward strategy for inspiring change! I was astounded the first time I heard Marshall Rosenberg name this blatantly obvious pattern. When approached with blame and criticism people usually defend themselves, which makes it harder to communicate. A more extreme example is yelling to feel heard. How does that usually work out? When we're on automatic, we end up employing strategies that have little chance of working or that backfire.

The pattern also gets inverted. We inflict that critical eye inward and blame ourselves. "It's my fault. I'm always . . . I'll never . . ." It's still the same game, just turned in the other direction: unmet needs equals someone's fault.

The Deeper Roots of Our Training

To understand how we approach conflict, we have to look deeper than intentions of blame or defensiveness. The roots of the blame game are in how we've learned to perceive difference.

Long before we learn about gravity in school, we know that if we let go of something at a height it will fall to the ground. This understanding is ingrained in our bodies through lived experience. In the same way, we learn much more than our mother tongue from our parents and society. As NVC trainer Miki Kashtan explains in her book, *Spinning Threads of Radical Aliveness*, we also learn a worldview.

Through repeated experience we form basic stories about who we are, how the world works, and what's possible in life. Depending on where and when we grew up, our class and social location, we learn certain things about what it means to have a male or female body; to have light- or dark-colored skin; to be part of a certain community, religion, or group; and so on. Perceptions of difference become as ingrained as the feeling of gravity, in spite of the fact that they're socially constructed.

Beneath all these layers lie ideas about human relationship that have been passed on by our family, culture, and society. We all learn a basic story that forms the underlying template for how we view difference and conflict. For most of us, it goes something like this: we are separate and there's not enough, so people tend to be selfish to meet their needs. When we examine this orientation to human relationship and its results on our personal lives and social institutions, the implications are staggering. Scarcity and separation are essentially a recipe for war.[1]

This is part of our unconscious communication training. It's unconscious because we didn't choose it. We absorbed it from the environment around us. We studied it very closely growing up—learning as much as possible about how our family system works, then how school works, and eventually how society functions. What are the rules? How do I take care of myself? How do I survive and find safety for my person, family, and community?

It's also unconscious because it generally wasn't intentionally chosen by those from whom we learned it. Just as no one chooses their mother tongue, no one chooses their conditioned worldviews. In most cases, our parents simply passed along their way of understanding the world—based on the society in which they lived and their social location—without questioning it.

We learn these lessons early in life. When our needs as children didn't align with the expectations of adults around us, what was the outcome? Usually someone got what they wanted, and someone didn't. Every time this happened, regardless of the outcome, we implicitly learned three things: (1) difference usually means someone wins and someone loses, (2) those with more power get their needs met more often, and (3) conflict is inherently dangerous because we can lose that which is important to us.

We see this play out every day in our public and private lives. Adults regularly use force with children when safety is not at stake, using their power to get children to behave in ways that are socially acceptable or convenient. "Couches aren't for jumping." "We have to leave now." This is how we internalize our default patterns. Instead of teaching children how to consider their own needs in relation to the needs of those around them (which is possible at ages much, much younger than we think, even with toddlers), we force children to do what we want because it seems more efficient, or because we lack the energy or skill to do it differently. As best we know how, we train our children to function in a society that is not centered around meeting human needs, often passing along the very mechanisms that create and perpetuate separation and competition.

Intertwined with these lessons come ideas of right and wrong, good and bad, should and shouldn't. When there is a disagreement or difference, someone is right and someone is wrong. To protect the well-being of others, we're taught to rely on external concepts of morality and obligation rather than being guided to recognize our innate ethical sensitivity or to rely on dialogue. As we grow up, these messages are continually reinforced through experience as well as through the media and entertainment industries.[2]

View Determines Intention

How we view things determines how we relate to them, which shapes our intention. If we view conflict as a dangerous affair, one of scarcity (of time, energy, resources, goodwill, or creativity) in which our only options are to win or lose, we play the blame game; we try to win by going on the offensive, or we try to protect ourselves. When we view things in terms of right and wrong, we are further compelled to judge or defend. If we see other human beings merely as objects in relation to our needs, aiding or blocking us from achieving our goals, we attempt to coerce, manipulate, or control the situation to get our way.

Based on our life experiences we form certain *views*. Those views engender certain intentions, which tend to reproduce the same experiences. Over time, our experiences and worldviews cocreate and reinforce each other.

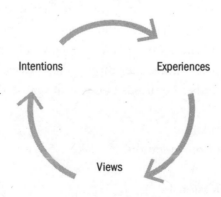

Intentions   Experiences

Views

FIGURE 1. CYCLE OF INTENTIONS

Principle: Our intentions, views, and experiences reinforce each other: views determine intentions, intentions shape experiences, and experiences confirm our views. Shifting our view therefore can change our intentions and our experience.

The table below outlines some of the fundamental, conditioned views we pick up in life and their most likely results.

VIEWS →	Lead to → INTENTIONS	Create → EXPERIENCES
Win/Lose Right/Wrong Conflict is dangerous, a problem, something wrong Others seen as objects in relation to our needs	Attack/Demand Protect/Defend Blame/Judge Coerce/Manipulate/Control	Fear, Anxiety Anger, Aggression Shutting down, Freezing Judgment, Rejection Disconnection Alienation

Four Habitual Ways of Responding to Conflict

Because of this conditioning, very few people feel at ease in the face of conflict. The word *conflict* literally means to "strike together." Its earliest form referred to armed battle![3] Our internal experience mirrors the meaning. When we believe one person's needs will be met at the expense of the other's, conflict is inherently threatening. We each tend to respond to this "striking together" of needs in one of several different ways:

1. Conflict Avoidance
2. Competitive Confrontation
3. Passivity
4. Passive Aggression

Each of these default strategies has its own logic, strengths, and dangers. Remember, these are learned, internalized behaviors; they're not our fault. They're deeply rooted patterns based on the painful socialization process and repeated life experiences. We use them because they've worked to some extent. The first step to shifting these patterns is to see how they operate in our lives. When we're more aware of them, we can begin to investigate and transform the underlying beliefs and emotions that hold them in place and start to make different choices.

> *Principle:* **Being aware of our habitual conflict styles allows us to transform the underlying beliefs and emotions that hold them in place and to make different choices.**

PRACTICE: Exploring Conflict Styles

As you read the following sections, consider which conflict style(s) you tend toward. What's your go-to strategy? Do you have different patterns with different people? What's the common orientation in your family? In your culture? Which strategies do those around you employ most often?

Conflict Avoidance

The default stance of conflict avoidance can be summed up in two words: *anything but.* This approach aims to circumvent or avoid addressing a conflict, sometimes at very high costs. We might change the subject, focus on positive things, ignore a problem, or flat out pretend it's not happening.

Conflict avoidance is at play when we decide to live with things the way they are to avoid the stress of a difficult conversation. It's the strategy of a family member who refuses to discuss another's addiction. It's operating when a colleague sidesteps our request by changing the subject or won't tell us that they disagree with our choices on a project.

The aim and hope of conflict avoidance is usually to keep the peace. One or more of the following unexamined beliefs often lie beneath avoiding conflict:

- Conflict is dangerous.
- Others will be offended if I bring up this conflict or discuss our differences.
- More harm will be caused by my trying to address this than letting it be.
- If I don't deal with it, it will go away or resolve itself.

Underneath this strategy are often needs for connection, safety, or belonging. Avoiding (or postponing) conflict can maintain harmony and temporarily preserve relationships. This strategy often comes with an ability to sense the needs of others but a failure to honor our own needs. It's usually supported by noticing and celebrating what's going well and a certain flexibility in adapting to difficult situations or sidestepping them, sometimes minimizing contact with the person with whom we have the conflict.

When employed unconsciously, this strategy can be dangerous. Chronically avoiding confrontation breeds resentment and can destroy relationships from the inside out. It can lead to feelings of mistrust, confusion, and even self-doubt, where we sense something is awry but it's not being named. Over time, forcing ourselves to ignore and suppress our feelings and needs can engender a kind of emotional deadness.

In situations that are emotionally or physically abusive, conflict avoidance can be self-protective or can enable continued harm, depending on the circumstances. In these situations, the fear and uncertainty of change can prevent us from addressing the abuse. Instead, we choose the security of what's familiar. When what's familiar is abuse, the consequences can be tragic.[4]

Competitive Confrontation

Another common response to conflict is competitive confrontation. Here, we are forceful and push for what we want, sometimes driving so hard that we're unable to see the other person's point of view. This approach is often characterized by a quality of aggression and an exclusive focus on our own needs. We might raise our voice, blame, judge, demand we get our way, coerce, or even threaten others.

This strategy is plastered all over the Internet, entertainment, and social media. It's presented as the strong, dominant, male energy. This approach drove my conversations with Aaron on that winter camping trip. It's at play when one family member directly coerces another to attend an event. It's there when a coworker demands we do things their way or responds to our request by pointing out our shortcomings. Politicians use this strategy regularly, denouncing their opponents with personal attacks rather than considered analysis of the issues. It also occurs when conflict avoidance reaches a limit and we flip to the other side.

The goal of this approach is to ensure our needs are met at any cost; the method is control or domination. Underlying beliefs leading to a confrontational approach can include:

- I'm on my own; it's "every man for himself."
- If I don't stand up and fight, I'll lose my power or be destroyed.
- Vulnerability is weakness; any empathy I show will be used against me.
- I'm right; they're wrong.

The strengths inherent in the competitive approach are assertiveness, directness, and often a clarity about certain aspects of our experience. While we can appear strong and courageous when working this approach, we often feel great fear and protectiveness beneath the surface. Unconscious use of this strategy frequently means being out of touch with more vulnerable feelings and relational needs. Confrontation is usually connected with needs for autonomy, agency, safety, and knowing that we matter.

This kind of confrontation is distinct from a direct, openhearted engagement with conflict that includes care for both people's needs. Instead, it's limited by its rigidity and can be dangerous in its disconnection from empathy. The costs of this approach are high. We may get what we want but compromise others' trust or lose relationships entirely. People may avoid us or refrain from being honest for fear of an argument. The lack of collaboration can result in a loss of creativity; the absence of honest feedback can develop into loss of intimacy. Competition also comes at a cost to our own well-being, leading to feelings of isolation, alienation, and ignorance of our own needs for connection and compassion.

Passivity

Passivity is the opposite of confrontation. Here, we give up what we want and acquiesce to whatever requests, needs, or demands are presented by those around us. Some people do this so automatically that they offer to give up their needs preemptively, at the slightest suggestion that someone else may have a different preference.

When using this approach, others may perceive us as easygoing, accommodating, and conciliatory or as a pushover. We might say things such as "It doesn't matter . . . whatever you want." Passivity can be coupled with a tendency to blame ourselves to avoid conflict: "You're right . . . I'm sorry, it's my fault. I should have . . ." A roommate using this strategy accepts others' preferences in their house. In a romantic relationship, a passive response shows up as one person regularly deferring to the other's wishes. The coworker being passive will say yes even when they disagree.

Passivity is different from conflict avoidance, as the aim is to defuse any potential conflict by *abandoning* our own needs or preferences. Some of the core beliefs that may be present with passive behavior are:

- If I go along with this, everything will be okay.
- My needs don't matter. I don't deserve to be happy.
- If I give others what they want, they'll like me.
- I've done something wrong.

Being passive is often an attempt to meet needs for belonging, harmony, safety, and connection. Its close cousin, appeasing, impels us to shape ourselves to please others. Those who default to appeasing are often highly attuned to the needs of others and skilled at adapting to difficult situations. Both passivity and appeasing require great internal strength (it takes a lot of energy to suppress one's needs), yet those employing these strategies often feel weak inside.

The limits of passivity are that we have fewer options for meeting our needs, beyond the spontaneous goodwill of others. Over time, repeatedly giving in to others can breed resentment. It can lead us to become so disconnected from our own feelings, needs, and desires that we forget how to discern what's authentic.

The passive approach to conflict, though it aims to enhance a relationship by smoothing things out, can diminish connection and beget dullness over time. Intimacy depends on being able to know one another. When we refuse to share our true feelings and desires for fear of conflict or rejection, we deny those around us the opportunity to get to know us more deeply.

Passive Aggression

This strategy is an indirect form of confrontation, masquerading as passivity. When employing this approach, we express our displeasure about a situation in a roundabout way, often with some degree of veiled hostility while verbally maintaining that all is well. It can look like conflict avoidance, but we are actually taking actions to express our anger or dissatisfaction.

When we're being passive aggressive, we might clean everything in the kitchen *except* our roommate's dishes, in effect saying, "Clean up after yourself!" In a romantic relationship, a partner being passive aggressive may agree to do something and then silently sulk or seethe to show their displeasure. We might agree to do a chore and either "forget" to follow through or do it so poorly that the other person is unlikely to ask again. In a professional situation, we might procrastinate, deliberately avoid certain aspects of our job, or do them in such a way that it creates problems and more work for someone else.

The aim of passive aggression is usually to find some way to meet our needs when we don't believe that engaging directly will help. Beliefs beneath this behavior include:

- I don't have a choice.
- My needs don't matter.
- There's no space for me.
- No one else cares about what I want.
- Speaking up won't make a difference; it could make things worse.

The strengths of passive aggressive behavior can be a sharp and intuitive understanding of relationship dynamics, an ability to stay connected to our own feelings and needs in situations that may not support our autonomy, and a certain creativity in finding alternate ways of self-expression.

Beneath this pattern is often a feeling of helplessness. Faced with the choice of abandoning our needs entirely or expressing them indirectly, we choose the latter, often with thinly disguised contempt rooted in our sense of disempowerment. Some of the needs that may be at the root of this behavior are having autonomy and choice, being seen or knowing that we matter.

The short-term gains of this approach also come at a cost. Passive aggression can erode trust in relationships, create enemies, and eat away at our sense of well-being. Ironically, the more we use passive aggressive behavior instead of engaging directly, the less empowered we feel to advocate for ourselves.

Loosening the Grip of Habit

When we are stuck in habitual, conditioned views of conflict, our attention becomes narrowly focused on a way of seeing that is rooted in negative experiences from our past. Our whole nervous system enters a familiar pattern, based on our ingrained views and corresponding intentions. We feel anxious, aggressive, or frozen. We may go on the offensive, backpedal, or zone out and pretend nothing is happening. We easily lose touch with our deeper values, the importance of a relationship, or our capacity to see things from multiple perspectives. The humanity of the other person can become obscured by our thoughts, beliefs, or emotions.

We each know the frustration of feeling locked into these habitual modes. (If you weren't at least a little tired of the blame game, you probably wouldn't be reading this book.) Yet we rely on our habitual strategies because they serve us. If they didn't work to some extent, we wouldn't use them. To shed these patterns, we need alternatives. Before we'll give them up, we need to develop other approaches that work at least as well.

Mindfulness can loosen the grip of our habits and create the possibility of choosing a different course. As soon as we become aware of what's happening, we can reorient the map (our views), call forth different intentions, and guide our energy in a different direction.

Handling these habits—in ourselves and in others—takes care, skill, and persistence. In the next chapter, we'll explore how to step out of the blame game with another approach to conflict: collaboration. When we can engage in true dialogue, balancing our own needs with openness and care for another's needs, we move beyond the framework of either/or, of separation and scarcity, and new possibilities emerge.

PRINCIPLES

Our intentions, views, and experiences reinforce each other: views determine intentions, intentions shape experiences, and experiences confirm our views. Shifting our view therefore can change our intentions and our experience.

Being aware of our habitual conflict styles allows us to transform the underlying beliefs and emotions that hold them in place and to make different choices.

KEY POINTS

Habitual views of conflict lead to default intentions of blame and self-protection, which constellate in four habitual patterns:

1. **Conflict Avoidance:** attempting to avoid addressing conflict
2. **Competitive Confrontation:** engaging directly with aggression or force
3. **Passivity:** yielding to conflict by acquiescing, giving up our own needs, or appeasing
4. **Passive Aggression:** engaging indirectly by expressing displeasure or hostility while pretending that all is well

QUESTION & ANSWER

Q: How can I stop being so defensive? I like the idea of being more curious and open-minded, but in practice I find it really hard to do.

The most important step, which it sounds like you're already taking, is to become aware of what's happening—to notice the default patterns. Try to view these habits with a kindly eye. Remember, they've protected and helped us for years. If you're out at sea and the only thing you have to stay afloat is a log, you're not going to let go until something better comes along. The concepts and practices in this book are like a stabler, nimbler raft.

Once you see the pattern, investigate its benefits and its limits. Seeing this clearly will increase your motivation to try the new tools. The trick is to start small. In strength training, you start with five or ten pounds, not one hundred. The more you have small successes, the more your nervous system will trust and remember there's a new way of doing this.

Q: My pattern isn't to blame or attack others, it's to blame myself. How can I work with this?

We can be so, so hard on ourselves! I certainly got a good dose of that conditioning.

There are two basic ways of working with this painful habit. The first is to build up internal resources to counter the harshness of self-criticism. Cultivate positive practices such as gratitude and self-empathy (chapter 9), as well as other methods such as self-compassion and loving-kindness meditation. These practices strengthen resilience. It's like stepping out of a burning house to breathe fresh air.

The second aspect involves putting out the fire, which means transforming the pattern itself. Learn to develop a relationship of empathy, clarity, and firmness with that critical voice. Translate self-judgments to hear the messages behind them (chapter 10). What feelings and needs are that voice expressing? We can use mindfulness to investigate the beliefs upon which the pattern may be resting. Often such habits have roots in early childhood, so it can be helpful to get support from another person to disentangle and heal some of those places. It's equally important to find ways to simply say no to the critical voice. When the blame is strong, compassion might mean cutting off the pattern. Interrupt it and redirect your attention in whatever ways you can to break the cycle.

where are you coming from?

I developed NVC as a way to train my attention—to shine the light of consciousness—on places that have the potential to yield what I am seeking. What I want in my life is compassion, a flow between myself and others based on a mutual giving of the heart.
—DR. MARSHALL B. ROSENBERG

HAVE YOU EVER persevered through a challenging situation with a friend and come out the other side with more respect for one another? Or worked out a disagreement with a loved one, finding that you feel even closer, with more care and affection?

Intimacy is born in conflict. Difference can bring us together and help us know one another. Friction can be creative and synergistic, leading to new ideas and perspectives. These kinds of conversations are characterized by very different intentions than our unconscious communication behavior.

What if there were a way to identify and support the conditions that lead to this kind of experience? A way to shift out of our habitual responses to conflict to a more helpful approach? This is one of the central questions behind Marshall Rosenberg's development of Nonviolent Communication. In the beginning of his seminal book, he writes:

Believing that it is our nature to enjoy giving and receiving in a compassionate manner, I have been preoccupied most of my life with two questions. What happens to disconnect us from our compassionate nature, leading us to behave violently and exploitatively? And conversely, what allows some people to stay connected to their compassionate nature under even the most trying circumstances?[1]

Rosenberg grew up in Detroit in the 1940s. During that time, he witnessed the race riots in which dozens of people lost their lives. These events, and his experiences of anti-Semitism as a youngster, seeded in him a passion for understanding the roots of violence. He discovered that our thoughts and speech play a huge role in our ability to stay connected to compassion. His method of NVC comprises a systematic training of our attention—relearning how to think, speak, and listen in ways that are more conducive to peace and harmony.

Instead of getting caught in habitual narratives of blame and judgment, in NVC we learn to identify the specific *observations* we want to discuss, our *feelings* about those events, the deeper human *needs* from which those feelings arise, and our *requests* for how to move forward together. We learn to listen in the same way, sensing what's beneath others' words. The entire system rests upon one core theme: creating a quality of connection sufficient to meet needs.[2]

This isn't about *what* we say but rather *where* we're coming from. It's about our intention.

When Daryl Davis Met the KKK

Daryl Davis is an African American musician and author who spent the first years of his life abroad. It wasn't until age ten, in 1968, that he discovered people could hate him for his skin color. While marching with his all-white Cub Scout troop in Massachusetts, people threw rocks and bottles at him. The incident sparked a lifelong curiosity about human attitudes. "How can you hate me when you don't know me?" he wondered.

Years later, after playing a gig in an all-white bar in Maryland, Davis was approached by a white man who said it was the first time he'd "heard a black man play as well as Jerry Lee Lewis." Davis shared that Jerry Lee Lewis was a friend of his and that Lewis had learned to play from black musicians. The two continued their conversation and over time became friends. The man eventually shared the names of local KKK leaders, whom Davis contacted and interviewed for a book he was writing.

Davis asked them about their views on various subjects and listened. At first, the Klansmen never asked Davis for his thoughts, believing he was "inferior." However, with patient, friendly conversation and through Davis's continual effort to create a real connection, they gradually became interested in his side of things. It was as if Davis's own warmth and respect slowly drew forth those very qualities in them.

In the end, he formed friendships with many Klansmen whose beliefs shifted after getting to know Davis. Many left the Klan and even gave Davis their robes and hoods. Over the course of his work, Davis has convinced—through dialogue and friendship—more than two hundred members of the KKK to leave the organization.[3] Daryl Davis may have never taken an NVC class, but he understands the power of intention. When we create genuine human connection, radical transformation is possible.

Enlightened Self-Interest

Intention is the single most powerful and transformative ingredient in dialogue. It shapes our verbal and nonverbal communication, directing the course of a conversation. If you take nothing else from this whole book, I hope you will take with you the importance the intention to understand, to come from curiosity and care, has in your interactions.

This intention to understand represents a fundamental, radical shift at the basis of our orientation to a dialogue. It involves weeding from our consciousness any blame, defensiveness, control, or manipulation and instead focusing on creating a quality of connection that is conducive to collaboration. Everything I share with you in this book is designed toward this end: creating more connection and understanding.

To make this shift, we need to see the limits of our habitual responses and the value of the intention to understand—its potential for transformation, creativity, and wholeness. There are two key principles that support this. The first runs through this entire book: the less blame and criticism in our words, the easier it will be for others to hear us. When someone trusts that we're actually interested in understanding them—that we're not manipulating things to get our way, that we're not trying to win or prove them wrong—they can stop defending themselves and just hear what we're saying.

Principle: The less blame and criticism, the easier it is for others to hear us.

From this perspective, it's in our best interest to come from curiosity and care. If we're rooted in this intention, our verbal and nonverbal communication sends the message that we're genuinely interested, which ultimately helps create the space to hear each other and work together.

This leads to the next principle: the more mutual understanding, the easier it is to work together and find creative solutions. This seems self-evident, yet we often lose sight of this simple fact. When we comprehend the deeper reasons behind what each of us wants, we can start to collaborate.

Principle: The more mutual understanding, the easier it is to work together and find creative solutions.

We're wired to feel joy when we give and to feel empathy in the face of suffering. Contributing to others is one of the most rewarding experiences we can have. This natural impulse is like an inexhaustible well of goodwill deep within the human spirit.

Because we feel joy in giving and compassion with suffering, when we fully understand one another we *want* to help instinctively. If I truly understand what's in your heart, why you want what you want, I am moved to find a way to work together. When I can help you see why something is important to me, priorities shift and there's more space and willingness to collaborate. (Just think of a time when you initially said no to a request, only to agree later when you better understood the situation.)

This approach to conflict is at the heart of nonviolent resistance. We have more power and integrity when appealing to the humanity of our fellow beings. This was the principle underlying Gandhi's work, the civil rights movement, and why Rosenberg named his method *Nonviolent* Communication. Taking this approach doesn't mean that we are passive, that we don't assert ourselves or take a stand for what we believe in. Cultivating the intention to understand makes us more effective by leveraging our connection to one another's humanity.[4]

A Different Way of Seeing

Davis's story, and the stories of many others who meet hatred, racism, and bigotry with love, points to a different way of viewing the world. It's a view that Rosenberg was seeking when he asked questions about the nature of compassion and violence. It depends on our ability to look for the humanity in each other, to see beyond our disagreements to something more essential.

All human actions are attempts to meet fundamental needs. Beneath our behaviors, preferences, beliefs, and desires are certain longings for physical, relational, or spiritual needs. We all have needs for safety, belonging, connection, and empathy. We have needs for meaning, contribution, creativity, or peace. (We'll explore this concept in greater depth in chapter 7.)

One finds this idea across many religious, spiritual, and contemplative traditions, as well as in the behavioral and social sciences. In Buddhism, it's put succinctly: "All beings want to be happy." It's the kind of wisdom that struck me as being right intuitively the first time I heard it. *What* happiness looks like differs from person to person, even from day to day, but at the root is an attempt to meet our needs.

Principle: **Everything we do, we do to meet a need.**

Remembering this perspective is one key to being able to come from curiosity and care. The view calls forth the intention. Whatever is happening, we can get curious about the deeper human needs and values beneath our words or actions. When we understand each other at the level of our needs, our similarities outweigh our differences. This, in turn, creates a generative, positive cycle of views, intentions, and experiences.

The great strength of this approach is that it's not limited to our intimate relationships. Whether we want to enjoy time with a friend, collaborate with a coworker, or build a diverse coalition, our genuine intention to understand has the power to create or enhance connection (for its own sake and in service of meeting needs).

To employ this in conversation requires a few things. First, we need to build our capacity to come from curiosity and care. We need to really

VIEWS →	Lead to → INTENTIONS	Create → EXPERIENCES
Win/Win Conflict is natural, a ground for learning We share universal needs Others have inherent value, independent of our own needs	To inquire/listen To care To collaborate To connect	Intimacy, safety Belonging Understanding & mutual respect Creativity, synergy

home in on what it feels like to have a genuine intention to understand so that we can bring our mind back there at will. Next, we need to train ourselves to notice when we're operating from our habitual tendencies. Last, we learn how to find our way back to curiosity and care.

Coming from Curiosity and Care

Every child is born with a natural desire to understand their world. Just as we have the innate capacity to be aware, we all have the capacity to be interested. Just as we can train ourselves in presence, we can cultivate the intention to understand.

To genuinely understand something requires curiosity and care. Curiosity means that we are interested in learning. Learning requires humility; we must be willing to not know. *To understand* means "to stand beneath." To comprehend anything, we need to put aside our preconceived ideas and be open to new ways of seeing.

Curiosity also requires patience. Conservationist and researcher Cynthia Moss shared that it took her twenty years of observing elephants, closely studying their habits and movements, before she began to realize how complex they were.[5] Such enduring patience can only arise when there is true curiosity, a deep intention to understand.

In order to be interested in something, to give attention, we also need to care. We don't pay attention to things we don't care about, and we don't care about things we don't pay attention to. This caring can be about many things. We might care about integrity, staying true to our values. We might care about peace and well-being. We might care about broadening our perspective. We might care about resolving conflict in our own lives in order to nourish hope that we can do better as a society. We might care about transforming the systems and institutions within which we live.

What's essential is the *quality of care* itself, goodwill connected to the empathic sense. It includes warmth, vulnerability, and flexibility. Care means that we are open to being affected by what we learn, that we are committed to seeing the other person's humanity, and that we are willing to include their needs in the situation rather than be rigidly fixated on getting what we want in exactly the way we want it. All of this is possible with practice.

PRACTICE: Coming from Curiosity and Care

Explore cultivating curiosity and care in conversation. Beforehand, reflect on your intention. How do you want to approach things? Where do you want to come from inside? See if you can find a genuine intention to understand the other person—their thoughts, views, feelings, or needs. How does it feel to be genuinely interested?

Try recalling this perspective when you are in conversation. What matters to this person? What do they long for or need? What is the effect when you are able to come from curiosity and care? As always, try this out in low-stakes situations at first.

Mindfulness and the Intention to Understand

Our ordinary relationship to experience is to judge and control it. Sit down and observe your own mind for a few minutes and you'll notice these tendencies firsthand. We react to experience by moving toward what's pleasant and away from what's unpleasant, judging the pleasant as good and the unpleasant as bad.

Through mindfulness practice we find that this habit is not only futile but also stressful and exhausting. We waste a great deal of our energy chasing pleasure and resisting pain, trying to control things beyond our sphere of influence. The basic shift we make over and over again in formal meditation is to cultivate the intention to understand experience rather than judge or control it. The more we explore this in mindfulness practice, the more readily we can make this shift in our conversations and day-to-day lives.

🔊 **PRACTICE:** Observing with the Intention to Understand

Take ten minutes or more for seated mindfulness practice. Do whatever helps you to arrive: orient; take some slow, deep breaths; relax into your sitting posture.

Let your attention settle with the sensations of breathing in and breathing out, allowing your breath to be natural. Whenever you notice your mind has wandered, gently let go and bring your attention back to breathing.

Pay particular attention to when your mind reacts to experience, liking or disliking what happens. When you feel something unpleasant, do you resist it, pulling away? When you feel something pleasant, do you try to hold on to it? When thoughts come, do you grow frustrated or berate yourself? Notice how your mind judges and tries to control the flow of experience.

Each time you notice this reactivity, cultivate an intention to understand rather than to judge. Whatever is happening, can you bring some curiosity and care to the experience? Try to notice the difference between when your mind is interested in the present moment and when it is reacting—pushing or pulling, leaning forward or manipulating. Which happens automatically? Which is more peaceful?

There are many ways to cultivate the intention to understand in the midst of conversation. For me, one of the primary ways of strengthening curiosity and care has been to integrate these qualities into my daily life. Try it out for a period of time—a day, a week, or more. Anything that occurs—an email, a conversation—simply aim to understand. "What matters here—to me, to them? What can I learn from this?" The more we remember this way of looking at things and feel a sincere interest in learning, the easier it becomes to approach dialogue in this way.

A Mindfulness Bell

One of my first communication teachers, Sandra Boston, has a great shorthand for remembering to use these tools: "Just say 'Oh!'" Whenever we find ourselves slipping back into our old patterns, we can use the friction we feel as a kind of mindfulness bell, "Oh—I have some tools here! I can handle this." We recall our training and bring up a perspective conducive to curiosity and care.

The first step is to be able to identify when we're on autopilot. We learn to recognize the attributes of being caught in our old habits and use those very signs as reminders to wake up out of their trance. Returning to presence, we find some inner ground. Then we get curious—first and foremost about our own experience. "What's happening here? Let me try to just understand this." Try this next practice whenever you find yourself defaulting to unconscious communication habits.

PRACTICE: Just Say "Oh!"

As you get more familiar with your default conflict styles, begin to study their signature in your body, heart, and mind. What lets you know you're on automatic? Here are a few common signs:

Physical

- Tightness in your jaw
- Tension in your limbs or body
- Shallow or rapid breathing
- Flushes of heat, sweating, or cold
- Feeling disembodied, ungrounded, or "up in your head"

Emotional

- Fear, anxiety, or a feeling of wanting to run away
- Irritation, anger, annoyance, or a feeling of aggression
- An urge to protect, explain, or defend yourself
- Feeling frozen, overwhelmed, or stuck

Mental

- Thoughts or images of anger, hate, or negativity
- Thoughts or images of hopelessness or despair
- Thoughts or images of worst-case scenarios

Verbal

- An increase in the pace, pitch, or volume of speech
- Reluctance to speak or respond; withdrawing verbally
- "But... that's not what I meant..."
- "You don't understand... You're not listening..."
- "Should... never... always... right... wrong..."

When you notice any of these signs, pause internally. Silently name what you feel and try to relax any tension or tightness. Recall that you have a choice about how to proceed. Use whatever method helps you lead with presence (finding gravity, the centerline, breathing, touch points). Then use one of the suggestions below to bring forth some curiosity and care.

These patterns aren't the enemy. In fact, noticing them can become the cue to return to presence. They also can be important signposts to investigate and uncover what's driving our own reactivity, which in turn brings more space and balance to engage in dialogue.

PRACTICE: Recalling Your Intention

To whatever degree possible, find a genuine intention to understand. You can silently ask yourself a question to seed curiosity and care. Here are a few suggestions:

- "What's happening here? How can I relax and find some balance?"
- "What if there were something to learn here?"
- "What if we figured this out and became closer?"
- "How can we start to understand each other more?"
- "What might work for both of us?"

- "Regardless of the outcome, how do I want to handle myself here?"
- "What's most important to me? What are my needs?"
- "What matters to them? What do they need?"

Let that simple intention guide what you say or do next, perhaps even expressing it explicitly: "I'd really like to understand what's been happening for you."

At first, putting down our old habits and finding sincere curiosity take time. With practice, we can learn to notice what's happening and shift our intention in a matter of moments.

A couple of years ago, my girlfriend and I spent New Year's Eve moving out of our apartment. We'd spent the weekend packing and had been carrying boxes and furniture down two flights of stairs for a couple of hours. It was getting late, we were both tired, and my back hurt—a perfect storm for losing presence and the intention to understand.

In typical male fashion, I took charge of loading the van, telling Evan what to bring down next or instructing her where to leave things, all with mounting irritation due to my exhaustion. At a certain point, responding to my tone of stress, Evan declared with frustration, "I feel like everything you say is criticizing me, telling me I'm doing something wrong!"

I immediately felt defensive. Everything inside wanted to snap at her, "I'm just trying to get this done!" Instead, I closed my eyes and just stood there breathing hard. I could sense she was in pain, and I didn't want to add more. I felt a wave of anger rise through my body, everything burning. I didn't want to act from that place and knew there would be time to share my side of things after I made some space for her. I kept breathing and put my attention in my lower body to ground myself. I felt my feet on the floor and the wave passed. I exhaled, and my breathing slowed as my fists unclenched.

"I hear you," I said, looking at her. "I'm sorry my words have had that impact on you." I paused, waiting to see how this landed. "Thank you," she said, still huffing a bit but softening. In one or two more short exchanges we understood each other, let go, and went back to loading the van—feeling more at ease and aligned.

I don't always catch the wave. But that time my training allowed me to notice the impulse to defend, return to presence, and come from a different place inside. Had I missed those signals and acted out of habit, I can imagine the argument that might have ensued.

Two Questions

Resisting the force of our old habits can be hard. We might see what's happening but lack the restraint to keep from acting it out or the energy to shift our intention. Maybe we're having trouble trusting that a new approach will work. In these cases, investigating our expectations and recalling our values can help.

Rosenberg had a succinct way of doing this. He encouraged people to ask two questions: First, "What do I want the other person to do?" Second, "What do I want their reasons to be for doing it?"

If we only ask the first question, we might use any strategy we can to get our needs met. We may blame them. We may manipulate, coerce, or even threaten in some way. (That New Year's Eve, I might have snapped, "Will you stop being so sensitive—I'm just trying to get things done.") While these strategies may produce results in the short term, they come at a cost in the quality of the relationship. We lose some of the other person's trust and goodwill.

If we ask ourselves the second question, we're much less likely to resort to these strategies. Do we want the person to change their behavior because they fear punishment or retaliation? Or do we want them to do something out of an intrinsic motivation, because they understand its value or why it's important to us?

These questions prime us to come from a very different place inside, to strive to create more connection. Our whole angle becomes, "Let's see if we can understand each other." In my situation with Evan, I wanted her to stay focused on packing *because she understood what was happening for me*, not because I'd won an argument or proved her wrong. Once we understood each other, moving forward was easy.

When we fall back on our habitual patterns, it's easy to make assumptions about another's intentions. A friend running late or a partner forgetting an agreement can take on much larger significance, implying that we don't matter. "If you knew how much this mattered you would . . ." or "If you loved me, you would . . ." Having the intention to understand opens new ways of seeing what's happening and may create alternative ideas for addressing the situation.

Using Force to Protect

There are situations in life where an immediate result is more important than collaboration and dialogue—mostly when safety is involved. When our primary objective is to protect our own or another's well-being, we employ what Rosenberg calls the *protective use of force*. If a child is running into the street, we shout or grab them, doing whatever it takes to keep them safe.

This is complicated terrain philosophically. Does the end ever justify the means, and if so, when? Who has the authority to determine that? As soon as we decide it's okay to use unilateral force "for their own good" or "for the greater good," we run the risk of abusing power and causing harm.

For the sake of our exploration, I want to point out a few key differences between Rosenberg's protective use of force and relying on our default habits. First, in Rosenberg's definition, we use force consciously rather than fall back on it unconsciously out of desperation or habit. Second, we use force without any malice, with the wish to protect rather than to harm. Third, it is a temporary, time-limited strategy. Last, we remain connected to the other person's humanity instead of seeing them as a problem or enemy.

Once all are safe, we can return to a more relational approach. Systems of restorative justice (as opposed to retributive criminal justice) are based on these principles. Once the immediate danger is removed, we can work to build understanding, creating the conditions for repair and more safety in the future.

The Power of Curiosity and Care: Aikido in Action

Aikido teacher Terry Dobson tells one of my favorite stories about embodying curiosity and care. Dobson is an ex-marine who'd been studying the martial art of aikido in Japan with its founder. Though his teacher stressed that aikido is a way of peace and reconciliation, Dobson was eager to test his training in combat.

One afternoon in Tokyo, a large, drunk day laborer stumbled into the subway, cursing angrily. He lunged at a woman and her baby, nearly hitting them. Dobson stood up and called out to the laborer, ready to defend the passengers. The man began hurling insults at Dobson, who provoked him further by blowing a kiss in his direction. Just then, from the other side of the train, a sharp voice called out, "Hey! Come here and talk to me."

A little old man sat on the other side of the car. The laborer turned and yelled, "Why should I talk to you?"

"What'chya been drinking?" the old man asked.

"I been drinking sake, and its none of your goddamn business!"

"Oh, that's wonderful," the old man said with delight. "Absolutely wonderful! I love sake too. Every night, me and my wife—she's seventy-six, you know—we warm up a little bottle of sake and take it out into the garden, and we sit on the old wooden bench that my grandfather's first student made for him. We watch the sun go down, and we look to see how our persimmon tree is doing . . ."

As the old man spoke, the drunk man's expression began to soften. "Yeah, I love persimmons . . ."

The old man asked, "I'm sure you have a lovely wife too?"

Tears began to stream down the laborer's face, who shared that his wife had died. He began to sob, "I don't got no wife, I don't got no home, no job, no money, nowhere to go. I'm so ashamed."

Soon the laborer was sitting beside the old man, his head in his lap, allowing his matted hair to be gently stroked. Dobson concludes, "What I had wanted to do with muscle and meanness had been accomplished with a few kind words. I had seen aikido tried in combat and the essence of it was love. . . . I would have to practice the art with an entirely different spirit. It would be a long time before I could speak about the resolution of conflict."[6]

This is the transformative power of coming from curiosity and care, of staying connected to each other's humanity in the face of aggression. Creating this kind of connection is a skill that takes practice. Leading with presence is the prerequisite and primary foundation. Having a genuine intention to understand is the compass that points us in the right direction.

PRINCIPLES

The less blame and criticism, the easier it is for others to hear us.

The more mutual understanding, the easier it is to work together and find creative solutions.

Everything we do, we do to meet a need.

KEY POINTS

Intention shapes our verbal and nonverbal communication and directs the course of a conversation. The intention to understand includes curiosity and care:

- *Curiosity* means that we are interested in learning and recognize what we don't know.
- *Care* is goodwill. It depends on our willingness to pay attention and our commitment to seeing one another's humanity.

Mindfulness practice helps us cultivate the intention to understand rather than to judge. We can train ourselves to notice habitual tendencies to blame and shift to the intention to understand with these practices:

- Consider inwardly, "What matters to this person?"
- Just say "Oh!" Notice any habitual intentions and get curious.
- Recall your intention.
- Ask yourself two questions: "What do I want the other person to do? What do I want their reasons to be for doing it?"

QUESTION & ANSWER

Q: How do you come from curiosity and care when you believe the other person doesn't have good intentions, when they're deliberately doing something to upset you or make things difficult?

It's not easy, especially if it's a contentious situation with little mutual trust. First, you need to find a way to handle your *own* experience with curiosity and care: get empathy from a friend, use self-empathy to relieve any distress, and get clear about your own needs. I also encourage you to hold your interpretation about their intentions lightly. We long to make sense of their actions, but our assumptions aren't always correct.

All of this frees up space inside to inquire, "What could they be longing for?" Remember, everything we do, we do to meet a need. Try to shift your perspective. Can you see their actions as strategies to meet deeper, more universal needs? This attempt to stretch your heart and imagine their experience can be transformative.

The last piece is to try to cultivate some compassion for the other person, which will ease your heart from any bitterness and open more possibilities in the relationship. As the saying goes, "Hurt people hurt people." I encourage you to try to see their vulnerability, pain, or insecurity that may be connected to their actions.

Q: I tried coming from curiosity and care and it didn't work. The other person wasn't interested in what matters for me. It seems like this stuff only works if both people are using it.

It certainly makes it easier! But it only takes one person to change the dynamics of a relationship or shift a dialogue. If one person changes their stance, it affects the shape and flow of the process.

There are many factors at play here. We may start out curious but lose touch with that genuine intention when under pressure. It requires practice and skill to stay grounded in challenging situations. We may repeatedly need to meet intense blame or anger with balance, hearing their deeper needs, defusing aggression, and sharing our point of view in a timely and helpful way. Finally, it's important to examine our expectations of what success looks like. If we're only interested in getting our way, then we're not really open to dialogue. We have to be willing to shift, to discover creative possibilities.

A colleague tells the story of two groups of women in Boston—a pro-choice group and pro-life group—who met regularly to discuss their conflicting views on abortion. In the end, none of them changed their views, but they built meaningful relationships of mutual respect. When the pro-life group heard through their network about plans for someone to bomb an abortion clinic, they sent a clear message that such actions were not welcome in their community. To me, that's success. Their views hadn't changed, but they were not willing to use violence as a strategy to meet their needs because they had learned to see the humanity of the other side.

Q: What about situations where you know your needs aren't going to get met? It's just not going to happen. How do you handle that?
It can be so difficult, so painful when our needs aren't met. A big part of using these tools is to find ways to handle those times in life by mourning our unmet needs. It can be very healing to allow ourselves to feel both the sadness and the longing. Finding tenderness with those feelings helps us learn to be at peace with our unmet needs, which brings more freedom to our lives.

Part of this process is differentiating between our needs and any fixation we have on a specific strategy. A lot of the time, this mourning is about the loss we feel over a *particular strategy* not being possible. One of the benefits of identifying our needs is that it gives us more choice. It gives us access to more creative options.

I also would encourage you to be fully conscious of the difference between what's actually happening and your predictions or beliefs. Sometimes when we tell ourselves, "There is no way so-and-so would . . ." we are trying to protect ourselves from the disappointment or pain of rejection. See if it changes anything for you to frame it this way: "I'm having trouble imagining a way in which they would say yes to what I want." This can feel more empowering and might lead to a different choice about how you engage. Or it might lead to a different internal experience, one based on clarity about the other needs you are choosing to meet by not making a request.

don't let the call drop

Listening with ears is less fine than listening with the heart.
—HSU-T'ANG CHIH-YU

LISTENING IS A cornerstone of dialogue and a powerful metaphor for spiritual practice. When we come from curiosity and care, we're willing and able to listen. We're opening a conduit that allows connection and understanding to happen.

There are so many ways to listen. We can listen to the content of what someone says, to how they're feeling, to what's important beneath their words. We can listen halfheartedly or wholeheartedly.

To truly listen depends on a kind of inner silence. It requires that we empty ourselves and make space to receive something new. I had a powerful reminder of this a few years ago when I had a disagreement with Jeremy, an old friend from high school.

"Bro—you're not listening!" he exclaimed.

We were standing in his kitchen and he was passionately upset. Though I no longer remember the details, I remember that I was only half-listening. I was waiting for him to finish so I could explain my perspective. Even though I was completely silent, making eye contact, and hearing every word, he could sense that I wasn't really taking it in. I was building my case, preparing to defend myself.

I took a deep breath. Closing my eyes, I let go of my interpretation, my desire to explain. There would be time for that later. I put all of that down for the moment and just relaxed into listening and trying to understand. I felt my feet on the ground and opened my eyes.

"Okay," I said. "Go on." As soon as I released my agenda to defend myself, the whole tone of the conversation shifted.

"Thank you," Jeremy sighed as he continued, sensing that I now was actually willing and available to listen. He went on to explain how he was feeling and why. I listened, really heard him, and acknowledged the truth of his experience independent of my own feelings or views: "Yeah, I get that's how you felt. I can see why you'd be upset."

Offering some words of understanding, things settled. I may have shared my side—I can't recall, and it didn't even matter much anymore. The vital shift had been letting go enough to hear him with genuine curiosity and care.

Learning How to Listen

To listen entails a fundamental letting go of self-centeredness. We have to be willing to put down our own thoughts, views, and feelings temporarily to truly listen. It's a wholehearted, embodied receptivity that lies at the core of both communication and contemplative practice.

Every conversation requires silence. Without it we can't listen, and no real communication happens. The silence of listening isn't forced or strained. It's a natural quiet that arises from interest. When you want to smell a flower, what do you do? You close your eyes, get close, and inhale slowly. Your mind grows still as you find the aroma. This is perhaps the most powerful way to listen: with full presence. As the poet and teacher Mark Nepo writes, "To listen is to lean in softly with a willingness to be changed by what we hear."[1]

The wilderness has taught me a lot about how to listen. The ancient steadiness of an old-growth redwood, the stillness of a high mountain lake, or the vibrant music of a stream—all have the power to quiet the mind and still the heart. In the face of such wonders, our mental chatter falls away. What remains is a state of pure listening.

We learn this kind of deep listening in meditation, discovering the stillness of awareness. With practice we can access it in the midst of conversation. The more we learn how to listen, the more available we become for others and for our life in general.

This is just as important for the wonderful moments as it is for the difficult ones. True listening allows us to appreciate the presence of a loved one or to let kindness touch us. When sharing affection or a hug, Evan and I will often gently invite one another to be present in this way, asking, "Are you letting it in?" This kind of receptive listening can nourish the spirit.

PRACTICE: Listening Wholeheartedly

All listening begins with presence. When in conversation, see if you can bring your heart's full attention to listening. Notice any tendencies to interpret, comment, or plan what you'll say next. Can you return to the simplicity of presence over and over again and just listen, letting go of these tendencies when they arise?

Don't Let the Call Drop

One of our primary aims in dialogue is to make a connection (to the degree necessary to handle the matter at hand) and then to do our best to maintain it. If we lose that connection, communication wanes or ceases altogether.

This is most apparent in heated arguments, when all attempts to acknowledge or understand one another can disappear. Instead, we end up layering one charged statement on top of another, never slowing down to check if we're actually hearing one another. The call dropped long ago but we're both still talking.

Much of the time, we maintain connection nonverbally, through culturally appropriate body language: facial expressions, eye contact, tone of voice, and so forth. We nod or say, "Mm hmm." We may tip our head to the side, narrow our eyes, or furrow our brow to indicate that we're losing the thread or to ask for clarification. A speaker may even insert simple yes/no questions: "Are you still with me? Does that make sense? You know what I mean?"

This can create a lovely call-and-response rhythm that strengthens the connection by confirming that listening and understanding are occurring. In this way, we use presence and intention to keep checking that we're connected with one another, that the call hasn't dropped. It's like keeping one hand on the wheel while driving to ensure that we don't drift out of our lane. Most of us do this intuitively and automatically; we can enhance our capacities in this area by bringing conscious attention to this process.

PRACTICE: Staying Connected

The next time you are in conversation, track the connection. Use the first two steps—leading with presence and coming from curiosity and care—to make a connection with the other person. Then listen and use body language, facial expression, tone of voice, or short verbal inquiries to check periodically if you're still connected. Anytime the call drops—if you sense a disconnect or misunderstanding—slow down and see if you can reestablish the connection.

Completing the Cycle

Checking informally through voice and body language helps us assess the general connection in a conversation, yet it relies on an unspoken assumption. If I ask, "Do you understand?" and you say, "Yes," all I really know is that you *think* you understand. As the saying goes, the single biggest problem with communication is the illusion that it has taken place.

To make sure the call hasn't dropped, we need a more reliable method, an authentic, lightweight way to confirm that we're actually hearing one another. When listening, we want to know that we've heard correctly, and when speaking, we want to know if we've been understood. In difficult situations, the need is even greater.

"You're not listening! You don't understand!" How many times have you said (or heard) this in the midst of an argument? Just because we're speaking the same language doesn't mean we understand each other. We say one thing, they hear something else. They say one thing and mean something else. It's amazing how quickly we can get entangled!

When someone says, "You're not listening," part of what they mean is "I don't feel heard right now." It's often a plea for empathy and a sign that we've lost connection. To get back on track we first need to reconnect. Let's look at two examples of how this might play out in a conversation.

PERSON A: "You're not listening!"

PERSON B: "Yes, I am! I heard everything you said."

PERSON A: "You're not listening!"

PERSON B: "It sounds like you're not feeling heard. I'm really trying to listen but let me try again."

OR, PERSON B: "Okay—I'd really like to understand more. What could I do or say that would help you to feel heard?"

Which conversation is more likely to move toward resolution? In the first instance, each person may feel less understood, which usually spurs us to assert our position more forcefully. This leads to less connection, more assertions, and so on. Most of us know how awful it feels to be caught in this kind of a vortex, how quickly things devolve and how painfully they can end.

Notice the difference in the second example, when we find some willingness to listen with empathy. Here, the speaker acknowledges the other person's experience and tries to reconnect. Doing this depends on our ability to lead with presence and come from curiosity and care rather than fall back into our default modes of defending or blaming.

The main tool here is using a verbal reflection to "complete a cycle" of communication. We listen, then get confirmation at key moments that what one person *hears* matches what the other person *meant*, that message sent equals message received.

A *reflection* is a restatement of or inquiry about what's been said to confirm understanding.

If you're ordering takeout, the restaurant employee repeats your order back to you to check that they have it correctly. In conversation, know when to reflect what you hear before you respond. If you say something important, ask the other person for a reflection so you know if they heard what you intended.

Reflecting before we respond is a fundamental building block of communication. It can make the difference between an effective conversation and an argument. When we complete a cycle, it feels good. It's satisfying

FIGURE 2

to get confirmation and know we're hearing each other. There's often a sense of settling, relief, or a spontaneous outbreath. And when we feel heard, we have more space inside to listen to someone else. In this way, offering empathy and listening to someone else is in our best interest.

Principle: **People are more likely to be willing to listen when they feel heard. To build understanding, reflect before you respond.**

Evan and I often rely on this tool to work through difficulties. I remember one time, early in our relationship, we sat on the couch discussing our different expectations around frequency of communication.

> EVAN: "I feel trapped, like you'll get angry if I don't respond immediately."
> OREN: "Sounds like you're feeling frustrated because you'd like more time to respond to text messages when you're at work?"
> EVAN: "Yeah, it's just not reasonable to expect me to reply right away."
> OREN: "And you want some understanding for the fact that you have other responsibilities that may be more important than replying to my text messages?"

Evan majored in environmental engineering and enjoys the clarity of science. At one point, after we'd settled into a rhythm of completing each cycle before moving on to a new piece of content, she exclaimed, "Wow! I never knew communication could be like math!" When we have the tools and the patience to hear one another and work something out, it can be exhilarating.

In addition to providing the relief of feeling heard, reflecting before we respond slows things down. It helps create understanding one step at a time—speaking, listening, reflecting—and gives each person time to integrate what's been said.

We may need to reflect many times in a given conversation before responding. It can take several cycles of empathic reflection before there is sufficient connection, particularly when someone is emotionally activated. If we stick with it, this kind of persistent empathy can have dramatic results.

PRACTICE: Reflect Before You Respond

Experiment with reflecting before you respond in a low-stakes conversation. After the other person shares something important, offer a reflection of what you heard to check that you understand. Do this when nonverbal confirmation is insufficient, when there is a lot of content, or when strong emotions are present.

Pointers

- Offer your understanding of what the other person has said in words they can easily relate to.
- Phrase your reflection as a *question* rather than a *statement*. You're checking to ensure you understand rather than telling someone what they said.
- Stay connected to genuine curiosity and care.
- Keep your language as natural and authentic as possible.
- Try this with celebrations and successes as well as difficult news.

Watch for signs of completing a cycle: a verbal affirmation, an outbreath, or some settling. Even if your reflection is not 100 percent accurate, it often leads to more connection because it gives the other person the chance to clarify or explain further what they mean.

Examples

STATEMENT: "I just can't believe she would say that. After all we went through..."

REFLECTION: "You're really stunned that she said that, huh?"

OR: "It sounds like you're really upset, trying to figure out what would motivate her to say that?"

STATEMENT: "I'm sick and tired of being the only one around here who does anything!"

REFLECTION: "Wow—you're totally fed up. You feel like you're the only one doing anything?"

OR: "You're really sick of this, huh? Are you wanting more teamwork or balance in the chores?"

Keeping It Real

What I'm encouraging here is different from what's often called "active listening." Many people learn to do this with stock phrases such as "So what I hear you saying is . . ." When we use a technique without being genuine, our speech sounds formulaic, which reduces connection. And we can miss the point. We get so focused on the technique that we forget to really listen.

It's essential right from the beginning to not lose sight of the principle beneath the training. Reflecting before you respond is a *tool* to build enough connection and understanding to collaborate. It's not a dogma: "Thou shalt always reflect before you respond."

Communication practice is not about what we say. It's about where we're coming from and how we say it. Let the sincerity of your intention guide your listening and your words. What would you say if you genuinely wanted the other person to feel heard? How would you check that you understood? How would you ask, if you genuinely wanted to feel heard?

It's also important to note that no matter how hard we try to be natural, there's often a period of awkwardness in learning anything. It takes time to find our voice and get comfortable with a new way of communicating.

The Roots of Empathy

At the heart of verbal reflection is empathy: an intuitive reaching to understand another's experience on its own terms. Without empathy, the reflection will feel empty.

Spend time with a giggling toddler or a puppy and something inside softens. Stand near someone who is angry or panicked and we feel it! This is the phenomenon known as *emotional contagion*. Babies begin to cry when they hear other babies crying. When we see that toddler or puppy hurting, something inside us quivers. We feel a compassionate impulse to reach out.

Today we are learning more about the neurological and evolutionary bases of empathy. Infants need empathic connection for their brains to develop properly. One of the most groundbreaking findings for the neurobiology of empathy was the discovery of mirror neurons, which provide an immediate kind of somatic empathy. Mirror neurons fire when we see another being perform an action. Part of our brain is silently enacting the movements of those around us as if we were doing them ourselves. This includes facial expressions. Our brains inwardly mimic the emotional expressions of others; they're wired for empathy.

Empathy is at the heart of listening. When I closed my eyes and took the time to really hear Jeremy, I was shifting gears to empathy. Empathy plays many functions: it can create healing and build resilience; it can stimulate healthy bonding; it can de-escalate strong emotions, facilitate understanding, and help resolve differences.

Empathy is the capacity to understand or feel what another person is experiencing from their point of view.

Empathy literally means to "feel into." While it can be expressed in many ways (silent listening, verbal reflection, touch, action), empathy is primarily *a quality of presence* in the heart. It's a receptive attunement to felt experience, our own and others'. We could say that empathy is a union of presence and the intention to understand. It's a genuine, caring interest that allows us to reach into another's world and understand their experience. Carl Rogers, one of the founders of humanistic psychology, described empathy in this way:

Empathy is a complex, demanding, strong, yet subtle and gentle way of being . . . it means entering the private perceptual world of the other and becoming thoroughly at home in it. It involves being sensitive moment to moment to the changing felt meanings which flow in this other person.[2]

This resonant, receptive faculty of empathy is one of the primary qualities that makes us human.[3] Given adequate safety, sustenance, and other basic needs, the natural tendency of the human being is toward empathy and compassion—to feel *with* another.

Roadblocks to Empathy

While empathy is innate, all sorts of conditions can hinder it. Most broadly, we learn not to be empathic through the socialization process. We are taught (by our family, culture, society) to fear or hate those different from us. We shut off our empathic capacity in order to fit in, to protect ourselves, or to get by in a world that is not structured to meet our needs.

Being disconnected from empathy comes at a high cost, as Miki Kashtan explains in *Spinning Threads of Radical Aliveness*:

To say, as I believe, that we are "hard-wired" for mutual recognition and empathy does not necessarily mean that we will always act in caring, compassionate ways. Rather, it means that to the extent that we ignore care and empathy and cultivate other emotional postures, we pay enormous prices: depression, apathy, nightmares, victimization, and anger on an individual level, and crime, neglect, and isolation on a societal level.[4]

Reclaiming our capacity for empathy is essential for well-being, for healthy relationships, and for effective dialogue. Many of the same things that disconnect us from presence will reduce access to empathy: being tired, stressed, or hungry; feeling emotionally activated, angry, or helpless; wanting something intensely or being attached to a specific outcome. Empathy can be blocked by strong views, fear, anticipation of pain, or burnout. There is even new research that suggests the more time we spend on electronic devices, the less empathy we feel.[5]

When we don't receive the empathy we want from others and don't realize (or forget) that there are things that can *block* empathy, we can make up stories to try to explain what's happening. We may assume there's something wrong with us, or with the other person, or that they don't care. Instead of believing these stories, we can recognize that the conditions for empathy to emerge might not be present. This leaves more room to come from curiosity and care, to identify those conditions and address them creatively.[6]

There are some fairly common ways we respond when we aren't feeling empathy. The psychologist Thomas Gordon calls them "communication roadblocks" because they hinder connection and understanding.[7]

PRACTICE: Identifying Roadblocks to Empathy

Take a moment to think about a time you felt frustrated or stuck. It can be something difficult (a relationship breakup) or mundane (getting the runaround at the DMV). Imagine telling a friend about it, then read the responses below.

BLAMING, JUDGING, OR CRITICIZING: "It's probably your fault. You always mess things up."

LECTURING, TEACHING: "You need to learn how to advocate for yourself. You should have spoken up ..."

GIVING ADVICE: "What you need to do is ... I know a great therapist ..."

WARNING, THREATENING: "You better take care of this soon or ... How many times have I told you ..."

ORDERING, DIRECTING: "Get over it. It's time to move on."

ANALYZING, DIAGNOSING: "The problem is ... I think there's a pattern here that may have to do with your childhood ..."

COMPARING, "ONE-UPPING": "You think that's bad? This one time ..."

DISTRACTING, SARCASM, HUMORING: "So, what are you going to do with your free time? Have you seen that new film?"

QUESTIONING: "Where were you? Why did you get involved with this?"

PRAISING, AGREEING: "You are the most generous, kind person I know ... You're right ..."

SYMPATHIZING, REASSURING: "Oh, you poor thing ... You did the best you could. It'll be okay."

How does it feel to not be received with empathy? Which of these types of responses do others in your life employ? On which do you rely habitually?

The difference between empathy and some of these responses can be subtle. Sympathy, generally regarded as positive, can contain a quality of pity that is marked by separation and a reluctance to encounter another's pain. Questioning can derail the speaker's train of thought. Praising and agreeing, while validating, may ignore another's emotions. Even reassurance can fail to offer adequate space to feel what's true and is often motivated by our own discomfort.

While some of these responses may be useful at the appropriate time, they are usually habitual and automatic, taking the place of genuine empathy. What would it be like, instead, to *feel into* the other person's experience? Maintaining presence, how might you respond from natural empathy?

With empathy, we join another in what they feel. It's often expressed more through our tone than specific words. We can say "I'm so sorry" with cool distance or with sincere concern. At its core, empathy seeks to know experience directly, on its own terms, without trying to fix it, change it, or explain it. This willingness to be *with* experience is the key to empathy.

Three Dimensions of Empathy

Maya Angelou once said, "If I had the power, I would make everybody an African American at least for one week; know what it's like."[8] What would be the effect if everyone in the United States knew *from the inside* the daily experience of living with brown skin in America? That kind of empathy could begin to heal the legacy of slavery and racism in this country.

True empathy is three-dimensional; it is at once cognitive, affective, and somatic. Cognitive empathy is about taking the other's perspective.

It's the ability to put ourselves in another's shoes and understand intellectually how a person feels. Affective (emotional) empathy means being able to feel *along with* the other person. It goes beyond a cognitive grasp of another's internal world to an emotional experience of it. Just as a stringed instrument vibrates with harmonic resonance, so too our heart can tremble in resonance with the suffering or delight of another.

The third kind of empathy is somatic empathy, which is the ability to sense another's experience in an embodied way.[9] This is a visceral, gut-level understanding. In his renowned book *Between the World and Me*, the African American writer Ta-Nehisi Coates describes a powerful somatic empathy in a letter to his teenage son:

> But all our phrasing—race relations, racial chasm, racial justice, racial profiling, white privilege, even white supremacy—serves to obscure that racism is a visceral experience, that it dislodges brains, blocks airways, rips muscle, extracts organs, cracks bones, breaks teeth. You must never look away from this. You must always remember that [it lands] . . . with great violence, upon the body.[10]

Deepening empathy is not merely a cognitive or intellectual exercise, though it begins there. It is an endeavor to inhabit both an emotional and an embodied understanding of another's experience. Without these complementary dimensions, our empathy will be incomplete. When cognitive empathy is divorced from affective empathy, it can be used to manipulate or harm others, even to make torture more effective. True empathy is the integration of all three of these domains. It can bring healing, resilience, and transformation.

Empathy challenges the view that we are separate and invites us to reach for our shared humanity with others. The first step is connecting more deeply with our own experience through mindfulness. Self-awareness is the basis for empathic connection. As we experience the inner landscape of our life with more detail and richness, so grows our ability to understand the inner lives of others.[11]

We then need to put down our own story, to step outside of our frame of reference. In describing the role of empathy in his craft, Broadway actor Okieriete Onaodowan put it quite eloquently: "To walk a mile in my shoes, you must first take off your own."[12] We stretch our heart and mind beyond our own views, opinions, and feelings to envision the inner world of another. We use imagination, creativity, and intuition to sense what it might be like to live inside their skin.

Listening with empathy is a primary way of coming from curiosity and care and a building block of dialogue. Here are three ways you can begin to practice bringing more empathy into your life that synthesize what you've learned in this chapter.

PRACTICE: Empathy

Try practicing this in conversations that aren't about you. It's often easier to access empathy when you're not under fire. Remember that empathy is not in the words; it's a quality of presence in your heart. Aim to understand the other person's experience and let the words flow naturally.

SILENT EMPATHIC PRESENCE: Practice listening completely, with the heartfelt intention to understand and "feel into" what the other person is saying. How is this for them?

PARAPHRASE: After listening, summarize the gist of what you've heard. What are the key features of what they've said? Sometimes simply repeating one or two key words can be enough.

EMPATHIC REFLECTION: After listening, check that you understand by reflecting what you hear is *most important* to them. This may include how they feel and/or what they need. What matters most to this person, beneath the story? How can you help them feel heard? Remember to phrase your reflections as questions, checking to ensure you've got it right.

There are many other ways to show empathy. We may express empathy through a kind word, with loving touch, or by sharing how we feel in response to what we hear. At times, we can show empathy by expressing interest with open-ended invitations, "Tell me more . . ." or "What else?"

My student Susan teaches high school art and told me the following story. Avery, a freshman who is usually cheerful and bubbly, began showing up early to class. Susan struck up a conversation and realized how much

Avery was struggling. They agreed to meet later that day to talk, when Susan had more time.

"I don't want to go to this school anymore," Avery said. She was thinking about dropping out. Susan noticed the impulse to go into problem-solving mode, an old habit of hers. Having just finished our week's lesson on empathy, she paused and decided to try listening instead. "Tell me more. What's going on?"

Avery began to open up. She was being bullied. She felt sad, alone, and depressed. Every time Susan noticed the urge to fix or solve, she attended to feeling the weight of her body and her feet on the floor, and resisted the temptation to offer solutions. Susan focused her attention on what Avery was feeling and reflected what she was hearing. Avery began to cry, oscillating between speaking, sobbing, and awkwardly making eye contact as if to check whether all of this was okay. There were a lot of tears, tissues, and long moments in which Susan simply held Avery's gaze.

Avery spoke more about her feelings of sadness, loneliness, and not feeling valued. "I've felt like this since first grade," Avery mentioned. "Was that the first time you felt so sad and alone?" Susan inquired. No, it started when she was three, when her dad left. They looked at each other, realizing they'd hit the root of her pain. Eventually they explored what Avery might need at school. They came up with some strategies to address the bullying. Avery decided to stay in school and to make a public art piece for the classroom about depression.

This is the power of empathy. We can receive each word expressed, each emotion revealed, with a listening heart. When we come from curiosity and care instead of our default, habitual communication strategies, healing and transformation are possible.

PRINCIPLES

People are more likely to be willing to listen when they feel heard. To build understanding, reflect before you respond.

KEY POINTS

The intention to understand is often expressed through listening, which involves temporarily putting aside our own thoughts, feelings, views, and opinions. We can listen in many ways:

- With complete, wholehearted presence
- To the content of what someone says
- To the feelings and needs beneath the content

Staying connected in conversation helps us build understanding and collaborate:

DON'T LET THE CALL DROP: Seek to establish and maintain connection in conversation.

REFLECT BEFORE YOU RESPOND: Confirm that you're hearing each other accurately before moving on. This "completes a cycle" of communication.

At the heart of listening is empathy, which includes:

- Cognitive empathy: seeing things from another's perspective
- Affective empathy: feeling another's emotions
- Somatic empathy: sensing another's embodied experience

QUESTION & ANSWER

Q: What if someone wants advice? Is that ever okay?

Of course. When someone asks for advice, you might try offering empathy first. I'll often say, "I'm happy to share some of my ideas, but first I just want to take in what you've said." I'll follow that with an empathic reflection of what I'm hearing and check if I've understood. This can help the other person process their experience and clarify what matters. I then circle back to inquire if they still want advice; sometimes it's no longer relevant.

If the tables are turned and you want to give someone advice, check first. Let them know: "I have an idea that I think might be helpful. Are you open to some advice?" This honors their autonomy, minimizes the chances that your input will be disempowering, and guards against giving advice as a way of soothing your own anxiety.

Q: I've been exploring these empathy tools with close friends and family and my new approach creates a lot of awkwardness. What do you do when others expect you to communicate in a certain way?

It can be confusing when our attempts to create more connection backfire. Part of what you're experiencing is the relational dimension of communication habits. They occur in a dynamic, so when we shift it affects others. It also may simply be the learning curve; it takes time to find an authentic voice with these tools.

Let go of the form and focus on your genuine intention to connect. What would help this person to feel heard? If someone is used to us showing care by asking questions or agreeing and we respond by reflecting their needs, that may throw them off. Try to tune in to what they want. When all else fails, let people know that you're trying something new that you hope will bring you closer. Ask them to humor you while you learn.

the third step
focus on what matters

THE FIRST TWO steps we've covered in this book set the stage for effective conversation: leading with presence makes everything possible; coming from curiosity and care points us in the right direction and guides the conversation. The third step, focusing on what matters, determines where we actually go.

This third step is about training where we put our *attention*. There are so many elements to a conversation. How do we sort out what's relevant from what's not? How do we determine what to address first? Training our attention is an invaluable resource in navigating these complexities.

I'd like to invite you to do a short experiment. First, place your attention in your hands and feel any sensations you notice there: warm or cool, heavy or light, dry or moist. Now put your attention in your feet and feel any sensations there: temperature, weight, texture.

Moving your attention from your hands to your feet illustrates a fundamental aspect of the mind: we can have conscious choice over where we place our attention. We use our hands and feet all day long, so we can put our attention there at will. This capacity to train our attention is the basis for the third step to effective conversation.

Marshall Rosenberg points out four key aspects of experience that, when clearly identified, help us stay connected to our humanity and support collaboration. Rather than being limited by blame, reactive judgment, and narrow interpretations, we learn to parse the actual *observations* that are most relevant to a situation, the *emotions* associated with those events, the deeper concerns and *needs* from which those feelings arise, and the specific *requests* that might move a conversation forward. In other words: What happened? How do you feel about it? Why? And where do we go from here?

In part three, we'll train our attention to discern and weave together these four components—observations, emotions, needs, and requests. As we grow familiar with these aspects of experience, we learn how they fit together like steps of a dance. We can use them to express ourselves more clearly and hear one another more easily.

Within this rich domain, the third step to effective conversation is extraordinarily flexible. Focusing on what matters can be a broad view of things or a narrow treatment of one aspect. We hone our attention to keep identifying what matters most in any given moment. This kind of skill gives us great freedom and flexibility in our communication, setting aside what's extraneous for what's essential. When we stay focused on what matters, we can say what we mean and build an effective conversation one step at a time.

getting down to what matters

Now here is my secret. It is very simple. It is only with one's heart that one can see clearly. What is essential is invisible to the eye.
—ANTOINE DE SAINT-EXUPÉRY

IMAGINE WHAT IT would be like if, no matter what anyone said or did, you were able to hear the deeper concerns beneath their words and actions. What would it be like to see into their heart and sense what they were truly longing for, to feel natural empathy for that person? Or to know intuitively what was most important *to you* in any given situation?

This is possible. It's the result of training our attention to identify human needs and values. It is a practice that is at once transformative, powerful, and liberating. It can take time and a certain discipline of attention to learn to see in this way, but it's entirely within our grasp and the results are profound.

In chapter 5 we explored one of the fundamental views at the heart of communication practice: *everything we do, we do to meet a need.* This is so core that I want to delve deeper into the implications of this perspective and the training of attention that supports it. To realize the transformative power of this view, we need to learn about needs and values. Being skilled at identifying needs and relating to them wisely brings more insight, freedom, and choice, allowing us to navigate even the most difficult relationships.

When I was first introduced to the concept of needs at a communication workshop in my early twenties, I was astounded. I'd been going through a fairly rough period: feeling lonely, struggling to find my place in the world, getting into conflicts with coworkers and family. Learning that there were real reasons behind my emotions was a revelation and a relief. I had found a new tool to understand behavior that made sense intuitively: we are each just doing our best to meet our needs.

In Nonviolent Communication and the work of many psychologists and social theorists, the term *need* refers to something very specific, different from ordinary usages. Colloquially we might say "I need you to listen to me" or "I need you to be on time." These are *strategies*—ideas about how to meet our needs. Needs are what matter beneath our strategies.[1] They are fundamental values that drive our actions. If I want you to listen to me, I may need understanding. A desire for more punctuality may be about valuing respect, teamwork, or efficiency.

> **Needs are the core values that motivate our actions. They're what matter most, the root reasons for why we want what we want.**[*]

We can think of needs as facets of our humanity. They are universal, positive qualities that animate a flourishing human life. We all share the same needs, though we feel them with varying degrees of intensity and have different strategies to meet them.[2] Anything that's tied to a specific person, place, time, object, or action is a *strategy*. Some strategies succeed, some do not. Some are wise, some are unwise. Any action can be understood as an attempt to meet many needs. We take a walk for health, relaxation, or to clear our head. Similarly, there are many strategies to meet a given need: we might relax by talking to a friend, going out, or doing yoga.

A Constellation of Needs

Abraham Maslow was one of the primary figures to introduce the concept of human needs in the modern era. In his formative theory of psychological health, he proposed a "hierarchy of needs," sometimes depicted as a

---

[*] Throughout this chapter I use the terms *need*, *value*, and *what matters* interchangeably to refer to this root aspect of human experience. While there are philosophical distinctions between a need and a value, here I am more interested in providing different ways of referring colloquially to the range of qualities that motivate us.

pyramid, with our most basic, physiological needs at the base; relational needs such as community, belonging, and respect in the middle; and higher needs such as meaning, fulfillment, and peace toward the top.[3] Maslow's work was further developed by fellow humanistic psychologist Carl Rogers, who went on to mentor Marshall Rosenberg.

The concept of a hierarchy of needs points to the fact that, in many situations, it becomes difficult to attend to higher needs when more basic ones aren't met. If we're stressed and tired, it may be harder to access empathy. Creativity may take a back seat if we don't have access to clean water, medicine, or physical safety.

Yet there is no *absolute* hierarchy of needs. There are countless ways in which we rise to the occasion above our basic needs. We may find patience to bear with a difficult conversation when we're stressed; parents and partners make daily acts of self-sacrifice for children and lovers; throughout history and to this day individuals find strength, compassion, and forgiveness in terrible situations of violence and poverty.

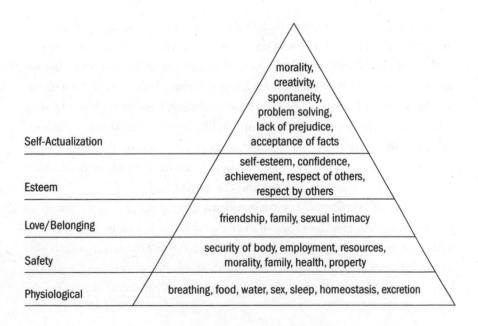

FIGURE 3. MASLOW'S HIERARCHY OF NEEDS

I am often moved when I think of people such as Nelson Mandela who, after twenty-seven harsh years in prison, unable to attend the funerals of his own mother and son, famously said, "As I walked out the door toward the gate that would lead to my freedom, I knew if I didn't leave my bitterness and hatred behind, I'd still be in prison."[4] Or I think of Etty Hillesum, a Jewish woman whose diaries and letters tell of her extraordinary inner transformation during WWII in occupied Amsterdam and later in a camp prior to being sent to Auschwitz. She dropped a note from the train en route to Auschwitz, where she died, which read, "We left the camp singing." Those five words speak volumes about the strength of the human spirit to rise above circumstances.

There is a deep well of resilience in human beings. We are not and can never be entirely self-sufficient, but we can develop our inner capacities of self-reliance to a tremendous degree.[5] Needs are fluid. There is no set hierarchy, universally or within the individual. Rather, our needs are a constellation of interrelated qualities within each of us. The ones we value most at any particular time are determined by a myriad of changing factors.

And yet, all of our needs matter. Human beings can survive for a few minutes without air; for a few days without water; and for a few weeks without food. When our relational and higher needs are not met, there is also real damage—it is just further delayed in time. Infants will die without loving touch. Children raised without sufficient care and empathy may struggle to form healthy relationships in life. Many of us must work hard to heal sufficiently from the absence of such core relational needs early in life. Adults can go only so long without human warmth and meaning before the mind becomes twisted and the spirit breaks.

The List of Human Needs in the following practice isn't intended to be complete. It indicates the range of needs we have as humans, any of which may be present at any time. NVC trainers have shared a version of this needs list with people all over the world, from all cultures and walks of life, asking, "Do you need these to thrive?" With small nuances, the answer is always yes.

Below is a partial list of human needs. Notice how it feels as you read each word. Which ones bring a sense of openness, joy, or relief? Are there any words that evoke discomfort or anxiety? Which needs are most important to you in your life? Does this differ in various roles—at home, at work, with friends?

List of Human Needs*

Subsistence

Physical sustenance
Air, Food, Water
Shelter
Health, Medicine
Physical Safety
Rest/Sleep
Movement

Security
Consistency
Stability
Order/Structure
Safety (emotional)
Trust

Freedom

Autonomy
Choice
Ease
Independence
Power
Space
Spontaneity

Leisure/Relaxation
Adventure
Humor
Joy
Play
Pleasure

Connection

Affection
Appreciation
Attention
Companionship
Harmony
Intimacy
Love
Sexual Expression
Support
Tenderness
Warmth
Touch

To Matter
Acceptance
Care
Compassion
Consideration
Empathy
Kindness
Mutual Recognition
Respect
To be seen or heard
To be understood
To be trusted

Community
Belonging
Celebration
Cooperation
Equality
Inclusion
Mutuality
Participation
Self-expression
Sharing

Meaning

Sense of Self
Authenticity
Competence
Confidence
Creativity
Dignity
Growth
Healing
Honesty
Integrity
Self-acceptance
Self-care
Self-connection
Self-knowledge
Self-realization

Understanding
Awareness
Clarity
Discovery
Learning
Making sense of life

Meaning
Aliveness
Challenge
Contribution
Creativity
Effectiveness
Exploration
Integration
Purpose

Transcendence
Beauty
Communion
Faith
Hope
Inspiration
Mourning
Peace (inner)
Presence

*Adapted and reprinted with permission from a version originally developed by Inbal, Miki, and Arnina Kashtan www.baynvc.org.

Cultural Myths: Independence, Self-Sufficiency, and Needs

We can feel great reluctance to acknowledge our own and others' needs. We may have many associations with the word *need*: weakness, dependence, selfishness, being "needy." I've inquired what someone needed only to be met with a flat and defensive shrug: "I don't need anything. I'm fine." I've heard those same words issue from my own lips as I struggled to protect myself from emotional pain or to maintain a facade of independence.

When we encounter others' needs, we may experience feelings of obligation, resentment, suffocation, or indifference. Depending on how we've been socialized, we may be highly attuned to others' needs and feel compelled to meet them (often at the expense of our own autonomy, freedom, or well-being), or we may be more focused on our own needs and feel threatened by others' requests (often at the expense of our sensitivity, connection, or intimacy). Almost all of us exhibit some complicated mixture of socially conditioned responses that vary depending on the context. Whatever one's particular style, it's tragically common for this kind of cultural training to result in feeling inauthentic, stifled or powerless in our lives.

Gender is a huge area in which this social conditioning occurs: our needs become limited by the reification of gender roles. For me, this was mostly the contemporary Western myths of masculine self-sufficiency ("I don't need anything"), meritocracy ("Anyone who works hard enough can succeed"), and hyperindividualism ("Decide alone and do it on your own"). From an early age, these stories shaped my experiences and expectations.

As a man conditioned by our culture's norms, I felt hesitant at times to acknowledge my needs for affection, intimacy and support. I also struggled for many years with feeling overwhelmed whenever I needed help. Unspoken assumptions at school and images in TV shows, movies, and comic books all presented an ideal of the independent hero conquering trials through his own strength. When things got hard, I held my emotions inside and tried to manage on my own. It took great patience (and countless reminders from those who loved me) to understand that we all need support sometimes, and that I could actually ask for help.

At some point I recognized that I can't do everything by myself. And perhaps more importantly, why would I want to? I saw that the illusion of independence, the fantasy of being a perfect masculine hero, separated me from others, while acknowledging my limits and asking for help connected us. It gave others the opportunity to see me and to contribute in meaningful ways.

For many of the women I am close to in my life, the messages they received growing up were more along the lines of caretaking ("Life's meaning is found in nurturing others") and self-sacrifice ("Giving is the highest good"). Many of them were socialized to ignore or negate their personal needs; they were taught to believe their needs didn't matter. (This was even more true for my grandmothers, who had less access to education and opportunity and gave up their entire lives for their husbands and families.) Female friends and colleagues have had to work hard to counter this social conditioning. The balance for them has often been in embracing their needs for autonomy, honoring the truth of their own experience, and trusting their ability to be assertive.[6]

Based on our culture and role in society, certain needs can become viewed as liabilities rather than as natural expressions of our humanity or innate values that animate our life. Many of the beliefs and stories we learn about our needs—though deeply ingrained and firmly held—are simply not true. They are at odds with the reality of our human existence. They're myths. Complete self-sufficiency isn't possible; complete self-sacrifice is rarely healthy when performed as a role.

As mammals, we are born physiologically dependent on those around us. All through childhood and adolescence, our nervous system is forming through relational bonds with adults. We are social creatures, and for millennia we have depended on the strength of close communities for our mental, emotional, and spiritual well-being, not to mention on the environment for sustenance. Every day—more so now than ever before in human history—we depend on thousands for our most basic necessities, from food and clothing to power and transportation. The use of money masks the vast interconnected web of relations upon which our lives depend, while at the same time revealing the depth and breadth of this web.

Similarly, the story of our great meritocracy in the United States—intricately tied to the myths of self-sufficiency and individualism—fails to account for the gross imbalance in access to resources and opportunities based on skin color, class, gender, sexual orientation, and physical ability, among others, as well as implicit biases for or against our success based on these factors.

The effects on our person, our families, and our society of operating under these myths are devastating. When we find ourselves struggling, when we feel depressed or lonely, where do we look for answers? Do we include in our malaise the devaluing of core needs such as connection and belonging? Are we cognizant of the spiritual poverty of modern culture? Do we include the disintegration of community and the incessant barrage of messages equating happiness with consumption and material success? Or do we blame ourselves and consider it a personal failing, wondering, "What's wrong with me?"

In place of recognizing our interconnectedness as humans—in place of the healing truth that we are inseparable from the rest of life, that we depend on one another and this planet for each breath, each sip of water, each morsel of food or love—we struggle to get by, thinking of ourselves as separate.

Learning to identify and be aware of our deeper human needs means coming to terms with all of this. It includes mourning the losses we as individuals and as societies have suffered and perhaps feeling anger at ways our institutions, culture, and the media perpetuate a widespread disconnect from our awareness of human needs. I wept when I realized how hard I'd been driving myself to "do it all" on my own, how unquestioned beliefs had prevented me from seeking support for so many years.

This process is about reclaiming our humanity. We *are* interdependent. However we have been conditioned, our needs matter. It is often our relationships that bring us the most joy and meaning, as well as the most pain and heartbreak. Thus, aspects of healing and wholeness often come through relationship. On a larger scale, we see that it is only by acknowledging our shared needs and collaborating that we will be able to solve the dire problems of our time. There are no individual solutions to structural problems.

This process of healing our hearts, reclaiming our needs, and working together to create a more just and equitable society begins with our ability to identify needs. We can use mindfulness and the intention to understand to inquire what matters most to us in any situation. The following practice builds this core capacity.[7]

🔊 **PRACTICE:** Sensing Your Needs

Think of something that happened recently that did not meet your needs. Remember to choose something that's not too difficult or it will be hard to learn the skill.

1. Identify what you *do* want, a specific strategy. What could have happened, what could have been said or done that would have pleased you?
2. Inquire: Why is that important? What matters about that to you? Or: If you had that, *then* what would you have? This is a way of investigating your needs. Don't think too much or try to figure it out cognitively. Listen inwardly.
3. Whatever response comes, ask one of the questions again. Continue asking that question and listening until you arrive at something that feels like a core value or need. You may feel settled or clear inside when you identify what matters most to you.
4. Shift your attention to this need itself, as a universal facet of being human, independent of the situation. Where in your body do you know that this is something important, something you want not just for yourself but for everyone? Can you appreciate the beauty and dignity of this need? Can you sense its innate value? What's that feel like?

You may find it easy to identify what you need, or things may feel quite opaque. It takes time to develop this skill. Be patient with the different thoughts and feelings that arise. What's important is the inquiry itself, learning how to listen for what matters with curiosity and care.

When we become aware of needs at this root level, something shifts inside. We are more directly in touch with a driving force in our life, and that will have an effect on the felt sense of our body. When we identify a core value or need, we may experience a somatic feeling of being settled, grounded, or clear. We can have a feeling of open spaciousness, an inner alignment, or a sense of energy and vitality.

Part of the trick in getting to this level is learning to be conscious of our needs in the positive rather than the negative. They're about what we *do* want rather than what we *don't* want. To gain proficiency with this skill we must work against the negativity bias—our evolutionary tendency to look for threats and focus on what isn't working. To create change—in our life, our relationships, our society—we need to imagine and identify new possibilities. Gandhi spoke of the "constructive program." Martin Luther King Jr. envisioned the "Beloved Community."

Training our attention to identify needs (our own and others') involves developing several different capacities. First, as we've already begun to explore, we expand our vocabulary for needs. The more familiar we are with these succinct words for needs, the more we notice them in our lives. Second, we train our attention to see life through the "lens of needs," from the point of view that all actions are attempts to meet needs. We practice shifting our perspective from strategies to needs again and again, until it becomes as easy as moving our attention from our hands to our feet.

The more we are able to differentiate between our strategies and needs, the more clarity and choice we have. Following a short NVC training in Israel, one participant reported a dramatic shift. He reached for a cigarette in the car and, having just learned that all actions are attempts to meet needs, paused to contemplate his choice. "If that's true, what am I actually needing in this moment?" He wanted to relax and take his mind off things. In that moment, he saw clearly many options to meet those needs that didn't compromise his health. He stopped smoking that day.

After a retreat I taught, a woman shared how her newfound understanding of needs transformed a difficult situation with her adult daughter. Her daughter was home for the holidays, had very little money for gifts, and sorely needed a few things herself. She felt ashamed and uncomfortable at the prospect of receiving more than she could give. They talked, and the daughter realized how joyful it would be for her parents to help. She saw how her needs for self-respect and autonomy were not mutually exclusive with her parents longing to contribute. The shame dissipated, and she was able to give and receive with more freedom.

Principle: **The more we are able to differentiate between our strategies and needs, the more clarity and choice we have.**

We always have choice. Even when external options are limited, we have a choice about how we respond to life internally. Things we tell ourselves that we "have to do" are choices to meet our needs. We may stay in a job we loathe because we value having a place to live or need to feed our children. We choose a strategy we don't like because it meets more profound needs. Becoming conscious of our needs can bring renewed energy and vitality, or it may prompt us to reevaluate our actions and make different choices.

PRACTICE: Seeing Life through the Lens of Needs

To familiarize yourself with this way of paying attention, dedicate a period of time—an hour, a day, or more—to practice viewing yourself and others through the lens of human needs. As your day unfolds, consider what needs you are trying to meet with your choices. As you observe others, consider: What matters to this person? What might be motivating them? Someone getting on a bus, agitated on a phone call, waving goodbye—what needs are they trying to meet?

Extend this inquiry to conversations you overhear, coworkers chatting, the news, and so on. Behind each statement, what matters? What might this person need? When is it easiest to identify possible needs? When is it more challenging? Notice the effect of attending to your own and others' experience in this way.

When we begin to see life through the lens of needs, something unexpected can happen. We may start to see how our commonalities outweigh our differences. Seeing needs is a doorway to compassion. We can understand the stories of blame and judgment we tell, words of anger and defensiveness from others, as expressions of unmet needs. Even extreme acts of violence can be seen as reaching for deeper needs—autonomy, freedom, empathy—however confused or distorted the strategy. As Rosenberg often said, "All violence is a tragic expression of unmet needs."

Awareness of needs is transformative. The internal mechanism that expresses our unmet needs as blame and judgment (of self or others) is based on our unconscious conditioning. Knowing which needs are at play, we shift into a wider field of awareness where new forms of understanding and creativity become possible. If I'm about to call someone "selfish," I can pause and inquire what I need. Instead of projecting my dissatisfaction outward as blame, I may recognize that I want consideration or more support.

The Power of Vulnerability

It's common to feel vulnerable or awkward discussing our needs. We can expand our capacity for authenticity while recognizing that the conditions to discuss all of our needs may not be present in every relationship. We can take care with what we share, with whom, and when. For example, sensing that someone lacks the capacity to meet our needs for empathy, we may seek empathy from others.

There are a few ways to develop discernment about sharing our vulnerability. First, it's essential to build close relationships of trust and mutual respect, in which we feel safe enough to explore needs. In a world that often does not acknowledge human needs, even one such connection is invaluable. For me, meeting a couple of folks in my early twenties who could see my pain and offer empathy was tremendously nourishing. It created enough space inside for me to break the cycle of isolation and start to open up to others.

Second, we can grow proficient at attuning to the level of vulnerability that supports understanding and collaboration, depending on the context. Evan spent time working at one hospital that lacked a culture of appreciation. She worked hard many hours a day, filling in when they were short-staffed and working holidays. Not being seen for her contributions brought up painful fears of inadequacy and distrust in her own value. At home, we could discuss her longing to be seen and to know that she mattered. At work, Evan chose to be less vulnerable. She framed the situation in terms of recognizing each person's contribution as a way to enhance motivation and teamwork. Instead of discussing her deeper psychological needs, she articulated shared values in the department for contribution, meaning, and teamwork in a way her manager was more likely to hear.

Third, we can transform our relationship to the experience of vulnerability itself, honoring it as a source of strength rather than a liability. To feel our vulnerability is to be in touch with reality. When we move beyond the discomfort, we find clarity and dignity. It is a great gift to be able to open one's heart and lovingly speak the truth.

Before I was born, my father fought in two wars, losing his younger brother in the second. Later in life, the trauma of these events and the pain of his divorce caught up with him. He grew obese, sedentary, and depressed. My mother, brother, and I each tried our best to offer support, empathy, encouragement, diet plans—you name it. Regardless of the intervention, he would always slide back into the same habits.

Out of options, I tried a different approach. During one visit back home, we sat at the dining room table as we usually did. I spoke from my heart, sharing the complete vulnerability of my feelings. "Dad, you know how much I love you. I want you to be here, to be in my life for a long, long time. And when I see the way you're living, I feel so scared. I'm angry, and worried, and helpless. I want you to take better care of yourself, and I've tried everything I know to do to help you and none of it has worked. I don't know what else to do, so I'm telling you this. What's it like for you to hear all of this?"

He looked at me and took my hand in his. He said that he understood, and that he didn't know what to say. We both shed a few tears. My words did not heal his depression nor his obesity, but it did bring us closer together. The anger and pain in my heart began to dissipate. We enjoy a warm and loving relationship to this day. When one speaks authentically, vulnerability carries tremendous power.

The Beauty of Needs

Over time, our relationship with needs matures. In the beginning we often think of them in a personal way. Needs belong to someone (me or you), and we measure them based on the extent to which they are satisfied. Evolution impels part of our mind to continually evaluate: Is my need met? How much? In this mode, our well-being is determined primarily by need satisfaction.

This approach limits our ability to navigate dialogue and constrains our inner life. It keeps us narrowly focused on ourselves and perpetually at the whim of circumstance. Regardless of our skill in communicating, much of life is beyond our control. Sometimes our needs are met; sometimes they aren't. Inner freedom doesn't come from being able to control outcomes; it comes from knowing our values, developing the inner resources to meet life with balance, and letting go.

This process of maturation begins with developing the capacity to be at peace with unmet needs. When life doesn't offer what we long for, we learn to mourn. We feel the pain of loss, great and small, with tenderness. This may include healing certain core wounds related to chronically unmet needs, often from childhood. When a need has gone unmet for many years, we may develop a quality of desperation around it. Being stranded in a desert, one becomes obsessed with water. At the first signs of moisture, we hold on for dear life! Even after arriving at an oasis, we may not trust there will be enough. Thirsty for love and affection, I suffered through the disintegration of many romantic relationships as I latched on to partner after partner with disproportionate intensity.

Turning inward opens the door to a new way of seeing. Our willingness to consciously experience an unmet need with awareness is transformative. After bringing empathy and compassion to the pain, we can learn to widen our perspective. Instead of focusing on the need's *satisfaction*, we can shift our attention to the need *itself*, independent of any conditions.

Needs have the fascinating property of being both personal and universal. They are personal in that we feel them intimately and experience directly the results of their satisfaction or lack thereof. Needs are universal to the degree that they are shared by every human. They partake of what it is to be human.

Every need also exists as a value that we carry within us, independent of whether or not it is satisfied. When we are in touch with our inner life in this way, a need's gratification is less salient than our awareness and appreciation of it as a value.[8] Each need, in the very fact of its existence, contains a beauty and a fullness in and of itself as an aspect of our humanity.[9] The need for peace is especially alive in times of war; a vision of equity and love is felt deeply in the midst of violent oppression.

This is an advanced level of awareness, yet when we touch this more universal dimension of our needs, we encounter great freedom. Whether or not our needs are met, we can still "meet" them—we can greet them face-to-face. When I directly encounter my need for peace—when I experience it as an ancient part of my humanity—I can feel it as a value within me whether or not it is fulfilled. This, paradoxically, allows me to advocate energetically for peace without burning out if I do not achieve a desired result, for my actions come from a place of integrity and inner alignment rather than a fixation on the outcome.

The question is not whether or not we have needs—needs are a fact of our existence—but rather how we relate to them. When our only perspective is a personal view of need gratification ("my needs" or "your needs" being satisfied), we tend to relate to them with a quality of grasping. Depending on our conditioning, we may overlook the reality of others' needs or erase the importance of our own. We may narrow our primary aim to gratifying certain needs and ignoring others, which often leads to conflict and tension. When we widen our view to a more universal perspective, to appreciating needs in and of themselves, we can remain fully committed to meeting both our own and others' needs, without being defined by the outcome. Letting go doesn't mean that we give up on our values, stop caring, or cease working for change.[10] It means that we recognize that the outcome of our efforts is not completely in our hands because in many ways we don't control the context.

We can explore developing this advanced awareness with more peripheral needs. For example, if others at work are too busy to offer appreciation for a presentation you gave, can you feel okay inside knowing that you worked hard, sensing your value for appreciation without *needing* it to be met? Try experimenting with the instructions below to shift your attention from the personal to the universal aspect of a need, from satisfying a need to experiencing its innate value and beauty.[11]

🔊 PRACTICE: Letting Go and Meeting Your Needs

Think of a situation in the last few weeks in which a need wasn't met. For this exercise, it's essential that you choose something that is low on the scale of difficulty in order to learn the skill of shifting your attention between the personal and universal aspects of a need. If you choose something that is too hard (think "water in the desert"), the emotional pain will likely hinder your learning.

Identify a key need in the situation. Inquire, "What matters about this to me? What do I want?" Listen inwardly, and then ask again, "If I had that, then what would I have?" Keep asking until you feel a settled clarity about the need or value for which you long.

Place your attention on the personal aspect of this need: the fact that it *hasn't* been met. You can say silently to yourself, "My need for _____ wasn't met." Notice how it feels to experience the need as a lack, something personal and unfulfilled.

Next, let go of the situation, the circumstances, and see if you can shift your attention to the need itself. Focus on the inherent value of this need as a universal aspect of being human. You can say silently to yourself, "I deeply value _____" or, "Just as I long for _____, so do all people need _____." Can you sense the beauty and dignity of this need? Can you experience its fullness, independent of whether or not it is satisfied?

If you have trouble sensing the universal aspect of the need, try to re-member (or imagine) a time when the need was met. Remember how it feels to have the need fulfilled. Then try to shift your attention to the universal aspect of this need as something you would want for all people.

Needs in Dialogue

Identifying our own needs and developing a balanced relationship with them form the groundwork for being able to express ourselves and engage effectively in dialogue. When we understand what matters most, we can de-escalate tension, nurture empathy, and support collaboration. The more we know our own needs and trust our ability to meet them, the more space we have to hear others. At the same time, identifying others' needs allows us to make heartfelt connections across differences. We gain the ability to sense the deeper values behind positions quite different from our own. Views that may seem incomprehensible on the surface become expressions of our shared humanity.

Conflict occurs at the level of our strategies. Understanding what's at stake can take us out of the strategy-based framework of the conflict, our polarized approach of either/or and win/lose, and generate more space to use our imagination and think creatively together.

On a recent communication retreat, Kristin recounted a recurring situation in which her mother corrected her parenting style, gesturing and making comments, in front of her son. Kristin felt angry and hurt. Past conversations had devolved into screaming matches about who was right. Exploring her needs, we identified that she wanted respect and support for her choices as a parent, and she also wanted her son to have a relationship with his grandmother. Contemplating her mother's actions, we surmised that she wanted to contribute to her grandson's learning and growth. Articulating these needs revealed new possibilities for engaging in a dialogue. Instead of arguing about their beliefs, she could imagine discussing parenting strategies and making agreements about what was nonnegotiable and where she was willing to flex.

Focusing on needs in conversation relies upon the very simple principle we've already seen: the more we understand one another, the easier it is to find solutions. When discussing any issue, it's helpful to keep this principle in mind. Our aim is to get all needs out on the table. Then we examine the situation together, from all angles.

> *Principle:* **The more we understand one another, the easier it is to find solutions that work for everyone. Therefore, establish as much mutual understanding as possible before problem solving.**

Such mutual understanding has the power to shift our position in a dialogue. When we understand one another's inner life, our priorities often reorganize. Contacting the universal quality of needs, the sense of identification with "my needs" or "your needs" can soften, and we experience the situation from a different perspective. All of the needs present matter, regardless of which person they happen to be located in. Out of this deeper connection, our need for compassion may rise to the surface and create the space for a different outcome.

Laura found herself overwhelmed and incensed at Thanksgiving one year when—in addition to cooking and hosting the dinner—she was volunteered by her husband to care for his elderly grandmother *both* the night before *and* the night of the holiday. In discussing the situation with him, she learned that he had struggled to find a way to make everyone happy and felt awful about "assigning" her this extra responsibility. His grandmother felt uncomfortable having a man look after her at night, and he couldn't figure out another way to get the family together. Seeing his inner conflict, Laura's anger shifted. They made some agreements about how to work together in the future and how to share the responsibilities for the holiday.

This outcome was possible because of a fundamental shift in Laura's approach to the dialogue from habitual conflict strategies to the intention to understand. Having done some training with me, Laura was able to check her assumptions and her impulse to blame and instead approach the conversation with curiosity. A key to this shift is valuing all of the needs present and letting the other person know that we are interested in finding a solution that works for both of us. When the other person trusts that we are genuinely interested in understanding what they want (not just getting our own way), we can begin to collaborate. The dynamic transforms from opposing forces to curiously examining a puzzle together, side by side.

> *Principle:* Conflict generally occurs at the level of our strategies— *what* we want. The more deeply we are able to identify our needs— *why* we want what we want—the less conflict there is.

Another student of mine, Noga, likes to meditate in the morning. Her roommate is often up early getting ready for work. Noga felt caught. Asserting her own need for quiet left little room for dialogue; not addressing the situation left her at the mercy of his schedule. A shift came when she realized that she genuinely valued *both* of their needs. She wanted some quiet and respect for her space, but she *also* wanted him to be able to get ready with ease, without feeling anxious or tiptoeing around the house. Knowing that she wanted to find a solution that honored both of their needs, it became much easier to have the conversation in an open and curious manner.

Making this shift rests upon our ability to identify others' needs. In the next exercise, we'll refine the practice of empathy we've already learned by focusing our attention externally on what matters most for someone else.

This practice contains three parts that develop our capacity to identify others' needs. Try this out in low-stakes conversations with friends.

1. Ground yourself in presence and the intention to understand. Find some genuine curiosity and care.

2. As you listen, focus your attention on what they might need. You might ask yourself silently, "What matters here? What's most important to them about this?"

3. At times, practice completing a cycle of communication by reflecting before you respond. Inquire in a natural way, "Is this what matters to you?" Remember, the intention of this question is to check that you understand rather than to analyze or tell them what they feel.

Notice how it feels to listen in this way. What does it feel like to check if you understand? Does it lead to more connection? What happens if your guess isn't totally accurate?

Focusing our attention on needs can feel awkward at first. Sometimes it's easiest to listen wholeheartedly and then consider what matters after the other person has finished.

Many people find that they feel more connected when listening this way. Offering an empathic reflection can produce visible relief. Similar to the somatic shift we feel when we recognize our own needs, another person may spontaneously exhale, sigh, or offer verbal affirmation— "Exactly!" At the same time, guessing what matters isn't about getting it right. It's not a performance test. It's about our genuine intention to understand. If we haven't understood correctly, the other person will clarify. Even when our guess is not accurate, it can still lead to greater understanding and may even reveal new layers of meaning that the speaker hadn't sensed.

Empathic listening is a gift we can offer in all situations. It can enhance the quality of any relationship, creating more trust and closeness in friendships, family, and intimate bonds. It's also essential when things get tense. Remembering to listen for needs in a conflict is like gaining a window into another's world. Negative images of the other person begin to crumble as we see their humanity: "Oh, they want . . . respect, support, ease . . . *just like me.*"

When we become aware of another's needs, our heart opens; something softens inside as we understand intuitively what matters to someone else. This is a very important point. If we can't support what we've identified in the other party, then we aren't connecting at the level of needs. If you can't get behind it and say "Yes, I want that for them," it's not a need. Needs are universal; they connect us. They are by definition something that we want for everyone, something to which we can internally say yes.

Authenticity and Needs

As our awareness of needs grows, we learn to find an authentic way to discuss this aspect of human experience. In conversation, stating needs in the positive, in a colloquial manner, can make it easier to establish connection and hear one another. Consider the examples in the chart below. What differences do you feel reading the statements?

Needs in the Negative	Needs in the Positive
"I can't stand it when things are messy and chaotic."	"I enjoy it when things are clean and tidy."
"I don't want to be trapped in our relationship."	"I want a sense of space and flexibility in our relationship."
"I don't want to be controlled or told what to do."	"Having some autonomy and freedom are so important to me."
"I don't want to feel sick or tired anymore."	"I long to feel healthy and well."

Notice how the negative constructions often imply a sense of blame, which can get in the way of being heard. The examples are also more colloquial, forgoing the word *need*. Below are some additional tips for how to refer to needs colloquially. As you experiment with these tools, try to find your own way of talking about needs and values.

Drop the Word *Need*

Because of our cultural associations, the word *need* may not be useful. Instead, try more natural phrases.

EXAMPLE: Instead of "Do you need more respect?" you might say, "Sounds like you really value respect?" or "You were wanting more respect. Is that right?"

ADDITIONAL PHRASES: "I/you love . . . value . . . really enjoy . . . long for . . . would be nourished by . . . thrive on . . . ." "X matters to me/you . . . is important to me/you . . . is fun for me/you . . . is meaningful to me/you . . . ."

Describe the Need with a Phrase

One-word needs are helpful for training our attention to get at the heart of the matter. To acknowledge the context and be more concrete, describe the need with a phrase.

EXAMPLE: Instead of "Sounds like you need more order?" you might say, "You really like knowing that everything is in its place, yes?"

State the Need in the Positive

Needs are about what we *do* want rather than what we *don't* want. Stating needs in the positive can be empowering and affirming and can move us toward creative solutions. Restate what matters in terms of what someone longs for.

EXAMPLE: Instead of "I hear how much you dislike getting mixed messages, huh?" try saying, "I hear how much you want clarity and directness, knowing you can take what's said at face value. Is that right?"

Ask, Don't Tell

Few people like being told what they are feeling, which can sound patronizing. When listening for what matters, pose reflections as questions—checking that you've understood—rather than tell the person what they said.

EXAMPLE: Instead of "You want to feel more engaged at work," make it a question: "Do you want to feel more engaged at work?" Or follow the reflection with an inquiry such as, "Is that right?"

Over time you will develop more facility with talking about needs in a natural, unforced manner. The foundation is learning to focus your attention on needs and values, what matters most to oneself or another.

Rosenberg teaches that, as we grow in skill and awareness, we can learn to hear every statement as saying "Please" or "Thank you." In some respect, we can boil the essence of any communication down to one of these two messages: "Please, meet my need" or "Thank you, you've met my need." Are we not always saying one or the other?

When we hear one another in this way, our heart responds with two profound emotions. "Please" gives rise to compassion, and "thank you" to gratitude. In these moments we experience our needs as fundamental expressions of our relatedness. Instead of being trapped alone to fend for ourselves, our lives have something to do with one another. Needs point to our interconnectedness with each other, the environment, and life.

PRINCIPLES

The more we are able to differentiate between our strategies and
    needs, the more clarity and choice we have.

The more we understand one another, the easier it is to find solutions
    that work for everyone. Therefore, establish as much mutual un-
    derstanding as possible before problem solving.

Conflict generally occurs at the level of our strategies—*what* we want.
    The more deeply we are able to identify our needs—*why* we want
    what we want—the less conflict there is.

KEY POINTS

Needs are the fundamental, root reasons for why we want what we want.
When we can identify our needs, we can:

- Connect: We all share the same needs, though we feel them with
  varying degrees of intensity and have different strategies to meet them.

- Choose: Becoming conscious of our needs can bring renewed energy and vitality and may prompt us to reevaluate our actions and make different choices.
- Transform Patterns of Blame and Judgment: Knowing which needs are at play, we shift into a wider field of awareness where new forms of understanding and creativity become possible.
- Collaborate: Work together to find creative solutions to as many needs as possible.

Training our attention to identify needs (our own and others') involves:

- Expanding our vocabulary for needs
- Training our attention to see life through the "lens of needs"
- Building close relationships of trust and mutual respect, in which we feel safe enough to explore needs
- Attuning to the level of vulnerability that supports understanding and collaboration, depending on the context
- Learning to be at peace with unmet needs
- Developing the ability to shift our attention from the personal to the universal aspect of needs, from a narrow focus on satisfying our needs to a broader appreciation for the beauty of human needs

QUESTION & ANSWER

Q: When I try to figure out what I need, I get lost, blaming the other person, feeling upset, planning what to say. Do you have any tips for this? We're working with decades of conditioning. If we're emotionally activated, the force of those patterns is even stronger. Give yourself time. Basic mindfulness practice, which steadies our attention, is a huge support here.

As you learn the associated skills of noticing feelings and making observations, you'll have more tools to disentangle things. The basic form of Nonviolent Communication—observations, feelings, needs, requests—provides a kind of road map to connect with our internal experience. The more you practice walking your attention through those steps, the more easily you'll be able to do it in real time.

Grounding all of this in your body is also very important. There is a conceptual component to needs, but they are also felt in our body as a gut-level knowing. Keep listening inwardly.

Last, I can't emphasize enough the importance of getting help from others. We learned to think and speak in relationship, and those patterns are best transformed in relationship.

Q: You talk a lot about collaborating to meet all of the needs present, but what about when the needs are in conflict? Or if there isn't a way to meet all of the needs?

Examine if it is actually the *needs* themselves or the strategies to meet them that are in conflict. More often than not, it is the latter. When our needs are in conflict—say, one partner wants closeness and connection, the other wants space and autonomy—then we work to deepen mutual understanding. To truly and wholly understand one another can bring transformation. Either person (or both) may shift because at that depth of understanding, one's need for compassion and contribution can outweigh the original need for space or connection.

In some situations, it's not possible to meet all the needs on the table. We can still find togetherness in valuing one another's needs and work together to meet as many as possible. When we're unable to think creatively enough to find a strategy that meets more needs, we can mourn that together. There can be a sense of connection and care in the experience of not finding an adequate solution.

Q: Can you say more about letting go of needs? I feel like I get stuck there.

"Letting go" of needs doesn't mean denying, rejecting, or getting rid of them in some way. It means transforming our relationship to needs from one of contraction and demand to one of receptivity and openness.

The first step is simply to know what your needs are. Then begin to examine your relationship with specific needs, one at a time. Are you grasping inside, *needing* a need to be met in a certain way? Are you pushing it away or rejecting it? Or do you have a sense of space around that need? Letting go of needs means that we accept our needs and aren't damaged if they aren't satisfied. We may feel sad or disappointed, but we have enough resilience to handle that. There's space inside to feel those emotions and mourn the absence of the object of our longing.

This shift happens slowly and comes from finding the balance and compassion inside to be with the tension and discomfort of grasping. If we're fixated and attached, start there. It feels awful to be gripped with desperation. If we can breathe gently with that experience, finding ways to calm and soothe the ache, it will begin to release and soften on its own. Again, with a lot of these areas, it's helpful (and sometimes necessary) to receive support from others. Get empathy for the pain of the longing. Brainstorm together other ways to begin to meet those needs and ease out of the narrow, tight space of clinging.

8

emotional agility

Feeling emotions is what makes life rich.

—DANIEL GOLEMAN

HUMAN LIFE IS a tapestry of changing emotions.

Our ability to relate wisely to this flow of emotions is among the most important skills we can develop. When understood, emotions give us valuable information about our own and others' needs, key input about our environment, and robust guidance for navigating conversations. Our emotions are our mind and body's age-old way of sending immediate, tangible messages to us about our relationship with the world.

How we handle emotions—our own and others'—can make or break a relationship. The intensity of our feelings can push us to say or do things that we later regret. Strong emotions can inhibit us from speaking the truth or sharing the things for which we long. Even our idioms point to the power emotions have to drive our behavior: we become "blind with rage," "choked up," "weak in the knees," "bent out of shape."

In a single day, how many emotions course through us? Though we have little choice over *what* we feel, we can have choice over *how* we handle our emotions. In this chapter, we'll explore emotions: where they come from, their role in dialogue, and how to develop emotional agility so we don't get slammed when the emotional volume gets turned up.

A Lesson of the Heart

In my midthirties, feeling unfulfilled by work and life in general, I had the privilege to step out of my routine and focus more intensively on my spiritual practice. I went to the monastery, and after a few months decided to take temporary ordination as an *anagarika*, the first step of Buddhist monastic training.[1]

When I told my Jewish mother about my decision, things didn't go well. The thought of her son "renouncing the world" with shaved head and white robes was more than she could handle. At one of the most important moments of my life she was aghast, bereft with anger and mourning.

We both felt deeply hurt. To her, I seemed to be rejecting everything she believed and had raised me to value: ethical action to make the world a better place. For me, her rejection cut to the core. I desperately wanted her to see the true intentions behind my choice. I tried my best to hear her, but the pain between us was too much to bear. She withdrew completely, refusing to speak with me for almost an entire year. Ouch.

I was ordained for two and a half years, during which I had plenty of time to contemplate our relationship: to cry, to forgive, and to heal. My mother and I eventually reconciled. We were able to talk about our views and feelings. Over time, she saw how my Buddhist training enabled me to help others in the world. In the end, we grew even closer. The process called forth powerful qualities in both of us: courage, honest vulnerability, patience, and humility. It taught me a lot about the willingness to feel and the gifts that wait on the other side.

The Middle Way

Emotions are rich and complex phenomena. They occur in our bodies and often include a mental or psychological component. As we'll see, the ability to distinguish the felt sensations of an emotion from our thoughts and interpretations is key in being able to handle and express emotions skillfully. For our purposes (and keeping with Rosenberg's language of NVC), I will use the two terms *emotions* and *feelings* interchangeably.[2]

Emotions are multifaceted, affective experiences felt in the body.

How we relate to our emotions falls on a spectrum. At one extreme, a tide rushes in and floods us. We get swept up and speak impulsively. In a flash of anger, fear, or pain, we can find ourselves lashing out, often harming the ones we love. We may be on the receiving end of harsh words, stabbed by "verbal daggers," as the Buddha once said. The cost of expressing our emotions reactively can be excruciatingly high. It can take weeks, months, or years to repair something that took seconds to say. Sometimes we never mend the rift. Less intense emotions can also take over a conversation, reducing our capacity to choose how we respond or making it harder to hear one another.

Seeing all of this, we may swing to the other extreme, suppressing emotions. Afraid they'll overwhelm us, damage a relationship, or complicate dialogue, we may try to ignore or avoid them. We pretend they're not happening or try to work around them. We may try to keep things bottled up until we snap or allow emotions to stay repressed indefinitely. Yet in spite of our efforts, emotions have a way of seeping into conversation, often in unproductive ways.

Unacknowledged emotions can make it harder to hear another person, leading to confusion or mistrust. Our body language, facial expressions, and tone belie deeper feelings. Emotions show up in our choice of words, in the quickness of a retort, even in our silences. We can create an entire story about someone else, their motives or views, all to try to make sense of an emotion that's under the surface.

Taking a cue from Buddhist teachings, the path through this murky terrain is the middle way between reactive expression and habitual suppression. Developing emotional agility involves three capacities: identifying emotions, finding balance with our internal experience of them, and expressing them openly without blame or judgment. The tools of mindfulness and the framework of NVC help us handle the intensity of emotions, to better understand them, and to channel their powerful energy toward more useful ends.

A Mythology of Emotions

In exploring this terrain, it can be helpful to examine how we've learned to relate to emotions. We each receive a kind of emotional inheritance.

Wherever we're born, we inherit generations of ideas, beliefs, and behaviors from our family, culture, religion, and society. Through the socialization process, we are given certain messages over and over again about what emotions we are allowed to feel and express based on aspects of our social location such as our gender, age, class, or race.

The fundamental template for understanding our emotions in the West began over two thousand years ago. Since the time of the Greek philosophers and the early Gnostics, aspects of Western philosophy and religion have posited a split between reason and emotion. The "passions" of the heart are seen as irrational and "base." They drive us to do harmful things and threaten the fabric of the social order, so they must be subdued, tamed, and controlled by reason.[3] Today, emotions are often associated with vulnerability, the feminine, weakness, and danger or with manipulation and subtle coercion.

This dichotomy set the stage for most of the ideas I was exposed to in public education. School is where we learn to reason. Emotions are generally unwelcome and rarely discussed, let alone integrated. As a child, how often did your teachers ask how you felt?

I grew up Jewish in the suburbs of New Jersey. At home I learned that it was natural to express a colorful range of emotions. At school I learned hard lessons about what was and wasn't socially acceptable. Sent out of class for raising my voice and cursing, I understood that it's risky to express anger. Shamed by a teacher and ridiculed by other boys for crying, I learned it's not safe to cry in public, especially not around other men. Although we each receive different messages based on our sociocultural location, almost all of us as children imbibe certain social rules about emotions based on our perceived gender: "Don't cry." "Grow up. Be a man." "Big girls don't cry."

We have been systematically trained to avoid and suppress our emotions. These rules are not merely theoretical. Their impact on us as individuals can be felt every day through a deadening of our vitality; in the shame, depression, and anxiety that are so prevalent in modern society; and in our inability to manage emotions in relationships.

In spite of these experiences, I was able to internalize the message that it was important to feel. My mother laid important groundwork by making regular efforts to encourage my sensitivity and emotional intelligence. The loneliness of being a sensitive, heterosexual man became an important motivator to understand and transform the emotional roles I inherited from society.

PRACTICE: Seeking Myths

Part of developing a wise relationship with our emotions is becoming aware of the notions we carry about them. Take some time to reflect on what you believe about feelings. What messages did you receive from your family, culture, religion, or society? What messages do you receive today through the media or your community? Which are explicit ("Don't cry") and which are implicit (through example or behavior)?

Make a list of the views and beliefs you notice. Are there certain emotions that feel more acceptable than others? As you move through your day, notice any fear of feeling your emotions or of others expressing emotions.

Reclaiming Our Right to Feel

These mythologies of culture, history, and religion would have us believe that our emotions are signs of a flawed nature; that they are abnormal occurrences that can be ignored, overcome, or explained away. Yet there is something deeper in us. We each receive an inheritance that is older, greater, and far more powerful than what our family, culture, or society bestows.

Our emotions are immutable expressions of our biology. They're as natural and essential to our life as our body's own immune system. Far from being irrational, we feel things for a reason. *If there's emotion, something matters.* Emotions are primary ways the body-mind sends signals about our needs. When our needs are met, we feel pleasant emotions. When our needs are not met, we feel unpleasant emotions.

Our feelings constitute their own unique form of experience and system of information. Any emotion is no more of a "problem" than the smoke detector in our house. When the smoke alarm goes off, we understand the signal and set about seeking its source. In the same way, we can learn to experience and understand our emotions as feedback signals about life. What are these signals telling us? Rather than taking them as imperatives to action, we can see them as information.

Of course, the feedback loops of memory, thought, and social conditioning can complicate the way we experience our emotions. Sometimes there's fire, sometimes there isn't. But we don't throw away the smoke detector just because the battery needs to be changed! We can learn to hear the wisdom in emotion.

From this perspective, all emotions are okay to feel. It's how we respond, what we do with them, that matters. When we're not aware of our emotions, or when we become flooded and allow them to take over, they can cause harm. What's problematic is *not the emotion itself* but rather our reactive expression of a feeling or our habitual suppression of it. When reactively expressed, the immediate harm is outward. When reflexively suppressed, the damage turns inward, with potential harm to others over time.

Our capacity to feel emotions emerges from millions of years of evolution and is deeply rooted in our neurobiology.[4] We are sensitive creatures built to feel things, touched both literally and figuratively by the world around us. The nerves that run throughout our body and viscera ensure precise and immediate feedback from our environment—sensory, mental, and emotional.

Volumes of research today illustrate the inherent value and intelligence of our emotional life.[5] From the cascade of hormones released to support healthy bonding between caregiver and child to the boiling of anger or the tremble of fear in response to a threat, the affective domain is an essential part of being human. When we understand emotions' natural purpose as a source of information, we can cut through the mythology we've internalized and allow ourselves to be aware of them and feel them more fully.

A Palette of Emotion

Mindfulness is the primary tool to develop our capacity to identify emotions (emotion recognition) and to feel them with balance (emotion regulation). Emotion recognition begins with noticing and naming what we're feeling—this is sometimes called *affect labeling*. At first, our vocabulary for emotions may be rudimentary. We may find we have just a handful of words to describe our feelings: happy, sad, mad, confused. It's like trying to paint with only a few colors.

PRACTICE: Reflecting on Feelings

Below is a partial list of feelings we experience when our needs are or are not met. Take some time to read it over and consider: Which feelings are most familiar? Which are least familiar? As you move through your day, what feelings do you notice in your own or other's experience? Name them silently. In particular, notice how your own emotions change over the course of one day, coming and going.

List of Human Feelings*

When Our Needs Are Met

Peaceful	*Loving*	*Glad*	*Playful*	*Interested*
Tranquil	Warm	Happy	Energetic	Inquisitive
Calm	Affectionate	Excited	Invigorated	Enriched
Content	Tender	Hopeful	Refreshed	Alert
Absorbed	Appreciative	Joyful	Impish	Aroused
Serene	Friendly	Satisfied	Alive	Astonished
Loving	Sensitive	Delighted	Lively	Concerned
Fulfilled	Compassionate	Grateful	Exuberant	Curious
Satisfied	Grateful	Confident	Giddy	Eager
Relaxed	Trusting	Inspired	Adventurous	Enthusiastic
Relieved	Open	Touched	Mischievous	Fascinated
Quiet	Thankful	Proud	Goofy	Intrigued
Carefree	Passionate	Exhilarated	Buoyant	Surprised

When Our Needs Are Not Met

Mad	*Sad*	*Scared*	*Tired*	*Confused*
Impatient	Lonely	Afraid	Exhausted	Perplexed
Irritated	Hurt, Hurting	Nervous	Fatigued	Hesitant
Frustrated	Unhappy	Startled	Lethargic	Troubled
Grouchy	Gloomy	Anxious	Indifferent	Uncomfortable
Agitated	Overwhelmed	Worried	Weary	Withdrawn
Exasperated	Distant	Frightened	Overwhelmed	Apathetic
Disgusted	Discouraged	Insecure	Fidgety	Detached
Animosity	Distressed	Anguished	Sleepy	Embarrassed
Bitter	Dismayed	Sensitive	Disinterested	Helpless
Rancorous	Disheartened	Shocked	Reluctant	Uneasy
Irate, Furious	Despairing	Apprehensive	Bored	Suspicious
Angry	Sorrowful	Jealous	Dull	Puzzled
Hostile	Depressed	Terrified	Blah	Unsteady
Enraged	Blue	Horrified	Mopey	Restless
	Miserable	Desperate	Heavy	Skeptical

*For additional feelings lists, see www.baynvc.org and www.cnvc.org.

These limits are often not just conceptual; they're also sensory—meaning our capacity to feel the nuances of our emotional life may be attenuated or atrophied. Years of shutting off or avoiding emotions can mute things.[6] This is completely workable. We begin by bringing awareness to our experience just as it is, wherever we are.

We all have a different relationship to emotions. It's common to not know how we feel, even to feel numb at times. Sometimes we may feel things quite intensely. There's no "right" way to be. What we're aiming for is the ability to identify how we feel in the moment, to clear the mental and sensory channels so that we receive the feedback from our surroundings and relationships.

Naming our emotions is a necessary foundation for mindful communication and the first component of emotion recognition. We refine this ability by feeling them in our body.

Have you ever stopped to examine an emotion directly? What is this surge of energy that can race through us like a hurricane? If you look closely, you'll discover that every emotion is a dynamic interplay of body, heart, and mind, a blend of sensations fed by thoughts and meanings.

A word such as *sadness* or *joy* refers to a rich world of inner experience. Sensation is a primary component of an emotion. Sadness may include pressure in our chest, a hardness in our throat, or heaviness in our eyes. Joy feels expansive, spacious, warm, or light.

Emotions also have embodied shape. Sadness lowers our head and droops our shoulders. Anger clenches our jaw and fists. Confidence lifts our chin. It works in the reverse too: assuming the bodily posture of an emotion stimulates its associated neurochemistry. Articulating the facial muscles into a smile can raise our spirits and standing tall can induce strength.

The more clearly we begin to sense the somatic experience of our emotions, the more alert and skilled we become at identifying what we are feeling. Over time, through patient mindful attention, our palette begins to expand. We go from just four colors to ten, then twenty, and eventually to a rich display. Like a painter with different tones of blue, lavender, and gray to paint the sky, we can learn to identify and feel the full range of our emotions.

Yet just because our palette is growing doesn't mean we know how to paint. We can be aware of what we're feeling and still be driven or oppressed by our emotions. Their intensity can transfix our attention and spin us around.

The next phase of practicing emotional agility is to learn how to manage them: to experience them in a nonreactive way. This is sometimes called *emotion regulation*, and it has more to do with internal balance than control. To return to the analogy, if emotion recognition expands our palette, emotion regulation teaches us to hold the brush properly.

Every emotion has a tone, a kind of primary "flavor" of pleasant, unpleasant, or neutral. This underlying agreeable or disagreeable tone is often what gets us going. It's what we crave, what we try to avoid, or what we resist feeling. Emotions can also have an energetic component, a sensory experience that spreads throughout the body. Anger often has a roiling, rushing feeling. Loving care can have a soothing, soft, or warm quality. Excitement and joy may be bubbly. Anxiety can feel brittle or jangled.

The tonality and energy of emotions tend to pull us in and push us around. It's our inability to tolerate the intensity of an unpleasant tone that sparks our reactivity. We can use mindfulness to notice this aspect of our feelings and stabilize our attention there, instead of being dragged along by the thoughts and stories that feed them. Rather than clamping down or cutting ourselves off from our emotions, emotion regulation invites us to feel them fully.[7] We develop the patience, strength, and spaciousness to let these waves of tone and energy wash through us without getting toppled by them.[8]

Our emotions almost always come with a story. While we may feel joyful or sad for no apparent reason, more often than not we are responding to something specific in our internal or external environment. This last dimension of emotions is the most complex: the thoughts, stories, and meanings associated with them.

The interplay between our thoughts and emotions is fascinating to explore. They often feed one another: thoughts and stories provide fuel for emotion, which in turn sparks further thinking and rumination.[9] Sifting through layers of thought, we usually find at the core of an emotion some meaning or belief that is connected to our deeper needs. Focusing on what matters means getting at the crux of this juncture, to any meaning and associated needs. Within sadness we may find the perception "I'm all alone" and a longing for companionship, friendship, or community. At the heart of shame may be the belief "I'm not good enough" and needs for self-acceptance, dignity, or recognition.

When I told my mother I was ordaining as a Buddhist monastic, storms of all these components—meaning, tone, energy, and sensation—tore through our hearts. To handle our emotions, we must develop the ability to notice these elements and feel them fully, to attune to all dimensions of an emotion without getting thrown by any of them. The more balanced we are internally, the easier it becomes to talk about our own and others' emotions.

> *Principle:* **Being aware of our emotions supports our ability to choose consciously how we participate in a conversation.**

🔊 **PRACTICE:** Feeling Emotions

Take some time to practice mindfulness and thoroughly explore the different components of an emotion. Begin by grounding your attention in your body. Steady your awareness with breathing and let things settle to whatever degree possible. Then call to mind a situation that brought up some feelings (nothing too difficult). Let it become clear in your mind. Use the steps below to explore any emotions present, one at a time:

EMOTION: Name the emotion. How do you feel?

LOCATION: Where do you feel it? Is it in your face, your chest, your back? Somewhere else?

SENSATION: What does it feel like there? What are the actual sensations you experience associated with the emotion? Is there pressure, tightness, aching, heaviness? Warmth, openness, lightness, flowing?

TONALITY: What's the overall flavor or tone of the emotion? Is it pleasant or unpleasant? Can you relax there, softening and widening your attention?

MEANING: Are there any thoughts, stories, or meanings associated with the emotion? If you had to boil it down to one word, what would it be?

NEEDS: To what needs is this emotion connected? What matters to you here?

Naming our emotions and identifying their components can help us self-regulate.[10] Using mindfulness to identify what's happening creates perspective. As soon as we name something, we're no longer completely identified with it; we have a relationship with it. With the space that's created by that perspective, the emotion can begin to settle.

Sometimes emotions are so powerful that we can't differentiate any of the above components, let alone tolerate them. Our mind and body flood with a surge of intensity. This can happen with pleasant emotions such as love or exuberance as much as with unpleasant emotions such as anger or disgust.

Here we can use mindfulness of breathing to soothe the intensity of strong emotions, fully appreciating the experience of the pleasant ones and bringing balance to the unpleasant ones. Just as we used a reference point in the body to anchor our attention for presence, we can use the breath or the body to steady our awareness amid the storms of strong emotions.

PRACTICE: Soothing Strong Emotions

The next time you feel a surge of strong emotion, try using your breath to calm and soothe your mind and body. Take a few slow, deep breaths. Feel the air filling your belly and chest as you breathe in. Purse your lips gently and breathe out long and slow, releasing your breath in a thin stream of air. Notice how your body feels, paying extra attention to any amount of settling or calming.

All emotions simply want our attention. They long to be known, felt, and released. As we observe our emotions, feeling them fully, we begin to see a deep truth: they are fleeting. Even as they send us important signals, they are like weather systems that come and go. The Latin roots of the word *emotion* literally mean "to move out." When we allow ourselves to consciously feel our emotions, they can do their job of helping take care of us. They inform our choices about how to respond to things and move on their way.

Hacking the Blame Game: Radical Responsibility

As we find more internal balance and stability with emotions, our ability to engage relationally grows as well. With a full palette and proper brush control, we're ready to paint. The last phase of emotional agility is to develop the capacity to hear and express them without blame. This is as much about how we *think* as it is about what we say.

One of the most pervasive and unquestioned myths about emotions is that *they are someone else's fault.* This notion is reinforced daily by the media and entertainment industries. "I'm angry *because you* . . ." This is our unconscious communication training at work, miring us in the blame game. I throw some blame and you toss it back, arguing and defending.

Our thoughts and words have the power to shape our experience. Taking responsibility for our feelings and extricating ourselves from blame involves keen attention to the very mechanisms of perception in our mind that generate and reinforce the blame game. The diagram below illustrates the logic behind the game. A friend is fifteen minutes late to meet you, and you say, "I'm so annoyed that you're late." Is this actually a direct cause-and-effect relationship, in which their actions cause your emotions?

FIGURE 4. THE BLAME GAME

On a different day you might have a different reaction. You might feel hurt, worried, or—if you've had a busy day—relieved to have a few minutes to yourself!

Our feelings are never caused *directly* by other people or their actions. There is a relationship, but it is an *indirect* one. The outward event is the *stimulus* for our feelings; it is a necessary but insufficient condition for our emotional response. The most direct root cause is how we relate to the event: our needs and values, represented by point B in the diagram below. This includes the context—our day, cultural conditioning, personal and social history, and expectations, as well as the stories we tell ourselves and meanings we fashion from the situation. All these factors are tied to our needs.

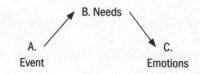

FIGURE 5. FEELINGS ARE A FUNCTION OF NEEDS

The blame game tries to hold someone else responsible for our emotional reactions, entangling us in argument. Can anyone *make* you feel something? How can you be responsible for my reaction? And vice versa, how can I possibly be responsible for your reaction?

We are each responsible for our actions and our reactions. Remember that our feelings are a function of our needs. To take responsibility for my reactions means training my mind to trace emotions back to the needs from which they arise. Every time my attention goes outward to blame someone, I can pause and investigate: Is this person solely responsible for my reaction? What meaning am I making about this event? What do I need? How is the broader context of my life, or my social location, structuring my experience?

When we step out of the blame game and take radical responsibility for our feelings, we carve the channels of our own freedom. If you are the cause of my emotions, you have power and I remain helpless. When we understand feelings as a function of needs rather than the direct result of another's actions, we reclaim our autonomy and agency. This is how humans facing brutal treatment, torture, or other horrors can feel compassion instead of hatred toward their oppressors. Our emotional life becomes an extension of our own values and a barometer for our needs rather than a liability or weakness we need to protect.

The Grammar of Inner Freedom

Have you ever tried to pull up grass to plant a garden? If you have, you know why activists call their work "grassroots" organizing. Our conditioning to blame others for our feelings is just as tenacious; it's a way of seeing that is deeply embedded in our minds.

There are a few telltale signs that you're playing the blame game, and a clear way to short-circuit it. First and foremost, watch for how our language constructs a narrative of blame. If you find yourself placing the cause of your feelings outside, thinking or saying, "I feel _____ *because you (they)* . . . ," turn it around and connect to your needs. As Rosenberg taught, use the following structure to locate the source of your feelings internally:

I feel _____ *because I* need / want / value _____.
You feel _____ *because you* need / want / value _____.

Note the parallel consistency of subjects: my feelings linked to my needs, your feelings linked to yours. Practice repeating this over and over again, until it becomes the default view of emotions in your mind. This will undercut the foundation of the blame game, making it easier to express yourself and to hear others.

Another way the blame game shows up in our language is by disguising thoughts as feelings:

I feel *like you* don't love me.
I feel *that this* whole thing is ridiculous.
I feel *as if* you're not listening.

Following the verb *feel* with *like*, *that*, or *as* will express a *thought* rather than a *feeling*—frequently blame, judgment, or interpretation. Similarly, following *I feel* with a pronoun or name will usually take us up into our head with analysis and evaluation:

I feel *I'm* no good at this.
I feel *they* keep putting things off intentionally.
I feel *Amy* isn't qualified.

These are indirect, alienated expressions of our emotions. They hinder our ability to be fully aware of our feelings, to express ourselves, or to hear others in ways that build understanding.

The last trick of the blame game is even more surreptitious. There are a variety of words in English that colloquially refer to emotions but instead express blame, attributing intention to another person. "I feel attacked" tells a story about what is happening: *you are attacking me*. What's more, it leaves out essential information about how I actually feel, which might be anything from afraid to hurt, angry, or confused. If we have the thought that someone is attacking us, here are a few examples of other ways we might express ourselves:

> "I'm feeling overwhelmed and confused, and would like to talk about this in a way that's easier for me take in. Could we slow down a bit?"

> "I'm a little taken aback and kind of stunned because I had no idea any of this was going on. Are you saying that . . . [empathy guess]?"

> "Ouch; that hurts. I really want to be seen for how hard I've worked on this. Can we take a few steps back and first review what's gone well?"

Each of these statements expresses our needs colloquially, adding context and authenticity, and ends with a request (something we'll explore in chapter 11).

PRACTICE: Noticing False Feelings

There are a range of words that fall into this category of "false feelings," that is, referring to an emotion by blaming the other person. In the list that follows, which of these do you find yourself using to express emotions? When you use that word, how do you feel on the inside?

False-Feeling Words

Abandoned	Diminished	Neglected	Treated unfairly
Abused	Dismissed	Patronized	Threatened
Attacked	Disrespected	Pressured	Unappreciated
Betrayed	Interrupted	Provoked	Unheard
Bullied	Intimidated	Put down	Unseen
Cheated	Let down	Rejected	Unsupported
Coerced	Manipulated	Taken advantage of	Unwanted
Cornered	Misunderstood	Taken for granted	Used

Translating Feelings—"How Do I Feel on the Inside?"

As you move through your day, pay attention to how you think and speak about your emotions. Be on the lookout for signs of the blame game: "because you," feeling "like or that," and false-feeling words. (Also watch out for the tendency to blame yourself for blaming!)

When you notice any of these, pause and ask yourself, "When I tell myself this, how do I feel on the inside?" Keep asking that question until you discern the actual emotions you are experiencing. Then try to connect your feelings to what matters. What do you value or need?

Listen to others in this way. Try to identify what they're feeling and, with a genuine intention to understand, consider what matters to them. What do they need that connects to these feelings? Try this silently at first, training your attention to identify feelings and needs.

If you find yourself caught in blaming perceptions, remember that they too are just another form of information, a particular way we've learned to become conscious of our needs. Shift your attention to the emotions beneath the words. Tune in to your feelings, and then listen for the needs to which they are connected. What matters to you?

Expressing Feelings

Speaking about his show, *Mr. Rogers' Neighborhood*, Fred Rogers once said to a US Senate committee that his aim was to "make it clear that feelings are mentionable and manageable."[11] This perspective lays the groundwork for being able to have successful, productive conversations about the things that matter, including our emotions.

When we've trained our mind in this way, we have a powerful technology to translate blame and judgment into the feelings and needs that move in the heart. Beneath "You're being cold," we hear the pain of longing for more affection or intimacy. Within the expression "Stop being so sensitive," we intuit frustration, perhaps a desire for more ease and flexibility. We learn to have empathy for others, regardless of how they're expressing themselves, and to share our own feelings openly in a way that others are more likely to understand.

Sharing our feelings and needs in this way can carry a lot of weight. Recently, my friend Sarah's mother died suddenly in the hospital. Lacking a clear diagnosis, her family made the difficult decision to conduct an autopsy. In handling the arrangements, Sarah had a challenging phone call with the funeral director, who scoffed at their choices and left out key scheduling information.

Disturbed by his lack of empathy, she asked to meet with the director in person. Sarah spoke openly and sincerely, in a nonblaming manner. "I am frustrated with the interaction we had yesterday," she said. "The loss of my mom has been incredibly challenging for my family, and it's really important to have as much clarity and ease as possible around these logistics." She explained that the decision to do an autopsy was very emotional for them. "For all of these reasons, I felt disappointed and frustrated by your responses to our questions." She encouraged him to respect the wishes of families and to interact with them with more compassion. By the end of the conversation, her clear, steady tone and openheartedness had its effect. The funeral director apologized, saying he understood and would try to communicate with more compassion in the future.

> *Principle:* **The more we take responsibility for our feelings, connecting them to our needs rather than to others' actions, the easier it is for others to hear us.**

> *Principle:* **The more we hear others' feelings as a reflection of their needs, the easier it is to understand them without hearing blame, needing to agree, or feeling responsible for their emotions.**

Just as with needs, talking about emotions can feel vulnerable. It's important to use wisdom in choosing when, where, and how to discuss them. This can vary widely depending on the context and culture. There's generally more bandwidth for talking about emotions in our personal life, intimate relationships, and friendships than in most professional settings. Yet when feelings are present, it's important to find a way to acknowledge and include them, regardless of the context. Otherwise they can start running the show beneath the surface.

When circumstances don't support discussing feelings openly, we can include them in conversation by understating them. To acknowledge anger without inviting too much vulnerability, try choosing words that reflect a lighter emotion or minimizing it with phrases such as "a little" or "kind of." For example, "Are you angry because you wanted things to go more smoothly?" becomes "Sounds like it's a little frustrating because you wanted things to go more smoothly?"

PRACTICE: Hearing and Expressing Emotions

Try acknowledging feelings in low-stakes situations. As you listen, reflect any emotions you hear in a natural, authentic way. You might simply remark, "Wow, sounds frustrating," or make an empathy guess, "Are you (feeling) . . . ?" When possible, connect the emotions you sense to needs, guessing at what matters.

When you feel emotions, ground awareness in your body. Give yourself some time to sense what's happening. Experiment with sharing your feelings and linking them with what matters to you. Can you be aware of your feelings as a reflection of your needs? Can you find ways to express them openly and honestly without blame, linking them to what you *do* want rather than what you *don't* want?

Being aware of our feelings and needs gives us more choice about how to respond to life. When our needs are met, we may savor, celebrate, or express gratitude. When our needs are not met, we can let someone know how their words or actions affected us, linking our emotions back to our own needs. When others express praise or blame, we can tune in to the feelings and needs they're experiencing.

When my mother and I finally reconciled, we were able to share how we felt and why. She wanted me to be happy, to live a life that she could understand and that was aligned with her values. I wanted to be seen, for her to have trust in my integrity and support for finding my own way. This understanding brought us so much closer.

In some circumstances, we may need to make a change or even end a relationship that is not serving us. Whatever course of action we take, we can choose to respond consciously rather than reactively, based on a clear discernment of our needs and an openness to dialogue.

We don't need to fear our emotions. We can learn to handle them with agility, listen to their signals, and find balance within their intensity. When we move beyond the binary options of avoiding and suppressing them or identifying with and acting them out, we allow emotions to flow through us as an integral part of being human. We can receive the information they offer about our heart, the deeper needs and values that trace the lines of our life.

PRINCIPLES

Being aware of our emotions supports our ability to choose consciously how we participate in a conversation.

The more we take responsibility for our feelings, connecting them to our needs rather than to others' actions, the easier it is for others to hear us.

The more we hear others' feelings as a reflection of their needs, the easier it is to understand them without hearing blame, needing to agree, or feeling responsible for their emotions.

KEY POINTS

We tend to relate to our emotions by suppressing them or getting entangled with them, yet emotions are a natural part of being human that gives us important information about our needs. Mindfulness is the primary tool to develop our capacity to:

- Identify emotions (emotion recognition), noticing and naming what we're feeling
- Feel emotions with balance (emotion regulation), having the space inside to appreciate the pleasant ones and tolerate the discomfort of unpleasant ones
- Hear and express emotions without blame (emotion expression), connecting them to underlying needs or values

Taking responsibility for our feelings and extricating ourselves from blame involve keen attention to the mechanisms of perception in our mind that generate and reinforce the blame game. We know we're playing the blame game when we:

- Construct a narrative of blame, placing the cause of our feelings outside
- Directly link our feelings to another's actions
- Disguise thoughts as feelings
- Use false-feeling words, words that refer to emotions but instead express blame, attributing intention to another person

QUESTION & ANSWER

Q: What if I don't notice any emotions or can't feel anything in my body?
This is quite common. We live in a disembodied society, so it can take time to feel our body and experience emotions. If our emotions weren't validated growing up, we may have learned to repress or avoid them. Or we may have shut ourselves off to our emotions after a traumatic event. Regardless of the cause, you can reawaken the ability to feel and develop a richer relationship with yourself and with life.

Notice that experience of "not feeling anything." Is it blank, empty, numb? Is it located in any particular area of your body? Stay with it; keep being aware. Movement, yoga, dance, or exercise can help. Speak with friends and ask how they think you might be feeling. Sometimes getting a reflection can help you recognize how you feel.

Last, talk to your heart. It sounds hokey, but it works. Tell your own unconscious that you're available to feel more. Before sleep or upon rising, say to yourself something to the effect of, "I'm interested in feeling my emotions. I'm here; I'm willing to feel." This plants a seed inside your psyche that can be the catalyst for opening to your emotions.

Q: I have the opposite issue. I feel so much I get overwhelmed easily. How can I work with this?
Noticing this pattern is the first step to shifting it. Being able to name what's happening is huge. Study the underlying dynamics. Are there particular situations that trigger the overwhelm? What helps you to rebalance? Use the practice for soothing strong emotions or the orienting exercise in chapter 3. Many of our emotional wounds arose in relationships, so it can also be healing to explore these patterns in a safe, supportive context with someone else, be it a friend, a mentor, or a professional counselor.

Q: We're not responsible for others' reactions, but we do affect each other. How do you handle it when you've done something that was hurtful without getting entangled in the blame game?

I want to be able to acknowledge when I've done something that doesn't meet someone else's needs and to repair any damage to the relationship. There's a difference between a heartfelt apology and taking on blame. The former acknowledges the impact of my actions and expresses my sincere care or regret. The latter interprets my intentions or makes a character judgment of me as being bad or wrong.

Q: What about when I really do feel manipulated or betrayed? What's the role of anger in mindful communication?

Anger is a completely natural emotion. It's a strong signal that our needs aren't being met. Evolutionarily it protects us when we perceive a threat in our environment. The destructive effects of anger come from how we handle it, not from the anger itself. When we can differentiate the stories of blame from our unmet needs, we can express ourselves more constructively.

Feeling "manipulated" or "betrayed" indicates that your emotions are colored by an interpretation about the other person's intentions. To honor the intensity of your experience without getting entangled in the blame game, see those words as information that points back to your feelings and needs. Investigate what's in your heart. When you tell yourself, "I'm being manipulated," how do you feel on the inside? What do you need?

Once this is clear, work on conveying the depth of your feelings without blame. Express the rawness of your emotions and connect them to what matters to you. If you can't find other words (and if you think the other person will understand), you could take responsibility for the blame by saying something such as, "I'm telling myself a story that you betrayed me." This indicates your subjective interpretation while leaving space for the other person's experience.

Q: What if I don't have time to feel my emotions during the day?

This is where formal mindfulness practice can be really beneficial. Taking time for contemplative practice gives us a chance to sort through the day so we're not carrying the residue of our emotional responses. It also sharpens our awareness and helps us build capacity. The more we explore strong sensations and challenging emotions "on the cushion," the more skilled we become at feeling and processing emotions "off the cushion" in our lives. Formal mindfulness practice also creates more space inside to tolerate the discomfort of unpleasant emotions without reacting, which enables us to respond in the moment with more care and thoughtfulness.

enhancing empathy and inner resilience

Learning to stand in somebody else's shoes, to see through
their eyes, that's how peace begins. . . . Empathy is a quality
of character that can change the world.
    —PRESIDENT BARACK OBAMA

THE COMMUNICATION WE'RE exploring in this book involves a deft
shifting of attention from our inner experience to the experience of
another. This flexibility confers great skill in dialogue and becomes
possible when we've trained ourselves in empathy.

In formal meditation, the rhythmic sensations of breathing in and
breathing out offer a reliable method to steady awareness and develop
mindfulness, concentration, and wisdom. In communication practice
(which is its own form of meditative training), awareness of feelings and
needs supports our ability to stay present, to express ourselves clearly, and
to hear others with empathy.

In the third step to effective conversation, sometimes empathy is what
matters most. As we've seen, empathic listening is what allows us to
actually hear one another. It is a potent source for healing and resilience.
It's such an indispensable aspect of communication that I'd like to explore
some additional ways to refine this capacity.

Letting in the Good: Gratitude, Joy, and Celebration

When we think of empathy, we often focus on handling pain, conflict, and
disagreement. Empathy does apply to handling difficulty, but it is also an
essential tool for enhancing goodness: deepening friendships, strengthening bonds, and appreciating the beauty of life. Empathy is the resonant

capacity of our heart. And when we turn this capacity to that which is nourishing, our heart rejoices. When I shared the news of my ordination as a Buddhist monastic with my family, I was longing for empathy for my joy—to be joined in my celebration.

This quality (called *mudita*, or "appreciative joy," in Buddhism) enhances our well-being and builds resilience. As I've heard it told, the Dalai Lama once said, "When you count others' happiness as your own, your chances of being happy increase six billion to one."

This ability to nourish the healthy aspects of our lives is an important, often overlooked aspect of healing. It can take courage to slow down enough to enjoy a success, take pleasure in a need met, or feel an affirming sensation. With practice, we can broaden our use of empathy to savor the good, cultivate gratitude for the happiness in our own lives, and celebrate the joy or good fortune of others.[1] Try the practices below anytime.

PRACTICE: Gratitude, Joy, and Celebration

Take time to contemplate something that you appreciate in life. Be as specific as possible: a meal you ate, a friend you saw recently. Let this circumstance come alive in your mind's eye. Notice any feelings of warmth, gratitude, or appreciation that arise. Where do you notice those emotions in your body? What's it feel like there?

Next, consider what needs of yours have been met. What matters about this situation, event, or person? Take time to savor the enjoyment of having your needs met. Like soaking in a bath, let yourself fully absorb this.

Turn this appreciative gaze outward. When you hear good news or spend time with someone who is enjoying happiness or success, tune in to their well-being. Can you celebrate with them? Notice any tendency to compare, contract, or believe that their good fortune somehow reduces the amount of happiness available to you. How would you feel if this person were your child? Can you stretch your empathy to celebrate their happiness?

Self-Empathy: The Strength of Tenderness

During that difficult period in my early twenties while working at a meditation center in rural Massachusetts, I felt increasingly lonely and isolated.

As contemplative practice drew my attention inward, I began to feel trapped in my desire for connection. I yearned for others to ask how I was doing, yet few were able to offer the kind of attunement I needed to feel safe enough to share. Every failure to connect reinforced the isolation and heightened my desperation to be seen. Being caught in this vicious cycle was paralyzing.

Pain can block empathy. When we are mired in our own distress, it can be difficult to let empathy touch us, let alone listen to others or offer them empathy. Without ways to handle our own suffering, communication becomes increasingly challenging.

Eventually I found one or two people who had the capacity to offer empathy in a way that I could receive. This eased the intensity of my longing and catalyzed a shift that continued to unfold for several years.

Sometimes, receiving empathy is the balm we need to heal. Through the care of others we learn to develop tenderness toward ourselves. Self-empathy enhances resilience, transforming our relationship with ourselves from harshness and judgment to kindness and self-compassion. It includes handling stress and emotional pain, finding peace with unmet needs, and healing our inner critic.

Not only does this make life more enjoyable, but it also gives us considerably more options in dialogue. Self-empathy strengthens patience. With a moment of mindful self-empathy, we can acknowledge our inner experience, put it aside temporarily, and create the space to hear someone else.

Principle: **Having empathy for ourselves increases our capacity to listen to others, whether or not they have the space to listen to us.**

◀)) PRACTICE: Self-Empathy

Use this meditation regularly to develop your ability to bring the caring attitude of empathy to yourself.

Begin by settling and establishing presence in whatever way feels authentic and natural for you—grounding in the body or taking some slow, mindful breaths. Next, call to mind a situation or event for which you'd like to develop self-empathy (nothing too painful to start).

What emotions are present? Feel their sensations in your body. If the emotion is strong, widen your attention to the rest of your body. Can you bring a quality of tenderness to any painful feelings?

Next, inquire about your needs and values, listening inwardly for what matters. Ask, "If I had that, then what would I have?" or, "What matters about that to me?" Inquire until you feel clear about your needs. Again, see if you can bring a quality of tenderness to how much you value this. Call forth all the care you can find for yourself and rest your attention with this feeling of kindness.

Finally, shift your attention to the universal aspect of the need or value itself as a facet of our shared humanity. Can you connect with any sense of wholeness, beauty, or dignity in this value?

The Riverbanks of Empathy: Dealing with Empathic Distress

There is an *empathy spectrum* in humans, a range of access to empathy and a range of intensity with which we feel it.[2] At times, empathy can come so easily that we feel overwhelmed or flooded by the depth of feeling. Indeed, one common cause of compassion fatigue is a kind of overidentification with the suffering of another, sometimes referred to as *empathic distress*.[3]

In these instances, the skill of empathy involves learning to manage our distress and sense our separateness. If we become overwhelmed, we lose the ability to engage skillfully. Out of self-protection, we may react in an attempt to manage our own pain or withdraw in fear of becoming lost in another's experience.

PRACTICE: Meeting Empathic Distress in the Body

The three kinds of empathy (somatic, affective, cognitive) provide a useful framework to build a strong inner container, like having riverbanks that support the flow of empathy.[4]

Try the following somatic exercises to regain balance:

- **Orient** to your surroundings to register physical safety.
- **Ground** your attention, connecting with gravity or another embodied

reference point (your centerline, breathing, or touch points such as your hands or feet).

- **Sense** the boundaries of your skin. Engage in any activity that stimulates the felt sense of your body, such as exercise, massage, gently squeezing your limbs, or a hot shower.
- **Notice** the physical space between you and the other person or notice the space around you.

In the affective domain, do your best to pause further input. For example, many people today suffer from empathic distress due to overexposure to intense worldwide suffering through the news media. Recovering and developing a more balanced relationship with empathy often includes limiting one's intake of news for a time.

In conversation, if you begin to feel overwhelmed or lose presence, find a way to skillfully pause the dialogue. Affirm your desire to stay connected, then share your need for a break. Here are a few examples:

- "I think I need a moment to gather my thoughts."
- "Wow, I'd like some time to take that in. Can we pause here for a moment?"
- "I'd really like to continue discussing this, and I'm feeling a little overwhelmed. Could we take a break and continue tomorrow?"

Once you've pressed pause, here are a few ways to integrate and digest what's been stimulated emotionally:

- **Receive** empathy from a friend or a mentor.
- **Engage** in self-empathy practice.
- **Soothe** strong emotions with formal mindfulness practice.
- **Balance** your activation with forms of healthy pleasure such as time in nature, art, or music.

Finally, in the cognitive domain, explore underlying beliefs that contribute to any overidentification with another's feelings. Talk with a friend and try to uncover any assumptions you have about your role in the situation, what it means to care, or how healing occurs. Here are a few of the common beliefs that may be at play:

- You may believe it's your responsibility to take care of others out of duty, fear, or an inability to handle your own discomfort with their struggle.
- You may identify with being a caregiver and feel disoriented by the possibility of stepping out of that role.
- You may believe that caring means suffering, that you can't genuinely have compassion for someone in pain and still be happy yourself.
- You may believe that you know what they need better than they do.
- If you sense that the other person doesn't have sufficient inner or outer resources, you may automatically take on more responsibility instead of supporting their agency or capacity for self-care.
- You may have other conscious or unconscious beliefs that oblige you to take on the other person's suffering.

These beliefs can be deeply rooted, compelling you to "fall in" to another person's pain out of your desire to help. Investigate what may be driving your own empathic distress. If you step back, you'll recognize that you have more to offer when you're balanced and well-resourced.

True empathy rests upon being centered. It arises from a deep trust in life and the innate intelligence of the mind and body. When we try to fix, change, or resolve another's pain (believing that we even could), we contribute to their fear and helplessness, effectively saying, "You can't figure this out, so let me do it for you."

In contrast, the empathic response allows experience to be just as it is. The acceptance, trust, and genuine care of empathy impart a sense of empowerment and often a healing power. As Carl Rogers wrote:

When someone really hears you without passing judgment on you, without trying to take responsibility for you, without trying to mold you, it feels damn good. When I have been listened to and when I have been heard, I am able to re-perceive my world in a new way and to go on. It is astonishing how elements which seem insoluble become soluble when someone listens. How confusions which seem irremediable turn into relatively clear flowing streams when one is heard.[5]

The key to this sort of balance is being able to maintain perspective. We recall certain fundamental truths. Being alive is inherently vulnerable; we all suffer and feel pain. Life is a series of ups and downs, with inevitable challenges and losses. We're ultimately not in control—we can neither prevent nor remove another's hardships. This is the wisdom of an elder. It lends equanimity and tenderness in the face of difficulty.

When our capacity for empathy is integrated in all three domains—when cognitive empathy is imbued with wisdom, when affective empathy is balanced with resource, and when somatic empathy is grounded in presence—the result is a resilience and poise in relation to pain and suffering. Our heart can resonate with the joys and sorrows of others without being overwhelmed.

Empathy without Agreement

When we disagree, we may resist opening our heart to someone else out of concern that having empathy means agreeing with their views or that it would be interpreted as such. Yet showing that we understand how someone feels or what matters to them is not the same as agreeing with their ideas or supporting actions that don't align with our values.

This is one of the great strengths of empathy: the possibility of finding connection without agreement. When we focus our attention on another's feelings and needs, it helps us tune in to their experience and connect with empathy. Try the following exercise to strengthen your capacity for empathy and enhance your ability to shift back and forth from your own experience to another's.

PRACTICE: Empathy Map

Use this reflection to explore a disagreement or prepare for a conversation. Begin with simpler, less emotionally charged situations, working up to more difficult ones. Draw four quadrants on a piece of paper as in the diagram below.

1. Explore your feelings and enter those in the upper left quadrant.
2. To what needs is each of those feelings connected? What matters

most to you? Explore your needs sufficiently until you feel a sense of settling. Enter those needs in the lower left quadrant.

3. Shift your attention to the other person and explore their feelings. Imagine what emotions they might be feeling. Enter those in the upper right quadrant.

4. Stretch your heart and consider their needs. What matters to this person? To what needs might their feelings be connected? If you don't feel support for their needs, then you haven't gotten to the level of their real needs. Inquire, "If they had that, then what would they have?" Enter those needs into the lower right quadrant.

5. Compare the two sides. Does anything shift for you? How might you approach the situation having done this exercise?

Empathy Map

My Feelings	Your Feelings
My Needs	Your Needs

Refining Empathy: Beyond You or Me

In this chapter we've explored several methods to navigate the interpersonal terrain of empathy: building an inner well of resources through joy, gratitude, and self-empathy; supporting empathy with strong riverbanks; and stretching our capacity to connect when we disagree. At the center of these techniques lies a fundamental willingness to be affected. Empathy challenges our notions of separateness. To open my heart to the joy or pain of another means that I am willing to feel, willing to be moved.

When I ended my time as a Buddhist monastic after two and a half years and returned to lay life, things got hard fast. In the space of one week, I contracted Lyme disease, left the monastery, and admitted my father to the hospital for systemic sepsis. My own health complications from the Lyme extended from weeks into months. At one point, when sharing my profound exhaustion with a good friend, she looked at me and simply said about the Lyme, "I'm so, so sorry that happened."

It was a moment of true empathy, of sincere and palpable caring. She was not "reflecting feelings and needs." She was not making an empathic guess or checking if she understood. Having allowed herself to feel my struggle, to sense my pain directly, she authentically expressed the truth in her own heart. In that instance I was no longer alone.

In the fields of counseling, psychology, and interpersonal communication we sometimes speak of "giving" and "receiving" empathy. As long as there is a concept of a giver and a receiver, a fixed sense of me and you, we are not inhabiting the full potential of empathy. True empathy transcends the duality between speaker and listener. Instead of engaging in an exchange, we enter a field of empathic presence—one of awareness, warmth, and care—in which all experience, regardless of its local identity as mine or yours, is known and felt. We enter that space by using whatever tools support our ability to open our heart to another's experience.

I believe our society and world today have a vast need for this kind of true, deep empathy. From our individual hunger for connection and healing to the urgent need to bridge political, class, and racial divides; from a growing global refugee crisis to the dangerous effects of climate change— empathy can extend our sense of identity beyond traditional borders, even beyond the human family to include other species and the biosphere as a whole. Fritz Perls, the psychiatrist who founded gestalt therapy, once said, "Contact is curative." Our ability to develop empathy and genuinely contact each other holds an essential key to our evolution as a species and survival as a civilization.

PRACTICE: Ways of Empathy

Below is a review of empathy practices. Experiment with these methods to access, share, and express empathy:

SILENT EMPATHIC PRESENCE: Offer your wholehearted, undivided attention to another.

PARAPHRASING: Offer your understanding of the gist of what the other person has said, summarizing their story or its key details.

EMPATHIC REFLECTION: Complete the cycle by reflecting before you respond, focusing on what's most salient in the moment. If feelings are what's strongest, offer an empathic guess of the other person's feelings. If their passion seems connected to what matters, guess at their needs. Practice the grammar of inner freedom by connecting their feelings to their needs. Do this as naturally as possible, being sure to phrase your guess as a question. You're checking that you understand rather than telling the other person their experience.

EMPATHIC EXPRESSION: Respond honestly and authentically from your heart. Let yourself take in what's been shared. How do their words affect you?

EMPATHIC/COMPASSIONATE ACTION: Allow yourself to respond with action. This could be touch, inquiring if they have any specific requests, or checking to see if the other person would welcome your support in other ways.

PRINCIPLES

Having empathy for ourselves increases our capacity to listen to others, whether or not they have the space to listen to us.

KEY POINTS

Empathy challenges our notions of separateness. To open our heart to the joy or pain of another means we must be willing to feel. To enhance our access to empathy, we can:

- Build an inner well of resilience through joy, gratitude, and self-empathy
- Manage any distress, potential for overwhelm, or sense of separateness by integrating all three kinds of empathy: somatic, affective, and cognitive
- Stretch our capacity to connect when we disagree by focusing our attention on another's feelings and needs

We can further balance empathic distress by:

- Taking a break from the conversation
- Getting empathy or practicing self-empathy
- Self-soothing through healthy pleasure (exercise, music, art)
- Exploring any beliefs that create obligation, entanglement, or distortion of responsibility with regards to another's pain

QUESTION & ANSWER

Q: When I empathize, am I just projecting my own experience onto someone?

This is the paradox of empathy, which asks one to be fully present, rooted in oneself, and simultaneously transcend one's own experience—to step outside of it and imagine another's inner world. In some ways, we're always referencing our own subjective experience to understand one another. Each of our experiences is unique, yet we have words for emotions and needs because there is a universal nature to them. While I can never know *exactly* how it is for you to feel sad, I can approximate because I've felt sad.

There's a kind of humility in true empathy. The absence of this quality says, "I know exactly how you feel." The presence of humility says, "I *can't* know exactly how you feel, but I care about what's happening for you and I will try to understand." This humility contains within it a deep respect and honor for another's experience.

Q: What's the difference between empathy and compassion?

The way I use these terms, *empathy* is broader and refers to the resonant capacity of the heart. It's a receptive quality that can attune to the full range of human experience, pleasant or unpleasant, joy as well as sadness. *Compassion* is a subset of empathy, referring specifically to care for suffering and pain. The receptive aspect of compassion is empathic attunement to the suffering. The active component of compassion is a readiness to respond in order to alleviate suffering. Both empathy and compassion depend on equanimity; we need balance and wisdom to be aware of another's inner experience without becoming overidentified with it.

Q: I keep trying to empathize with my teenage daughter, but it doesn't seem to help. I'll say, "I hear how much you really want to go out tonight, but I need to finish this work so I can't take you." She just gets angry or says that I don't really care.

I'm glad you're making an effort to use these tools with your family. I have more hope for our world when I think about children learning these skills.

I see a couple of things in your approach that indicate why your daughter might not feel seen or heard. You seem to have already come to the conclusion that there isn't a way to meet both your needs and her needs. Having a fixed outcome in mind leaves less room to connect and collaborate. This shows up in how quickly you move from empathy to your own needs.

Separate offering your daughter empathy from expressing your needs. Give her your full and complete attention, reflecting her feelings and/or needs until she feels heard. *Then* share your side of things and propose brainstorming to find something that works for both of you. Maybe she helps you and then you take her? Could she take a cab and work later to pay you back? Even if you can't find a way to meet all of the needs, listening and being open to collaborating will likely strengthen the relationship.

how to raise an issue
without starting a fight

The ability to observe without evaluating is
the highest form of human intelligence.
—JIDDU KRISHNAMURTI

WE'VE EXPLORED THE process of listening at some length—using
presence and intention to meet others with a balanced and open mind,
identifying emotions, sensing needs, and developing empathy. These practices enhance our ability to listen, and they form the basis for speaking.

Whenever I teach mindful communication, I generally introduce tools
for listening before speaking for a few reasons. First, it's often the bottle-
neck in conversation. When neither person can listen, understanding ceases
and conversation can break down. Second, it's how we learn to speak.
Every infant learns to speak by hearing the sounds, rhythm, and syntax of
their native language. When we train to listen, we begin intuitively to learn
how to articulate ourselves.

Now let's talk about the other side of the equation: self-expression.
How do we say what we mean? To say what we mean requires *knowing*
what we mean. We must be able to listen inwardly and get clear about our
experience. What do we want the other person to know? And how can we
communicate that fully and authentically, in a way that they can hear?

The core of Rosenberg's Nonviolent Communication model—observations, feelings, needs, and requests—offers a powerful template to investigate our own experience, thoughts, and emotions and to determine the
essential components we wish to communicate. Before discussing our
feelings and needs, we may need to get on the same page about the events in
question. Making observations helps us talk about the *context* of a situa-

tion. When we don't make observations, we can end up arguing about stuff that doesn't matter or just feeling confused about the topic of discussion.

In this chapter we shift our attention in the communication dance from listening to speaking. We'll explore the role of making observations in conversations, look at some tools for training our attention to observe clearly, and learn how to translate judgments into useful feedback.

What Are You Adding?

The Buddhist teacher Sylvia Boorstein tells the story of calling a Zen meditation center to register for an upcoming retreat (this was in the days before online registration). She reached the receptionist, who explained she would need to speak with a man named Steve who had already left for the day. She called back the following day, only to find that she had just missed Steve again, and was told to try back tomorrow when Steve would be in by 9:00 a.m. The next day she dutifully called shortly after 9:00 a.m. only to be told by the receptionist, "I'm so sorry. Steve is stuck in traffic."

Feeling frustrated, Sylvia exclaimed, "Well, I guess this means I'm not supposed to sit this retreat!" The receptionist replied rather dryly, "No, it means Steve's not here."

We can jump to conclusions so quickly! Joseph Goldstein describes an interview with a student on a meditation retreat who had been noticing tension in his jaw. He began to weave a story, telling Joseph, "I'm such an anxious person, always so tense and uptight." Joseph responded, "It sounds like you noticed your jaw was tight." The student continued, "I've always been high-strung. That's probably why my relationships never last. I'll never have a long-term relationship because I'm so anxious . . . I'll always be alone." Again, Joseph pointed out, "It sounds like you experienced a feeling of tightness in your jaw; the rest is thinking."

Experience is one thing; what we add to it is another. Knowing the difference between these two is the key to talking about what happened in a way that builds understanding.

> *Principle:* Stating clearly what happened, without judgment or evaluation, makes it easier for someone to hear us and to work toward a solution.

Have you ever tried to have a conversation only to find yourself in the middle of an argument in less than one sentence? Maybe you begin, "I wanted to talk about how messy the kitchen's been lately—" and before you can get another word out the person is defending themselves or accusing you of being a neat freak. "What just happened?" you wonder.

If we lead with a subjective interpretation that the other person doesn't share, they're likely to challenge it. The blame game thrives on interpretations: "messy, ignored, attacked." Clear observations allow us to discuss events with less chance of an argument.

You also may have had a corollary experience: someone approaches you and launches into a diatribe, visibly upset. You're confused, caught off guard. You may think to yourself, "What are they talking about?"

Without an observation, we are left on our own to puzzle things out. Observations provide a shared reference point. They give us a context to talk about our feelings and needs in a way that the other person is more likely to recognize without needing to argue.

An *observation* is a concrete, specific, and neutral statement of an event, of what we see or hear in our environment, distinct from evaluation or interpretation.

Referring to what happened clearly and neutrally makes it easier to get on the same page. We can cover a lot of ground in dialogue just by sifting through interpretations, judgments, and evaluations and building a shared understanding of events.

Seeing Clearly

My good friend Hanuman knows something about separating observations from interpretations. One afternoon in Boston, he met an attractive young woman while waiting at a crosswalk. They had a short but warm connection, and they exchanged numbers. A few days later he called and left a message. After a couple of weeks, when he didn't hear back, he decided to call again. More time passed with no response. Hanuman stuck with his observations: he'd felt a genuine connection when they met; he'd left a few messages and hadn't heard back. That's all he knew.

Over the next few months, he called a few more times, leaving short, friendly messages with an open invitation to connect. Months later, the phone rang. She'd been doing her residency, pulling all-nighters, and said she was so glad he kept calling. They went kayaking and ended up dating for over three years.

It's natural to interpret and draw conclusions from our experience; it's part of how we navigate life. Our brains continually evaluate, discerning safety from danger, friend from foe. Clear discernment is useful. Reactive, automatic, or habitual judgment is not. The problem is when we evaluate without awareness, mistaking our interpretations for reality. Conflating observations and evaluations creates stress internally and can wreak havoc in our relationships. We can interpret a single facial expression to mean anything, spinning an entire narrative of antagonism without even checking if we understood in the first place. The mind jumps so quickly from an event to an interpretation that we easily miss the fact that these are two separate things.

Mindfulness is often defined as awareness free from distortion or bias. It illuminates the process of interpretation, clarifying the difference between our direct experience and the stories we tell about it. One Buddhist text enjoins the practitioner to discern "in the seen, just what is seen; in the heard, just what is heard."[1] We can use mindfulness to deconstruct our beliefs and interpretations. Applying careful attention, we tease apart the actual events—specific data in our environment—from the added layers of thought, perception, and reactivity.

Clearly knowing this difference can be profound. Many of our most painful core beliefs and psychological patterns are rooted in unseen, unquestioned stories about who we are, how others see us, or what life can offer.

The basic building block of this process is to identify what happened as directly as possible. To determine if something is an observation, ask yourself, "Could this be caught on film?" A camera registers movement and sound. It can't record someone "behaving coldly." It can't demonstrate someone "never" or "always" doing anything. Does a video camera record someone "ignoring me," or does it record one person walking past another while looking ahead?

Another key metric for making an observation is the likelihood that it might bring up defensiveness. Remember, if we're interested in creating understanding, our overall aim is to use language that leads to connection. How might you state this neutrally, so that the other person can recognize it without taking issue? "When I saw you walk in and turn on the TV" is less likely to trigger an argument than "When you ignore me."

The classical form of NVC for training attention to make observations is, "When I see / hear . . ." Beginning with the pronoun "I" rather than "you" shifts the focus from the other person to our direct experience. Verbs such as "see" and "hear" help us focus on the specific event rather than our interpretations. (This also indicates that we might remember events differently.)

Here are a few pointers on making observations:

- Use mindfulness to discern the raw data of what happened.
- Separate what you actually know from assumptions or interpretations.
- To check, ask yourself, "Could this be caught on film?"
- Avoid words that exaggerate or interpret: *always*, *never*, *ever*, *whenever*, *rarely*.
- State your experience in the first person, "When *I* see/hear/ notice . . ." rather than "When *you* said/did . . ."
- Determine if you are confident the other person would recognize this without growing defensive. If not, refine it further.

Below are some examples of the difference between an evaluation and an observation. Evaluative terms are indicated in italics. Which is more or less likely to build understanding?

Evaluation	Observation
"You *rarely* come home on time." "You're *always* late."	"I noticed you came home twenty minutes after you said you would . . ."
"You're so *amazing*."	"When I see the things you've accomplished . . ."
"When you're *rude* to me . . ."	"When I hear you say that . . ." "When I hear you say, 'Whatever' and look away . . ." "When I see this certain expression on your face . . ."

Once we've made an observation, we link that to our own internal experience—our feelings and needs—to share where we're at inside. These three components—an observation, a feeling, and a need—provide a simple map to say what we mean, discerning inwardly and sharing outwardly how we're doing. *What happened? How do you feel about it? Why?* Training our attention to identify these specific components gives us clear and powerful information to state our experience.

PRACTICE: Getting Concrete

Think of a recent situation that has some significance, positive or negative. Consider the following questions:

OBSERVATION: WHAT HAPPENED? Try to be as specific as possible. If you were to state this to the other person, would they agree with your description or get defensive?

FEELINGS: HOW DO YOU FEEL? What emotions are in your heart? See blaming thoughts or false-feeling words as information to uncover your emotions.

NEEDS: WHAT MATTERS? For each emotion, listen inwardly and connect it to your needs. Try to become conscious of what matters in terms of what you *do* want rather than what you *don't* want.

Does doing this reflection give you more clarity or shift how you might discuss these events with the other person?

Part of making observations is recognizing that there is often more than one perspective on a situation and that our observations will almost always be colored by our subjective experience. A well-known Buddhist allegory illustrates just how limited our perspectives can be. A king gathered a group of blind men, asking each to feel a different part of an elephant's body. One held the ear, another the tusk, a third the tail, and so on. When asked if they knew what they touched, each responded with confidence: "It's a basket . . ." "It's a plowshare . . ." "It's a rope . . ."[2]

We can be so certain of our observations, assuming that we see the whole picture. This goes beyond the personal level, in which our vantage points differ based on our subjective individual experience, to the collective level, in which our differing experiences of systemic oppression, power, and privilege can yield divergent observations. My own privilege, for instance, can blind me to certain group dynamics.[3] At one conference, a female colleague gently pointed out how my quickness to speak first reflected a lack of awareness of the power dynamics inherent in my position in society. I observed that there was a period of silence, and then I spoke. She observed that none of the people of color present had spoken yet, and a *white male* spoke following a temporary silence. I only saw things from the individual perspective, while she observed through a wider lens. Given the dominance of white male voices in almost all aspects of society, my choice to speak first can be seen and understood very differently from a systemic perspective than from an individual one.

Not only do our observations vary, but our interpretations of their *impact*—the meaning we assign them—also differ greatly depending on the context. A female student of mine recently complained of an ongoing situation at her legal firm in which a peer, male colleague regularly offers her unsolicited feedback. He observes his actions on the personal level, loosely aware of an intention to contribute. She experiences his actions within the context of a lifetime of being treated as inferior by men and from the collective, historical perspective of patriarchal oppression of women. She can see his intentions, but he is blind to the impact of his actions. To fully build mutual understanding and address the situation, he may need to acknowledge her frame of reference and understand his actions in a wider context. Similarly, some may view the success of an African American individual (Barack Obama, Oprah Winfrey) as proof of the American dream and the eradication of racism, while others understand the same observation as an exceptional accomplishment within a larger context of struggle. Bringing humility to the way we view an event and recognizing the possibility of other perspectives can help widen our view and open the door for more understanding.

The Ladder of Inference

When we're unaware of our interpretations (and the context upon which we base them), we tend to state them as facts, presenting our way of seeing things as reality. This can spark arguments and leave little room for dialogue.

To communicate effectively, we need to investigate the very process of perception whereby our feelings and needs color events. Just as we bring a keen observing attention to the specific events around us, we can bring a radical honesty to the interpretations we add to an experience. The more aware we are of our judgments and evaluations, the more flexibility we have with how we express ourselves.

Chris Argyris, a prominent business theorist and author connected to Harvard Business School, devised a visual metaphor called the *Ladder of Inference* to map the process of how we make interpretations and jump to conclusions.[4]

You can see a version of his model in figure 6. At the bottom of the ladder is all observable data: the wealth of images, sounds, thoughts, feelings, and sensations that constitute our life. (Internal events, such as

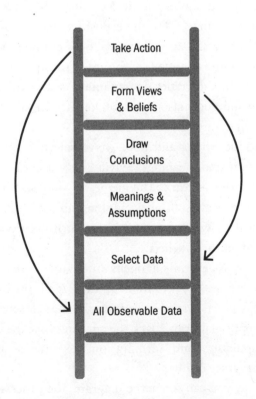

Take Action

Form Views
& Beliefs

Draw
Conclusions

Meanings &
Assumptions

Select Data

All Observable Data

FIGURE 6. THE LADDER OF INFERENCE

thoughts and feelings, are also part of this data, since observing our internal experience is essential for skillful communication.) From this pool of information, our mind naturally selects certain data as more or less relevant. For example, if we're having a conversation in a restaurant, we focus on the words of our interlocutor and filter out other conversations and ambient sounds.

However, we tend to select data based on our views and biases. The negativity bias, whereby we attend more to perceived threats in the environment, is one example. In the classic roommate dynamic, the person who likes things neat usually notices only the behaviors of their roommate that *don't* match their preferences for cleanliness and overlooks times they are tidy or make contributions in other ways. This selection process itself is a form of interpretation, skewing our perspective.

An essential part of strengthening romantic relationships is countering these tendencies by bringing attention to the goodness that exists, building what psychologist and author John M. Gottman calls a system of "fondness and admiration."[5] Are there positive aspects of our partner's behavior, actions, or personality that we take for granted? What would be the effect of paying more conscious attention to those attributes instead of focusing solely on the difficulties or irritants? As we explored in the last chapter, savoring the good also improves mental health, resilience, and emotional well-being.

From the specific events and data we've selected, our mind begins making assumptions and meanings. Sylvia says, "I guess this means I'm not supposed to sit this retreat." The meditator shares, "I've always been high-strung." The process continues climbing up the ladder, as effortless as a monkey in a tree. We draw conclusions, form fixed views, and then speak or act based on those beliefs.

This whole process generally happens automatically, usually under the radar of our awareness. We are, by definition, ignorant of our assumptions. Mindfulness practice teaches us to look more closely at these inner workings of perception; it draws back the curtain to see the wizard of consciousness manipulating and forming our experience into the neat categories that structure our life.

What's more, as you can see in the diagram, the process has feedback loops. Our views and beliefs make it more likely that we will select certain data. Our very choices and actions affect what data we have access to, determining who we spend time with, what events or activities we attend, and so forth.

This process occurs collectively as well. The news and entertainment media are powerful societal filtering mechanisms, selecting and presenting data based on what sells. The algorithms driving social media create online filter bubbles in which we are exposed only to information that confirms our preexisting views. The effects of these biases become lodged in our consciousness. Consider the effect on a young gay person when none of their school classes celebrate examples of LGBTQI adults or the effect on people coming from impoverished families of seeing only stories of financial success on TV.

The implications of how this process operates in our lives are dramatic and far reaching. These filters narrow our views, fueling fear and antagonism by eliminating opportunities to build diverse relationships. As Martin Luther King Jr. said in a speech in 1962:

> I am convinced that men hate each other because they fear each other. They fear each other because they don't know each other, and they don't know each other because they don't communicate with each other, and they don't communicate with each other because they are separated from each other.[6]

We can use the Ladder of Inference to catalyze our awareness. When we are embroiled in conflict, we are often high up on the ladder, locked in views about one another, our motives, or intentions. Painful emotions also can drive us up the ladder, as we attempt to make sense of another's actions. The specific distinctions between various "rungs" is less important than becoming aware of how high up we are on the ladder and growing skilled at traveling back *down* so we can make observations that the other person will recognize.

PRACTICE: Using the Ladder

As you move through your day, pay attention to your inner narrative of thoughts. When you notice interpretations about yourself or others that are higher up on the ladder, see if you can come back down. What are the actual events to which you are reacting?

Pay attention to conversations. Notice when you or others are higher up on the ladder. What are the specific data points in question? What would be the effect of shifting the dialogue to these specifics rather than the interpretations?

Translating Negative Judgments

Coming down the ladder isn't always easy, especially with strong, negative interpretations. In their raw form, such reactive judgments are likely to embroil us in argument. We can release ourselves from their grip and step out of the blame game by uncoupling judgments from specific observations, our feelings, and the needs associated with them. This gives us more options to talk with the other person and can transform the narrative of blame that often makes it difficult to hear one another.

> *Principle:* Translating judgments into observations, feelings, and needs can yield valuable information about what is and isn't working and provide clues for how to move forward.

In training ourselves to make observations, we are cultivating a commitment to honesty. When we consider the difference between an observation and an evaluation, which is true? Is he really "being rude" or would it be more truthful to say that he did or said something that you didn't enjoy, that didn't meet your need for respect? Is it accurate to say that "you're never affectionate" or that "you're not as affectionate *as I would like*"? When we're honest in this way, there's less to argue about and more room to hear one another.

The first step to translating negative judgments is to recognize our judgment, honoring it as a vital piece of information. Judgments and evaluations are just one way we've learned to communicate what's happening inside. They are reflections of our own unmet needs.

PRACTICE: Transforming Judgments and Evaluations

Use this exercise to work with judgments you may hold about yourself or someone else. Begin with a situation that isn't too difficult, to get a feel for the process. You can use this activity to prepare for a conversation or, as it becomes more familiar, during the flow of a conversation.

Begin by settling your mind and becoming aware of your breathing. As genuinely as possible, connect with your intention to come from curiosity and care. Call to mind a situation in which you have some judgments you'd like to transform, then:

NAME THE JUDGMENT: Say the judgment aloud or write it down. Let yourself really feel it. If there are many, choose just one to explore. Remember that this is a valuable piece of information that expresses something that matters to you.

INVESTIGATE: What was the actual event, the one direct observation to which you are reacting? If there are several, choose one on which to focus first.

OBSERVE: Can you make an observation, as clearly and neutrally as possible? Could this be caught on film? Would the other person recognize this without arguing?

FEELINGS: What emotions do you feel in relation to this event? Take some time here, allowing yourself to feel fully. If the original judgment returns or new judgments arise, acknowledge them and return to feeling your emotions.

NEEDS: Listen inwardly for your needs. What matters to you here? What is it you *do* want rather than what you *don't* want? Are there different needs connected to different emotions? Sift through things until you arrive at one or two core needs. For what do you long?

REFLECT: Review your observation, feelings, and needs. How does this affect your experience of the event? Repeat this process for any other judgments you have, one at a time.

Ideally we do the work of translating our evaluations into observations, feelings, and needs before we speak. Sometimes, particularly if we are in a lot of pain, we're unable to do that work of translation. In these situations, it can be helpful to seek empathy from a friend or mentor. Sometimes, a trusted companion can help us identify our emotions and the powerful values being stimulated underneath those feelings.

If we still can't get to an observation (or if we don't have the time or energy to do so), we can take responsibility for our evaluations by acknowledging their subjectivity, which leaves room for the other person's experience. In other words, we can make an observation of our own evaluation. Here are a few examples of how we might separate observations and evaluations, taking responsibility for an evaluation or judgment (indicated in italics):

- "When I hear you say that, *I'm telling myself that you're judging me.*"
- "When I hear that you offered to help, *I think that you are being too kind.*"
- "*I've rarely seen him* make a decision without changing it at least once."
- "*I find* him *attractive.*"
- "*I think she's great.* We get through the agenda when she facilitates the meetings."
- "*I don't think* he'll stay in the job more than a few weeks."
- "*I can't remember a time* when he followed through without a reminder."

Praise, Feedback, and Gratitude

Translating judgments into observations, feelings, and needs is a flexible template that can bring clarity, richness, and meaning into many domains of our lives. Praise is a common form of positive judgment. While it may feel pleasant, we learn very little from being praised. What's more, praise places one person in a position of power over another, determining the value or worth of another's actions. Instead, we can name the specific actions we are celebrating and which needs of ours have been met.

PRAISE: "Great job! You're so amazing."

TRANSLATION: "When I heard you got the job, I felt so amazed at what you've been able to accomplish." [colloquially sharing needs for growth or meaning]

We also can use this format to give one another accurate feedback, sharing what did or didn't work (the observation) and why (our needs). In professional situations, it's often most useful to frame the needs in terms of a team's shared values or goals.

> *Principle:* **When giving feedback, be specific about what is and isn't working and why, which makes it easier to learn.**

In intimate relationships, we may express our enjoyment and care for one another with the tender words "I love you." While this can express a certain depth of feeling or strength of commitment, it can be even more meaningful to elaborate. What do we mean? Are there specific traits, words, or actions to which we're responding? How do we actually feel, and why? Consider the richness of a statement such as, "When you hold my hand I feel so safe, warm, and at ease. I'm so glad to have you as a companion in my life."

When our needs are met, we have the opportunity to express the fullness of our gratitude. This practice gives us a method for doing that, for opening our heart and celebrating our relationship by sharing the details of how someone else has contributed to our life. We may have to stretch beyond our comfort zone to speak so openly and authentically, but it pays off in an enriching quality of connection.

PRACTICE: Expressing Gratitude

The next time someone does something you enjoy, let them know. Instead of saying "Thank you," take a risk and share the fullness of your appreciation. Be specific about what they said or did, how you feel, and why. Speak from your heart. Focus on conveying why this mattered or how it contributed to you (as opposed to simply following the structure of the form).

As we learn these tools, it's common to start to think that there is a "right" way to communicate. "Stop praising me . . . That's an evaluation, not an observation! You're using a false feeling!" The more we think there is a right and a wrong way to speak, the further we move away from genuine curiosity and care.

The point of these practices, the ultimate aim of refining our thoughts and crafting our words, *is to create understanding and connection* in service of meeting needs. If you find yourself wondering, "Is this an observation? Can I say this in mindful communication?" take a step back and reconnect with your intention. Consider, "How might the other person hear this? Is it likely to lead to connection and build understanding?" If the answer is yes, go for it! If not, find another way to express yourself authentically that the other person is more likely to hear.

The Courage to Speak

It's not always easy to speak up and say our piece. We may have had difficult experiences of not feeling seen or heard or even may have been actively silenced. It can take patience, courage, and support from loving friends and community to find our voice.

Recognizing the source of these challenges—internally or structurally—can be freeing. Karen works internationally around issues of sustainability and rural development. She's good at what she does, but she can find it challenging to identify her needs and express herself at work. After one coaching session, she realized that growing up, her family consistently dismissed her point of view. She had learned to mistrust her own experience. This insight helped her begin to heal the pain beneath her frustration, opening new possibilities of self-expression.

I've mentioned my own struggles with speaking up. I learned to sing and play the guitar around the same time that I encountered NVC. These worked together synergistically, helping me find my voice literally and figuratively. As I sang, I could feel the constriction in my throat and chest begin to loosen. The relaxation carried over into the interpersonal domain, giving me the courage to share my feelings and needs and bridge the chasm between myself and another.

Personal challenges to self-expression are often compounded by structural issues. When we belong to a group that has been historically oppressed, we often internalize the impact of generations being systematically ignored, punished, and even murdered for speaking up. Tragically, this can leave those of us in society whose voices most need to be heard least equipped to speak up, which continues the cycle of invisibility and oppression.

Having a critical awareness of the context of our individual life experiences can bring powerful inspiration and insight to free ourselves from any sense of personal failure. We can seek support to heal the inner pain of this legacy and work with others to transform the systems that perpetuate the dynamics that prevent us from being heard. It takes time, and it requires steady support to transcend the external and internal obstacles. Despite it all, even deep-seated patterns can change, giving way to a great freedom and clarity of self-expression and a commitment to everyone's liberation.

PRINCIPLES

Stating clearly what happened, without judgment or evaluation, makes it easier for someone to hear us and to work toward a solution.

Translating judgments into observations, feelings, and needs can yield valuable information about what is and isn't working and provide clues for how to move forward.

When giving feedback, be specific about what is and isn't working and why, which makes it easier to learn.

KEY POINTS

Tips for making observations:

- Use mindfulness to discern the raw data of what happened.
- Separate what you actually know from assumptions or interpretations.
- To check, ask yourself, "Could this be caught on film?"
- Avoid words that exaggerate or interpret: *always, never, ever, whenever, rarely.*
- State your experience in the first person, "When *I* see/hear/ notice . . . ," rather than "When *you* said/did . . ."

- Determine if you are confident the other person would recognize this without growing defensive. If not, refine it further.
- Use the Ladder of Inference to consider whether you are observing or evaluating.

QUESTION & ANSWER

Q: I have one relative who gets really aggressive and yells whenever they're upset. How can I make an observation without them getting even angrier?

I'm hearing how much you'd like to find a way to talk with this person that minimizes the chance of angering them. No matter how we say something, we can't control another person's reaction. All we can do is come from a wholesome intention and approach the situation as skillfully as possible.

You may want to begin by getting empathy from a friend. If you feel heard and understood, you can bring more clarity and balance to the situation. Then find a time to talk about the pattern when it's *not* happening, which increases the likelihood they'll be able to hear you. I suggest leading with something that you enjoy about the relationship or framing the conversation in terms of what you'd like to build on. For example, "I'd so like for us to be able to spend time together at family gatherings in an easeful way."

When dealing with patterns, begin with a specific instance. To make an observation, you could describe their behavior in reference to your own manner or preferences: "Some of the ways you expressed yourself were very difficult for me to hear. I felt scared and overwhelmed. Can we talk about how we handle things when we disagree?" Listen to their side of things and see if you can brainstorm how to navigate the dynamic together.

Q: I feel really awkward when I state an observation, a feeling, and a need. Even when I manage to get it out, it's so unnatural that it leads to less connection rather than more!

The form is a skeleton, not a script; there's no need to follow it rigidly. Use the components in whatever order feels authentic, recognizing that it takes time to make this your own. We are retraining our attention to see more clearly. In the beginning, feel free to stick to the principles and just track these components silently.

Marshall Rosenberg was fond of saying, "Don't confuse what's habitual with what's natural." I believe it is more natural for us to be conscious of feelings and needs than to blame one another. We learn to blame and judge. When infants are hungry or in pain, they cry; they don't blame their parents. The words feel unnatural because we haven't practiced.

Q: What if I can't translate a judgment? I see that I'm evaluating, I'm even aware of my feelings and needs to some extent, but I'm still blaming the other person inside. How do I deal with being stuck like that?

Blame feels so true sometimes, doesn't it? The power of a judgment is directly proportional to the intensity of our feelings and needs. The stronger our emotions and the deeper our needs, the fiercer the judgment. It's our mind and heart's way of letting us know, "Hey! This is really important!"

Getting empathy is one of the best ways to transmute that energy. Find someone who can really listen and offer a genuine reflection of your experience, without agreeing, reassuring, or trying to fix, solve, or strategize. In some cases, depending on the relationship, you might be able to get that support from the person you're judging. If they have some tools, acknowledge that you're stuck in a judgment and ask for their help. If they're able to listen and offer empathy, it can be very healing.

Q: How do you deal with people who won't acknowledge certain facts, who have different data or "alternative facts"? How do you have a conversation when part of the issue is that you can't even agree on an observation?

If these tools only work when we agree, they would be very limited. Their power is in the possibility of creating connection in any circumstances. Focus on the needs. Getting alignment on shared values is what enables us to have meaningful conversations. The real work is in establishing that mutual framework, criteria for the solutions we devise. For example, if we are policy makers and can't agree on the science of climate change, we can still explore our requirements for a viable economy, a wise use of resources, and so forth.[7]

When we care deeply about the issues, such dialogues are by nature challenging. It's therefore important to do as much inner work as we can ahead of time. Get empathy for any pain, fear, despair, or anger you have about the impact of the other person's views. Then try to see their humanity. Stretch your heart with empathy. Try to make sense of their choices, to reach for the deeper needs behind what may seem incomprehensible on the surface. This can create an important bridge in hearing one another and can protect us from devolving into reactivity.

You also can explore the disagreement directly. You might inquire, "I'm guessing we both care about having accurate information, and that we share the view that good data can help us make more informed decisions?" I imagine most folks would agree. You might continue, "I know for me, one of my concerns is the belief that your data is biased, and I'm guessing you have the same concern about what I'm presenting?" From there, you might have a richer conversation about your shared concerns and strategies for examining the data.

Q: Sometimes I'm not willing to make neutral observations, especially if someone has caused harm. If someone said something racist or made a microaggression, I don't care if they get upset or defensive. Why should I go out of my way to make it easy for them to hear me?
I'm hearing your fierce commitment to being fully authentic, as well as the clear recognition that you're not responsible for their feelings or reactions. I'm guessing all of that is heightened by the historical dynamics of racism beneath the personal level in that sort of interaction.

Making neutral observations doesn't mean tamping down one's authenticity or "being nice." Nor is it about taking care of the other person or tiptoeing around their feelings. Saying things neutrally is a *strategy* to meet needs—needs for understanding, clarity, connection.

If your goal is to give this person some honest feedback or change their behavior through dialogue, then the question becomes, what's most effective? What's most likely to create understanding and inspire change? When someone has done something that hurts us, our tendency is to react—to throw that pain right back at them. These tools offer a method to share your experience in a way that opens the other person's heart and catalyzes a shift in their consciousness. The aim is to be fully authentic and caring at the same time, sharing the depth of your feelings without blame. Making an observation can serve that end.

11

if you want something, ask for it

The human hand must open to receive, but also to give, and to touch. The heart must open as well to give and to touch another heart.

—LYNNE TWIST

A LITTLE WHILE ago I was speaking with Laela, a meditation student who has chronic pain. She lives with her parents, who were in the process of moving. She needed to pack her belongings but was in the midst of a flare, her joints and muscles burning with pain. Just lying down hurt, let alone packing boxes or lifting things.

After listening and offering some empathy, I inquired, "Laela, may I ask you a question? Why don't you ask for some help from your folks or a friend?" Strange as it may seem, she had never thought to ask. We spent the rest of our conversation exploring the assumptions and beliefs that had kept this most basic, simple possibility hidden from her awareness. I could relate to her resistance. Having often felt invisible as a child at our family dinners, it took me many years to muster the courage to speak up and ask for someone to listen.

Being able to make requests is the last core component of training our attention to focus on what matters. In conversations, requests move things forward one step at a time, building understanding and proposing solutions that may work for everyone. In this chapter we'll explore the different kinds of requests we can make and some of the conditioning that gets in the way.

The Gift of Needs

"I don't want to impose. I'd rather not burden them."

"I can handle it; I'll be okay."

"It's no big deal. I wouldn't want them to feel obligated . . ."

Sometimes it can feel easier to shoulder a burden on one's own than try to navigate the awkwardness, fear, or discomfort of asking for help. Our intentions may be quite wholesome: we genuinely *don't* want others to feel obligated. We respect their autonomy, time, and energy and want to ensure that they feel free to say no.

These values needn't prevent us from making requests. In fact, they enable us to make truly effective requests that support collaboration. When we're unable to take into account another person's needs, we make demands. It is our lack of skill in *expressing* these values and navigating the responses that trips us up. Similarly, if we can't come up with more than one strategy to resolve a situation, our request may bear a quality of desperation that challenges the other person's sense of choice. Beneath all of this, our fears, beliefs, and vulnerability can stop us from asking.

Making a request is about finding a way to meet needs. To ask is to acknowledge our interdependence, which opens us up to disappointment or rejection. We may have had experiences that have taught us it can be dangerous, shameful, or futile to ask for what we need—so why bother? Alternatively, we may have learned that giving is the only way to get our needs met or that help from another can only come laced with hidden agendas and strings attached.

As we've explored, our belief in cultural myths of self-sufficiency or the idealization of individual achievement can further limit our ability to seek support. On the collective level, entrenched systems can give rise to feelings of futility and despair or make violence seem like a viable strategy. These messages and experiences often leave us with complex and confusing relationships around how to meet our own and others' needs or how to work for change.

My heart breaks to see how our culture, society, and upbringing twists and complicates one of our most basic, beautiful, and natural impulses: the impulse to give and receive. Spend time with a child (who is rested and well-fed) and you know the joy they feel at giving, sharing, and helping those around them.[1]

Contributing to one another is one of our most fundamental drives; doing so brings joy. Consider the ease or uplift you feel when engaging in simple acts of kindness such as holding the door, smiling, or greeting someone. Recollect the last time you helped a friend in need—not because you *had to* but simply because you *could*. Felt pretty good, right?

Rather than being a burden, needs can be gifts. When we are able to negotiate the dance of choice and willingness, respecting the limits of one another's time and energy, all needs become invitations to experience the joy of giving and receiving.

🔊 **PRACTICE:** Reflection on Giving and Receiving

Reflecting on how it feels to give and receive can transform your relationship with asking for what you need and helping others. Take some time to settle into your body and allow your attention to gather with the sensations of breathing. When you feel ready, reflect on the following questions.

Recall a specific time when you helped someone in your life, not because you felt obligated but simply because you wanted to. Contemplate how it felt to lend a hand. How does it feel to remember it now? How would it have felt if you learned later that they needed help but didn't reach out?

Next, recall a time when you needed help and someone was there for you, a time when you trusted that they were helping not because they felt obligated but because they genuinely chose to help. How did it feel to receive their support? How does it feel now recalling this?

Recognizing how it feels to give and receive freely, what gets in the way of asking for help when you need it?

A Little Secret

In my early twenties, a good friend passed along a piece of advice he'd received from his dad. Upon graduating from high school, his father had said, "I'll tell you a little secret to life: if you want something, ask for it."

This is the central principle behind making requests.

Making clear requests is fairly uncommon. Listen to any conversation and see how often a speaker ends a statement by asking for what they'd like to hear back or see happen next. How many times have you shared something important, only to have the other person take the conversation in a totally different direction? Without telling someone what we'd like to hear back, they are left to guess or to respond however they please.

Principle: The clearer we are about what we want and why, the more creative we can be about how to make it happen.

By contrast, following a statement with a request lets others know how they can help and offers a concrete idea for where to go next in the conversation. It's illuminating to see the power of making requests. As one student of mine commented, "What was most frustrating was realizing that I wasn't getting what I wanted simply because I wasn't letting others know what I needed."

A *request* is a question about one's willingness to perform a specific action to meet needs. Requests are strategies and are distinct from demands.

"No Spilling": Making Requests

Some time ago, I was at an airport waiting to board a plane and saw a mother with two little girls. The older child, no more than five or six years old, was holding a large drink with a straw. The mother said to her, with agitation in her voice, "Don't spill it!" I watched the young girl's body tighten with anxiety, trying to figure out how to prevent further rebukes by "not spilling" the drink.

How might it have been had the mother said, "Sweetie, that's a big drink and I'm concerned it might spill. *Can you hold it carefully with two hands?*" With such a request, the daughter would have had specific instructions for what to do, making it clearer and easier to meet the request.

Requests gauge another's willingness to help or agree to our strategy. To make this as clear as possible, it's best to formulate requests with three qualities:

1. **Positive:** Requests state what we *do* want rather than what we *don't* want.
2. **Specific:** Requests are concrete and doable rather than vague or abstract.
3. **Flexible:** Requests are distinct from demands; they offer a suggestion for how to move forward, with openness to other ideas.

Making requests can be challenging, but we've already been developing the skills to do so. Our ability to make a request *positive* is based on our capacity to identify needs and then to offer a strategy that might meet them. Making a request that is *specific* rests upon our ability to find clear observations, concrete behaviors we are seeking. And the *flexibility* that is at the heart of a request comes from understanding our needs, being sensitive to the needs of others, and being creative enough to find more than one strategy to meet all of the needs present. Here are a few examples that illustrate these qualities.

NOT POSITIVE: "Don't talk to me that way!"
AS A REQUEST: "Would you be willing to lower your voice, or can we take a break?"

NOT SPECIFIC: "Will you love me more?"
AS A REQUEST: "When you come home, can you try to remember to look me in the eyes and say hello? It would mean so much to me."

NOT FLEXIBLE: "We have to talk."
AS A REQUEST: "Can we find some time to sit down together and talk about things? Or, if not, do you have ideas about how we can sort this out?"

PRACTICE: Listening for Requests

As you move through your day, pay attention to the presence or absence of requests. How often do people (yourself included) let others know what they'd like to hear back? When is it implicit? When a person does make a request, is it positive, specific, and flexible?

Kinds of Requests: Asking for Empathy

There are two basic kinds of requests in conversation: requests that aim for connection and requests that propose a solution. *Connection requests* check that the line hasn't dropped, in effect saying, "You still there?" They complete a cycle of communication, confirm that the message sent was received, and water the seeds of trust and goodwill. *Solution requests* propose concrete strategies to address both of our needs and make agreements about going forward.

In simple situations, solution requests may be sufficient. "How about this? Any way you could find time for XYZ?" With more challenging issues we need to lay some groundwork before discussing solutions. After all, another person's willingness to collaborate is based on the quality of understanding and connection we've established. In chapter 7, we touched on the importance of building understanding, trust, and goodwill before proposing solutions.

> *Principle:* **The more we understand one another, the easier it is to find solutions that work for everyone. Therefore, establish as much mutual understanding as possible before problem solving.**

When it's not clear from the context or body language that the other person has understood, when things are particularly charged, or if it's important for us to feel understood, it can be helpful to ask for a reflection. Here are a few examples.

Connection Requests That Ask for a Reflection / Empathy

- "Can you tell me what you're getting (from what I said)?"
- "I'm not sure I was totally clear. What are you understanding?"
- "Could you tell me your understanding of what matters to me? Knowing that would really help me to feel understood."
- "I'd like to make sure we're on the same page. What are you taking away from this?"

If we have a sense that the other person is with us, we may simply want to know how they're responding.

Connection Requests That Ask for a Response/Information

- "How is it for you to hear all of this?"
- "What do you think? How do you feel about that?"
- "What can I say or do that would help you to feel more understood?"

Making connection requests isn't always easy and doesn't necessarily come naturally. It can feel awkward at first, and it takes practice. Yet with time, letting others know that we're interested in hearing one another can be a powerful way to come together.

In my twenties, my father and I grew quite close thanks to my persistent use of these tools. I explained how I wanted him to know more about my life and how meaningful it would be to have him just listen. He would agree but then inevitably interrupt to offer advice or to explain why I "shouldn't feel that way." I patiently heard these replies as expressions of his care and then reminded him that what would be most nourishing to me was his listening attention. He would listen, and I would check every now and then to see if he was still with me. Periodically, I asked how he felt about what I'd shared. After feeling heard, I usually was more open to his advice.

My attempts at creating connection with family weren't always so graceful. Another casualty of my early attempts at NVC was my paternal grandfather. Sabba, as I called him, grew up in Poland and moved to what was then British Palestine in his late teens. When I knew him, he was mostly blind, living in the house he had built for his family.

One of the last times I saw Sabba, I sat by his bedside as my dad translated. I shared how much I loved him, and how much I would miss him when I went back home. I carefully ended each sentence with a request, asking him what he'd heard me say. After a short time, my grandfather's face became very dour, clearly upset. "What's wrong," I inquired? My father explained, "He says he's not a child; he understands what you're saying."

In my zeal to build connection, the awkwardness of translation, and communicating across cultures, I failed to recognize that he was hearing me just fine. I hadn't developed an intuitive feel for when to ask for a reflection, when to ask for a response, and when to trust my gut and just let things be. If I could go back, I would have simply spoken from my heart and then asked him two questions (both connection requests). First, "How is it for you to hear all of this, Sabba?" And then, "Is there anything you'd like me to know?"

In the end, we sorted it out. I apologized and explained where I was coming from. I believe he heard how much his strange American grandson loved him.

PRACTICE: Making Connection Requests

When speaking, consider what you would like from the other person. Do you want to be heard and understood? Do you trust that's happening sufficiently? If not, try venturing a request for a reflection. This could be as simple as "Do you know what I mean?" or as specific as "What are you getting from what I just said?" If you want information about how the other person is responding inside, ask.

Trust your ability to gauge the level of understanding and connection that is present, reading cues of eye contact, facial expression, and body language. When you make a connection request, do so in a way that is natural and authentic to you. If it's someone close to you, you might even tell them you're experimenting with something new and ask if they would be willing to give it a try with you.

When we're unable to arrive at a deeper level of personal connection, it's still essential to discuss the underlying needs and objectives in a situation before hammering out specific strategies. Without an understanding of what's at stake for both of us, the solutions we create are less likely to address all of the factors or to come from a place of true willingness. The transition from building mutual understanding to problem solving is therefore key.

Requests That Move toward a Solution

- "Is there more? Anything else you'd like me to understand?"
- "Would this be an okay time to shift to talking about where we go from here?"
- "Do you have any ideas about what might work for both of us?"

When exploring strategies, the more creative we can be, the more likely we are to find a viable solution. If and when you reach an agreement, to maximize the chances of success, be sure to check if the other person has any concerns or reservations.

> *Principle:* **Have ideas for strategies that meet as many needs as possible, which invites others to look for creative solutions.**

Flowers for My Table

The most essential component of a request is the intention behind it. A request contains an inner orientation of flexibility that takes another's needs into account and is distinct from a demand. Essentially it is a proposal: "How about this?" It is a *continuation* of the conversation, our best guess at where to go from here. A demand, on the other hand, is the end of a conversation; it's how we use force or coercion to get our way when we don't see other options. Requests invite collaboration; demands threaten consequences. We can indicate the collaborative nature of a request with the inflection of our voice or with specific words, signaling our willingness to explore other options and our desire for information about the other person's needs. Here are a few examples of ways you might begin a request:

- "Would you be willing to . . . ?"
- "Could it work for you to . . . ?"
- "How would it be for you to . . . ?"

Marshall Rosenberg had a poetic way of capturing the spirit of making requests: "Ask others to meet your needs like flowers for your table, not air for your lungs." If I ask you to do something with desperation, how much choice will you feel? How much joy in agreeing? How will it feel if I ask with openness and ease, as if to say, "Wouldn't this be nice?" This depends on transforming our relationship to our needs and framing our requests around the joy of meeting them. Returning to the classic examples of roommates or romantic partners, notice the differences between the requests below:

- **AIR FOR LUNGS:** "Would you *please* wash your dishes and wipe the counters? I need more order in this house!"
- **FLOWERS FOR TABLE:** "Would you be up for washing your dishes and giving the counter a quick wipe down after you eat? I feel so much more relaxed when the kitchen's clean and tidy."

- **AIR FOR LUNGS:** "I need more time together. When are we going out again?"
- **FLOWERS FOR TABLE:** "It's so sweet for me when we have quality time. Could we look at our calendars and see when we can schedule another date?"

Even when the needs at stake are pressing, we have more leverage when we can create connection and make requests that consider the other person. A female NVC practitioner awoke in the middle of the night with a strange man standing in her bedroom. Trained in nonviolence, one of her first thoughts was, "My safety and this man's safety are interconnected." Refusing to see this person as an enemy, understanding that their safety depended on her ability to create connection, she spontaneously asked him what time it was. Caught off guard, the intruder looked at his watch and replied with the time. "How did you get in?" she asked him. A window had been unlocked. Trying to make sense of his breaking in, she ventured a guess, "Oh, it must be cold outside tonight?"

They spoke in that tense situation for a few minutes. She learned that he had nowhere to go. Eventually she explained that there was a guest bedroom down the hall, linens in the closet. He could spend the night if he wanted, and if he left in the morning before she was up, she would not call the police. They agreed, and he left her room. This is an extreme example, and few of us know how we would respond in such a situation. I'm not advocating this approach in a potentially dangerous situation without significant training in nonviolence! Yet the example is instructive with regard to how radical the effects of intentional communication can be: in the face of fear and potential violence, she remained able to see his humanity and make requests that accounted for both of their needs.

Providing Context

Whenever we make a request, if the other person doesn't understand why we're asking or how it will contribute, they're less likely to want to help. This is as true for connection requests as it is for solution requests, for mundane situations as for substantive ones. If it's not already clear, we need to let the other person know *why* we're asking; we need to give them a *reason* to say yes.

A simple example: My partner asks me in the morning, "Are you going to eat this for lunch?" I feel confused. Depending on the context, my response would differ. "I'd really like to take this for lunch today, were you planning on eating it?" is a different question from "I'm afraid this is going to spoil. Will you eat it, or shall I?"

Here's another example. Notice the difference between asking for a reflection with and without context:

WITHOUT CONTEXT: "Can you tell me what you heard?"
WITH CONTEXT: "I just said a lot and I'm not sure it all came out the way I meant. Can you tell me what you heard?"

WITHOUT CONTEXT: "Could you tell me your understanding of what matters to me?"
WITH CONTEXT: "I'd really like to feel heard right now. Could you tell me your understanding of what matters to me?"

A Complete Way of Communicating

Observation, feeling, need, request; what happened, how we feel about it, why, and a suggestion for what's next—this is the classical structure of

Nonviolent Communication. It provides a road map to say what we mean and to hear others. The first three components—observations, feelings, and needs—answer the basic question, "How are you?" In sharing this we invite one another into our felt experience: "Here is what's happening for me." Requests answer the question, "How can I help?"

Expressing an observation, a feeling, and a need carries a lot of weight. If we share that level of detail without making a request, the other person is likely to hear blame regardless of our intentions or words. Consider the following statements with and without a request.

WITHOUT A REQUEST: "When I heard you wouldn't be home until eight, I felt so disappointed and frustrated. It's really important to me to have some time together in the evening."

WITH A REQUEST: "When I heard you wouldn't be home until eight, I felt so disappointed and frustrated. It's really important to me to have some time together in the evening. Can we talk some about how to balance your responsibilities at work with my hopes for our relationship?"

WITHOUT A REQUEST: "I heard music coming from your apartment last night around eleven, and I got pretty frustrated. My earplugs didn't help. I work early and need to get a good night's rest."

WITH A REQUEST: "I heard music coming from your apartment last night around eleven, and I got pretty frustrated. My earplugs didn't help. I work early and need to get a good night's rest. Would you be willing to turn the music down or use headphones after ten on weeknights?"

Our intentions appear vague in the absence of a request, leaving the other person to figure out what we would like from them. Most of us are so conditioned to hear blame that that's the first interpretation we make. Offering a request lets the other person know why we're bringing this up and proposes how they can be helpful in this moment.

Demands, Hearing and Saying No

The difference between a request and a demand isn't in our words; it's in how we respond when the other person says no. If we can meet a no with curiosity—"Oh, why not? What do you need?"—then we were genuinely making a request. If we respond with anger, self-righteousness, or a guilt trip, then we weren't really asking in the first place, were we?

As we've explored, using guilt, blame, or demands to meet our needs comes at a cost in goodwill, trust, and the quality of relationship. Even if we get what we want in the short term, we pay a price in the long term. Most people respond to demands by reacting: submit or rebel. Neither is based on true freedom and autonomy. Even if they agree, their inherent motivation will likely be compromised. Here, asking ourselves Rosenberg's two key questions can dissuade us from making demands and guide us to a more collaborative approach rooted in curiosity and care:

- What do I want them to do?
- Why do I want them to do it? What do I want their *reasons* to be?

This second question is not an attempt to control the other person or manipulate them. It's a way of reconnecting with our deeper intentions of curiosity and care, of remembering how good it feels when others *choose* to meet our needs because they understand how it will contribute to us.

Our ability to hear (and say) no without losing connection is essential. Hearing no can be one of the most vulnerable parts of making a request, especially when we are asking for something important. For beneath any request, however small, is a hidden question: "Do I matter?" Hearing no can challenge our sense of agency, frustrate our hopes, stimulate disappointment, or touch painful wounds.

In these instances, the practice of self-empathy is an important component in having the resilience to stay engaged and not take things personally when someone says no. If we can pause, sense our needs and any deeper longing to know that we matter, we can bring more openness, patience, and curiosity to the dialogue.

The ability to say no is a sign of a healthy relationship. If someone always says yes, we can't know if they are genuinely agreeing or doing so out of fear, shame, or obligation—all of which can lead to resentment, mistrust, or lack of follow-through. On the contrary, when someone says no, we can trust that they mean it when they say yes!

We can also view no as a source of information rather than a dead end. After all, saying no is in and of itself a strategy to meet some need; it indicates that there is something else more important preventing them from saying yes to our request. Instead of taking it personally, we can listen for the yes behind their no. This doesn't mean assuming that they are saying yes to *our request*. It means that they are saying yes to *something else* that is more important to them. If we can identify what that is, we have more options to work together creatively. To what *other* needs are they saying yes? Can we find another strategy that meets all of the needs present or a way to sufficiently address their needs such that they can say yes to our request?

PRACTICE: Hearing No

When someone says no, try to get curious. Check if you are open to other strategies to meet your needs and if you genuinely want the outcome to work for the other person. Here are some ideas for additional requests to continue the conversation:

- "I'm curious to know why not? Could you share more?"
- "What's leading you to say no?"
- "Can we take some time to brainstorm ideas that could work for both of us?"
- "Do you have other ideas?"
- "What would you need to know, or what could I do, to make it possible for you to say yes?"

You may find yourself on the other side of the spectrum, struggling to honor your own limits and say no to requests. Overriding your own needs to help others can lead to burnout, depression, resentment, or lopsided relationships. This can come about for many reasons. You may fear disappointing others, want to avoid the discomfort of a difficult conversation, or have trouble trusting that your own needs matter. You may genuinely want to help but chronically overestimate your inner resources.

There are ways of saying no that maintain connection, honor your needs, and protect against misunderstanding. If you say no without affirming their needs in some way, the other person may interpret your response as not caring about them. Instead, try to separate your response to their *strategy* from your care for their *needs*; that is, share your understanding of their needs and express your interest in finding a way to meet them. Let them know why you are saying no and propose an alternative, or invite them to do so.

PRACTICE: Saying No

The next time someone asks something of you and you're not willing to agree, try to stay engaged in the process of dialogue. Here are a few examples of ways to say no while maintaining connection:

- "I'd like to say yes, and here's what's getting in the way of that right now."
- "I hear how important this is to you, and I'm not seeing how I can make it work given that I also have a need for ... Could we explore some other options that might work for you?"
- "I can't agree to that without a significant cost to myself in terms of ... [my other commitments, my need for rest ...]. Would it work for you if we tried this instead?"

A Cycle of Giving and Receiving

When we're able to make requests, hear no, and gently persist with care, beautiful things can happen. I used what I learned from Sabba to help my student Laura find closure with her grandmother.

Laura teaches mindfulness, and her ninety-two-year old grandmother had been an important source of inspiration throughout her life. Every time Laura tried to share her appreciation, her grandmother would grow uncomfortable, change the subject, or gently deflect Laura's words. In her humility and desire to make space for others, she was unavailable to receive Laura's gratitude.

I coached Laura to reframe the conversation from trying to *give* something to her grandmother to making a request. "Grandma, there are some things I'd really like to share with you. It would be so meaningful to me to have you listen. Would you be willing to sit with me for a bit? It would be such a gift." Her grandmother was delighted to offer this simple gesture of presence. Laura spoke of how meaningful their relationship was and of how her grandmother had been a role model for her all these years. They shared some tender moments of appreciation and even a few tears. By making a request, Laura had helped her grandmother see how receiving appreciation was a gift to both of them.

PRINCIPLES

The clearer we are about what we want and why, the more creative we can be about how to make it happen.

The more we understand one another, the easier it is to find solutions that work for everyone. Therefore, establish as much mutual understanding as possible before problem solving.

Have ideas for strategies that meet as many needs as possible, which invites others to look for creative solutions.

KEY POINTS

In conversations, requests move things forward one step at a time, building understanding, connection, and proposing solutions that may work for everyone. To transform our relationship with making requests and receiving them, we can see requests in the following ways:

- Making a request is about working together to meet one another's needs.
- Needs are gifts, invitations to experience the joy of giving and receiving.
- Expressing our needs through requests lets others know how they can help and offers a concrete idea for where to go next in the conversation.

- Being skilled at making requests includes supporting others in asking for what they need, being sensitive to and intuiting requests they may have.
- Hearing (and saying) no can be a sign of a healthy relationship and points to information about other needs that are preventing someone from saying yes.

We can say no and still maintain connection, honor our needs, and protect against misunderstanding by:

- Affirming another's needs
- Sharing our understanding of their needs and expressing our interest in finding a way to meet them
- Letting them know why we are saying no and proposing an alternative or inviting them to do so

QUESTION & ANSWER

Q: I've been using these tools, and I am getting a lot of feedback that I'm being self-centered, controlling, or pushy. What am I doing wrong?
When we become aware of our needs and start making requests, we can sound a bit demanding. Check if your requests are flexible. Are you coming from an attitude of "You should do this"? Also check that the other person understands that you're genuinely willing to hear no.

When we have these tools, we also take on an extra role in conversation. We're no longer solely an advocate for our own needs. We simultaneously become a facilitator, advocating for the other person's needs as well—because we value their needs as an integral part of a healthy relationship, recognize our own needs for compassion and contribution, and understand that their willingness is a key ingredient in the success of any agreements we make.

You may need to make an extra effort to communicate as clearly as you can that you are genuinely interested in finding something that works for both of you. We can't control others' perceptions, but we can do our best to let them know that we would like to take their needs into consideration.

Explicitly invite them to share: "I'd love to hear more about what's important to you. What would work for you here?" Find requests that make it easy for them to say no or that invite them to share more information. For example: "I only want you to say yes if it really works for you . . ." or "I don't want you to feel obligated; it's okay if you say no."

Q: I'd like to be able to make requests, but things happen so quickly I kind of freeze. Even when there's space, I wouldn't know what to ask for.
There is a certain amount of retraining our nervous system to feel more ease in conversation. Start by using the tools of presence to handle your inner experience and find the courage to speak. Feel your feet on the ground and bring some attention to your posture, which can boost your strength. Start small, building confidence in less challenging situations.

To make a request, we have to be aware of our needs too, to know what we want. Try memorizing two or three simple requests that you can use any time. Find an authentic way of making a basic connection request for a reflection or a response, and practice until you can say it without thinking. Try rehearsing a request for some time to think, such as "There's something I'd like to say. Can you give me a moment to gather my thoughts?"

Q: "Would you be willing . . ." sounds so formal and stilted. Why not just say "Please"?
Remember, it's not about what you say but where you're coming from. The words help train our *attention* to stay aligned with the *intention* of the principles. "Please" can carry a lot of connotations. Most of us are socialized to say "please" and "thank you" whether or not we actually mean it. Sometimes "please" codes as a veiled demand. For these reasons, I suggest you find other ways to indicate your flexibility, such as "Would you/could you" or "How would it be for you . . . ?" These phrases tend to carry less cultural baggage.

Q: How do I tell the difference between when to bring something up and make a request and when to just let go or deal with it on my own?
I'm interested in flexibility, cultivating the capacity to do both. Letting go isn't mutually exclusive with making requests. I hope it's clear that the less

attached we are to getting our way, the more room we actually have to make requests and engage in dialogue.

Consider your conditioning and practice going in the other direction. If you're someone who tends to work everything out on your own inside, risk speaking up and inviting others to hear what's in your heart. If you're more vocal and tend to look outside for resolution, balance that with some introspection. See if you can find some spaciousness inside and how that changes your perspective on the situation.

Q: What about when someone isn't interested in engaging? I've made several requests and it's either "No" or radio silence.
It can be so painful when the other person is not willing to engage in dialogue. It seems to touch some ancient, deep-rooted need for belonging, even a fear of exile from the tribe. I think most of us need a lot of tenderness and care in times like that.

We can try to empathize with the feelings or needs behind their silence which, in effect, has become their only message. In some circumstances, this can create the conditions to reengage in dialogue. In my own life, I've seen that sometimes we just have different expectations. The other person may need more time before they are ready to talk. For me, it's been incredibly important in such situations to get support and to turn inward and call upon my own resources for healing and resolution. With patience, we can find a lot of compassion for ourselves and forgiveness for others. In the end, the process can be deeply freeing.

bringing it all together

WHEN THE THREE steps to effective conversation are functioning together, dialogue can feel like dancing. We relax. We take turns speaking and listening with ease, shifting our attention back and forth as if to the rhythm of music. Leading with presence grounds us and gives us more choice in how we relate. Coming from care and curiosity, we create the conditions for collaboration and understanding. Focusing on what matters, we identify what's actually important.

Other times, conversation feels more like mountain climbing than dancing! We trudge uphill with a heavy load, picking our way around obstacles, stumbling over dicey terrain. We interrupt, skip ahead, or jump from one topic to another.

Life is complicated and messy, and learning to be light on our feet takes practice—whether we're dancing or climbing a peak. We need to be prepared to lose the rhythm, rub sore feet, tend to a few blisters, and stumble every now and again.

In the last part of this book, we'll explore how things fit together in the arc of a conversation and how to handle challenging situations. We'll learn how to move nimbly, knowing when to dance, when to trek uphill, and when to stop and rest. We'll also learn how to follow the larger movements of a conversation, how to shift and move with the changing focus from me to you, and how to manage the different threads of information that can arise.

12

the flow of dialogue

This life is a thump-ripe melon, so sweet and such a mess.
—GREG BROWN

A GOOD FRIEND of mine, Amanda, called me to ask for some advice about a tricky conversation. She'd recently spent some time with a friend. After a week of camping and a rushed departure, Amanda's four-year-old son had a meltdown in the car on their way to the airport. The friend intervened (without permission) and later emailed Amanda some unsolicited parenting advice.

I offered Amanda some empathy for how frustrated she might be feeling and asked if she longed for more respect for her choices as a parent. Then we took things apart and strategized how best to approach the conversation. There were several layers: their friendship, the other woman's genuine desire to contribute, Amanda's need to receive support in a way and at a time that works for her. We identified each of the different topics, clarified her needs, the requests she could make, and finally discussed some ways to open the conversation to start off on the right foot.

The three steps to effective conversation—lead with presence, come from curiosity and care, and focus on what matters—form the foundation for how we show up, the way we engage, and what we discuss. It's also important to be able to zoom out and have a broader view of the conversation as a whole. Where do we start? How do we shift from one topic to another or from my perspective to yours?

The Steps of the Dance

Dialogue is a lot like dancing. It takes time to learn the basics, but when we are conversing smoothly with someone else, it can be magical. Old friends and new lovers can talk for hours, moving effortlessly through the steps of that ancient dance. We speak, we listen, we dwell together in contemplation or wonder, in celebration or mourning.

Just as the in- and out-breath anchor our awareness in meditation, just as feelings and needs ground our attention in conversation, three basic "positions" choreograph our dance of dialogue. I mentioned these briefly in chapter 1, and I'd like to return to them now with the added richness of all that you've learned.

In any given moment of a conversation, we can speak, listen, or rest in presence. *We express*: we speak from the heart, sharing observations, feelings, needs, or requests openly and honestly, with as little blame as possible. *We receive*: we listen from the heart, with curiosity and care, hearing the human feelings and needs beneath another person's words. *We rest*: we bring presence to the whole process, pausing to settle and integrate as needed.

These are the basic moves of the dance. All communication comes back to these three options: express honestly, receive empathically, or return to presence.[1]

It can be healing to feel that rhythm of give-and-take and work through a challenge. We find a flow as we shift attention back and forth, hearing one another and allowing things to settle. Many students report how transformative just one successful conversation can be. In sensing the rhythm of that dance, something in our nervous system learns how to participate in the process of creating understanding with another human being.

PRACTICE: The Dance of Dialogue

Simplify your focus in conversation and return to the basics. Allow the details of all that you've learned so far to be in the background. Lead with presence, come from curiosity and care, and consider the choice points between speaking, listening, and resting with presence. Can you find the rhythm of give-and-take in conversation, the dance of speaking, listening, and resting?

Framing a Conversation

Beginnings are delicate. How we start a relationship or a conversation can have a significant effect on its trajectory. (Starting a date with "You're late" will probably influence how the night unfolds.) Yet so many factors feed into any one moment that it can be hard to know where to start.

The behaviors of complex, dynamic systems are highly sensitive to what are known as initial conditions, the value of certain variables at the beginning of a process. Human beings are complex, dynamic systems; the pre- and perinatal periods of a child's life can have a dramatic impact on their long-term psychological and physiological health. A conversation is also a complex, dynamic system. It's a living, breathing process. We can use a tool called *framing* to set the initial conditions for a successful exchange.

> *Framing* summarizes an issue or area of discussion in a broad and neutral way, often in terms of any shared needs, goals, or values.

Framing gives someone a general indication of the territory we'd like to discuss in a neutral or positive way. Like putting up the scaffolding for a house, it provides structure and outlines areas to be filled in later. Framing can be particularly helpful when the issues are loaded, and specific observations are likely to embroil us in the heat of a challenge. It also can provide an opportunity to gauge another person's willingness to converse, align us with one another, or introduce a metalevel discussion concerning how we're going to talk about things.

The first and most essential aspect of setting initial conditions is agreeing to have the conversation. If we are too focused on the issues, we can forget to negotiate this most basic aspect of relating. Is this the right time to talk? Is it a good place? Here are two examples of introducing a topic with and without framing.

WITHOUT FRAMING: "When I heard you say 'stop being so self-centered' I felt so hurt. I really wanted you to know how much it would mean to me if you came to the event. Can you understand how I might have felt?"

WITH FRAMING: "I wanted to talk about the conversation we had yesterday to see if we could understand where we each were coming from a little better. Would you be up for that?"

Instead of quoting the most painful observation, the speaker refers to the conversation more generally, suggests some shared needs, and frames things in terms of "we." Each of these aspects can create alignment and togetherness at the outset of a dialogue. Here are two more examples of an initial request for dialogue:

- "Would you be willing to take some time to have a conversation with me about . . . ?"
- "Could we sit down and look at what we both need, to see if we can find a way to work this out?"

There are many ways to frame a conversation to create a sense of togetherness and shared purpose. Depending on the context, different facets may be more or less useful.

Options for Framing

BROAD VIEW: State the situation in a broad, neutral way that lets the other person make an informed decision about entering the conversation without getting into potentially contentious details.

FEELINGS: Share your vulnerability, naming feelings that may stimulate compassion.

SHARED NEEDS: Include any shared needs, goals, or benefits of the dialogue. State things in terms of "we" rather than "I."

APPRECIATION: Are there bonds you share that would support goodwill, curiosity, and care? Begin with appreciation for the other person, what you enjoy about them or your relationship.

Here are some examples of how you might use each of these options.

FRAMING FEELINGS: "Some of our interactions recently were a bit difficult for me. I'm struggling to sort them out, and wonder if we could take some time to talk about what happened?"

FRAMING SHARED NEEDS: "Could we revisit that last interaction? I'd love to find a way for us to both feel understood and supported."

FRAMING APPRECIATION: "Our friendship is so important to me; I really appreciate having you in my life. What happened last week was difficult for me and I'd like to find some resolution. Would you be up for talking?"

Each of these examples offers a different way of creating alignment as you enter a conversation. Use discernment to determine which tool is best suited to any given situation.

Principle: **Stating how a conversation can contribute to both of us helps create buy-in and willingness.**

Tracking in Conversations

Navigating a conversation can feel like trying to follow an overgrown trail through the woods. It takes patience and careful observation. You lose the path periodically, only to pick it up again later. While every conversation is unique, there are certain universal patterns. To shepherd a dialogue toward resolution, we track its *process*—what kind of conversation we're having, where we are in that, who has the center of attention—and we track its *content*—the specific topic we are discussing and if it's complete.

Tracking **means following specific pieces of process or content in a conversation.**

At the most basic level, there are two kinds of conversations—*relational* and *logistical*; they often coexist as layers of a single conversation. The relational domain includes our quality of connection, our emotions, and the ways in which we're relating. The logistical domain encompasses whatever problem we are trying to solve concretely and any agreements we make. In Amanda's situation, the relational conversation was about how she felt in response to her friend's interventions, the kind of trust and support she wanted, and her friend's motivation for giving advice. The logistical conversation was about what to do next time a parenting issue arose.

Trying to resolve a logistical conversation without addressing underlying relational issues can be confusing and complicated. We're discussing something concrete but keep getting snagged because there's an unnamed subtext of emotions. If Amanda only discussed strategies about parenting practices without acknowledging her underlying concerns, the conversation would likely feel tense and edgy. (At times, we may choose to focus solely on the logistical level because there is insufficient trust, safety, or willingness to address the relational domain. In these cases, having internal clarity about the relational issues can bring more balance and centeredness to how we interact.)

Similarly, mistaking a logistical issue for a relational one can lead to confusion. My mother was visiting recently, and I asked Evan if she would help make the guest bed. She promptly walked into the other room and began doing something else! Puzzled (and slightly annoyed), I went to help my mother make the bed myself. I later learned that she simply hadn't heard me. Had I mistaken this logistical miss for something relational, I might have created painful interpretations or sparked an argument.

It's generally helpful to try to deal with relational issues first. In complex situations, if we need to shift back and forth, being clear internally about which we are discussing can help us navigate the changes with more ease.

As we've already seen, successful conversations also have two main phases: building mutual understanding and problem solving. There can be a lot of pressure to jump prematurely to solutions. *Let's just figure this out already!* Whether we are dealing with a relational issue or a logistical one, the more understanding and trust, the easier it will be to create a lasting solution.

We can track which phase of the conversation we are in and study when and how to make transitions. Before moving from mutual understanding to problem solving, we ensure that we've gathered enough information to understand one another. Usually, there is a sense of settling or renewed energy when it's time to brainstorm solutions. Here are some questions to consider before problem solving:

- Do you have all the information you need?
- Are both of us clear about the needs and objectives that are present?
- Is there an overall sense of both people feeling heard or understood?
- Does the other person trust that you are genuinely interested in what will work for them?

Here are some requests we can use in making this transition, which build on the "Requests That Move toward a Solution" in chapter 11:

- "Do you have a sense that I understand what matters to you here? That I get your side of things?"
- "Is there anything else you think would be important for us to consider?"
- "I'd like to find something that works for both of us. Can you sense that?"

Establishing trust is crucial. If we can show that we're genuinely interested in collaborating, there will be more willingness and creativity to brainstorm. We build this kind of trust one step at a time, showing empathy, hearing and reflecting the other person's feelings and concerns.

PRACTICE: Tracking Process in Conversation

The next time you are trying to work something out, consider what kind of conversation you are having: Is this a purely logistical matter, or are there relational aspects? If both are present, see if you can sort out the relational before handling the logistical level. When moving between the two, try to be clear inside about what you are discussing.

Focus on building as much understanding as possible before transitioning to problem solving. Bring particular attention to that shift from one phase to another, checking to ensure you are both ready to look at solutions.

Who Has the Floor?

Tracking what kind of conversation we are having and where we are in that conversation are broad, macro level skills. To flow with the dance of a dialogue, we also need to be able to track smaller movements. The most basic of these is tracking what I call the *center of attention*, or who has the floor.

In every conversation there is a center of gravity that shifts back and forth between the interlocutors. This is broader than just who's speaking or listening. It's about sensing which person most needs to be heard in any given moment and bringing awareness to how we navigate those changes. If we are careless about shifting the center of attention, grabbing it back and forth between us, this can lead to mistrust, complexity, and a lack of empathy.

> **In conversation, the *center of attention* is the party on whom attention is focused in any given moment, the one who "has the floor."**

The general guideline is to listen first. Whenever possible, offer the center of attention to the other person. Shift the focus back to yourself after they feel heard and complete, when they're more likely to have space to listen.[2]

Using empathy, you can build understanding and check if the other person feels understood. Keep asking two basic questions: "Did I get it? Is there more?" You may need to offer several rounds of empathy before someone feels heard enough to give you the floor and listen. Check if the person is willing to shift the focus by making a request:

- "Is there anything else you'd like me to understand?"
- "I'd like to share a little about how I'm feeling. Do you have some space to listen?"

Taking care with this transition can go a long way to building trust and repairing damage in difficult conversations.

Principle: **Whenever possible, check if the other person feels understood before moving on to a new topic or shifting the center of attention to your own experience.**

Of course, our patience and empathy have limits. If we lose the ability to listen, we can respectfully bring the center of attention back to ourselves. Remember, there are no hard rules in communication. Our job is to stay grounded and present, connected to our good intentions, and to respond to what's happening as skillfully as possible. This is about using mindfulness to be aware of what's happening in our own internal process. Are we still present? Are we able to stay connected to a genuine intention to understand? If not, what do we need to do to reconnect? Would shifting the center of attention help?

We can lose the ability to listen for many reasons. There may be more information than we can follow, we may begin to feel full and lose the ability to track our own thoughts or feelings, or there may be something so pressing inside that we need to speak to get some relief before we can listen more. If we can't listen, *that's* what's most important. If we can't hear the other person, pretending to continue to listen won't serve either of us.

In these instances, we need to interrupt—not because we *don't* want to listen but rather because we *do want to listen*; we recognize that if we don't interrupt we won't be able to do so. The more heated the conversation, the more care needs to be taken when interrupting. To reduce the chances that the other person will take offense, we lead with our intention to connect. Here are a few examples of interrupting skillfully—notice how each begins with an affirmation of the connection:

- "I want to hear the rest of what you're saying and I'm starting to lose track. Would it be all right if we paused so I can summarize what I'm hearing so far?"
- "I want you to continue, but I'm a bit confused. May I ask a question?"
- "I want to keep listening, and I'm having trouble because there's something I want to clarify. May I respond for a moment?"

In the first two examples, even though we are interrupting, the center of attention stays with the other person. In the third example, we propose shifting the center to ourselves by letting the other person know that we need to express something before we can continue listening.

If we have the floor and the other person shifts the focus back to themselves, we have two options. We can follow their lead, letting go of our piece for a moment as we listen and offer them some understanding, or we can acknowledge the shift and request to keep the focus with us: "I hear that, and I'd like to finish what I was saying first. Could we take a few more minutes to complete this piece before moving on?"

PRACTICE: Tracking the Center of Attention
Who has the floor? Notice when the center of attention shifts from one person to another. What is the effect when that shift happens smoothly with consent or abruptly without consent? Practice shifting the focus consciously by checking if the other person feels complete, by making a request, or by interrupting skillfully if necessary.

Tracking Content

Most conversations have more than one piece of content to discuss. In Amanda's case, she'd had several interactions with her friend around parenting, including an email exchange, and needed to discuss the relational issues at play. Tracking all of that can be tricky. The course of a conversation often seems more like a labyrinth than a trail. It twists and turns, breaks off, and loops back on itself.

If we're unable to track these elements, we can find ourselves entangled in a mess. Tracking skills help us keep an eye on both the general trajectory of the conversation (what phase of dialogue are we in; who has the floor) as well as the actual content we're examining. To do this, there are a few more tracking skills to flow with the dance of dialogue.

Just as someone may jump ahead to problem solving, many times people will introduce new topics before completing the one that's already on the table. I call this *splintering* because it's a way that conversations can fracture and break apart. We start talking about one thing that then diverges into two, then three or four, and soon we can't even remember where we began.

When a conversation splinters, it gets complicated quickly. Issues rarely get resolved because there are too many things on the table at once without any of them being completed. If we get off topic or jump ahead, we need to be able to *redirect* the conversation—to gently guide it back on course. In challenging conversations, this requires extra care and sensitivity to minimize the chance that the other person will interpret our efforts as controlling or as a challenge to their autonomy.

> *Splintering* introduces new pieces of content before the current topic is complete.

> *Redirecting* gently guides a conversation back to a chosen phase or topic.

Redirecting is similar to interrupting skillfully. First, we affirm or acknowledge what the other person has said so they don't think we are dismissing their point. Then we state our desire to return to the previous topic. Here are a few examples of redirecting:

- "Thank you. I'm glad you mention that. Before we go there, I'd like to say one or two more things about . . ."
- "I appreciate you bringing that up. I want to discuss that in a minute, but first I'd like to touch on a few more things related to . . ."
- "Yes, that's important. Can we finish talking about this first, and come back to that in a moment?"

The basic tool of reflecting before we respond to complete a cycle of communication helps prevent splintering. Instead of letting a topic hang in the air, we use empathic reflections to ensure that understanding is happening. When we apply this consistently in conversation, we build a sense of momentum and cooperation.

Just as we feel a somatic shift when we complete one cycle of communication, we often experience a felt change when we complete a larger topic or thread in conversation. There can be a sense of settling, an outbreath, or a spontaneous feeling of energy when we both recognize "Okay, that's that! This is a good place to pause or to shift." Even if an area isn't completely resolved, we feel it when we arrive at a place of some shared understanding around an issue.

PRACTICE: Tracking Content

When there's more than one issue on the table, pay attention to which piece of content is being discussed. If the conversation splinters, jumping ahead or introducing a new thread in a way that doesn't seem helpful, try redirecting. Affirm the importance of what's been said and gently request to return to the previous issue.

As you discuss an issue, reflect before you respond in order to complete the cycle. Try to close each loop in a conversation, seeing if you're on the same page before moving on to a new area.

Say What You Mean: The Power of Being Succinct

The last tracking skill is essential in creating understanding: being clear about what and how much we say. When we feel passionate about something, or if we don't feel heard, we often repeat ourselves. Yet the more words we use, the less understanding we usually get. We all know what it's like to be on the receiving end of a monologue, how easy it is to feel overloaded and lose the ability to digest what the other person is saying.

> *Principle:* **We have more clarity and power when we use fewer words with more sincerity. Speaking in short, succinct chunks makes it easier for others to understand us.**

We can distinguish between two types of self-expression, *chunking* and *flooding*. Flooding is the experience of opening the gates and letting it all pour out! Our inner world doesn't gather and collect before we share. We may speak for several minutes at a clip without taking a break or checking if the other person is still with us. Chunking is the ability to share information in manageable pieces, one or two at a time. This makes it easier for the other person to take things in and gives us the opportunity to check for understanding and complete the cycle.

Flooding is when we repeat ourselves, try to say everything all at once, or share more information than the other person can process at once.

Chunking is when we speak one piece of content at a time, in small, manageable parts.

We each have different ways of expressing ourselves. Some of us prefer to know what we want to say before we begin, others of us like to discover what we mean through the process of dialogue. In my Jewish family of origin, we often show our love by interrupting one another. In my Buddhist community, we tend to express care through speaking more slowly or pausing. Regardless of our personal style or culture, it's helpful to be conscious of the amount we're sharing and the other person's capacity to take it in, so we can adjust accordingly.

To be succinct rests upon the ability to discern what we want to communicate and on the capacity to be self-aware as we speak. The discernment aspect of speech is a training in understanding and organizing our inner world. This begins with deliberate practice and culminates in more spontaneous, clear communication. The act of verbal expression (literally to "push out" words) is a process whereby something gathers within and is then offered without. It is to comprehend our inner life, allowing thoughts and feelings to coalesce and form into discrete words and phrases.[3]

Give yourself time to gather your thoughts, discern your feelings and needs, and formulate what it is you wish to express. Recall that we communicate to create understanding, to "make common" what is unique and personal. Instead of asking yourself, "What do I want to say?" you might consider, "What do I want the other person to understand?" The clearer you can be about what specifically you would like them to know or hear, the easier it will be to articulate in chunks. Eventually you will learn to do this in real time.

To curtail the runaway train of words that can tumble out of our mouths, we use presence to track our own level of stimulation. This internal tracking can remind us to pause periodically and check with the other person to see where they're at.

When we can chunk information and stay attuned to completing the cycle, we begin to enter the flow of dialogue. We speak, check, and build understanding. When listening, we can guide the conversation with that same rhythm, interrupting to stay connected, helping to ensure that the other person gets the understanding they want and need.

There is a wonderful saying (often attributed to Albert Einstein) that gets at this skill: "Everything should be made as simple as possible—but not simpler." Tracking the content of a conversation is about paring away what's extraneous and attending to the essence of what's being expressed by ourselves or another.

PRACTICE: Chunking Information

To increase the chances that you'll get the understanding you seek, consider what it is you'd like the other person to understand before you speak. If there is more than one point you'd like to make, or more than one thing for which you'd like empathy, break it down into chunks. When you speak, track the amount of information you're sharing. Stay grounded with presence, pausing periodically to check if the other person is still with you.

Entering the Flow of Dialogue

The third step to better conversation is focusing on what matters. To do this, we need to train our attention to notice and identify the range of possibilities of what might matter in each moment. Which of the three basic positions in dialogue is needed: expressing clearly, receiving empathically, or returning to presence? Within the specifics of the conversation, is there an observation to clarify, a feeling to express or receive, a need to acknowledge, or a request to make? What's needed to keep things on track? Do we need to redirect or interrupt so that we can stay connected? Or do we need to practice chunking, breaking something complex down into more basic components so that we can get to the heart of what matters?

It can seem like a lot, but the practice boils down to one central question: What is most salient? In each moment, at each step of the way, what's most important? If we've taken the time to train our attention to notice each of these components of conversation, what matters will be clear.

When Amanda spoke with her friend, she started by framing the situation more broadly and getting agreement to have the conversation. She made some observations, shared how she felt and why, and asked for understanding. Though she didn't receive the empathy she had hoped for, having clarity about her needs helped her navigate the conversation. Her friend got a little defensive, but Amanda was able to address the relational side of things enough to make some logistical requests around the advice-giving in a respectful and caring way. Her friend understood and agreed to do her best to honor Amanda's wishes.

You don't have to have it all figured out or even know what to say next. You just need to show up, come from curiosity and care, and focus on what matters. Trust what you notice and use the tools as a road map to proceed.

Try to relax and find the flow of dialogue, that rhythm of moving between basic presence, speaking, and listening in a fluid and natural way. Lead with presence and trust your genuine intention to understand. Let this be your guide. Continue to train your attention in the tools and practices I've shared, but don't be afraid to let go and trust the principles behind them. Conversation is a living, dynamic activity. Trust the process and follow what's alive in the moment.

PRINCIPLES

Stating how a conversation can contribute to both of us helps create buy-in and willingness.

Whenever possible, check if the other person feels understood before moving on to a new topic or shifting the center of attention to your own experience.

We have more clarity and power when we use fewer words with more sincerity. Speaking in short, succinct chunks makes it easier for others to understand us.

KEY POINTS

In conversation, notice how you can shift between speaking, listening, and resting in presence. Learn to track the different parts of a conversation:

- Relational level: your connection, emotions, and how you're getting along
- Logistical level: any concrete problem you're trying to solve
- The center of attention (who has the floor?)
- The specific topic or thread you are discussing
- The tendency to splinter (introducing new topics) and the possibility of redirecting (returning to complete the previous topic)

QUESTION & ANSWER

Q: I get tripped up by the speed of conversations. I find it difficult to switch between listening and trying to be aware of what I'm feeling.

It takes time to learn how to shift back and forth with the flow of conversation. It's a little like learning to drive a manual transmission. At first there are so many things happening; every time you try to shift gears the car starts jerking back and forth! Over time your feet, hands, eyes—your whole mind and body—learn how to work together to operate the vehicle. It's the same with these tools. If it feels overwhelming, just stick to the basics: lead with presence, come from curiosity and care, and focus on *one thing* that matters. From there, you can slowly add in the other components.

Q: Sometimes it's easier to pretend that I'm listening than to interrupt and deal with the awkwardness of telling the other person I'm not interested. What would you recommend?

We're not always interested to listen, even with the people we love. The question is, what kind of relationships do you want in your life? Do you want them to be based on mutual trust and honesty or on some level of deceit, however minor? If someone were pretending to listen to you, would you rather they carry on the ruse or be real with you? Our time, attention, and energy are some of the most precious resources we have in life. Why waste them pretending to listen? Is it really worth the price to avoid the discomfort of interrupting?

There's a balance between being honest and showing care. If possible, discuss the dynamic when it's *not* happening so that you're not feeling impatient or frustrated while talking about something sensitive. Begin by framing the conversation with shared needs or appreciation. Talk about the quality of connection you'd like to experience and some ideas for how you can create that together. Or, if you're no longer interested in spending time together, have the difficult conversation with as much tenderness and compassion as you can.

Q: What about when interrupting is seen as disrespectful? I can do that with my American friends, but in other cultures it would be regarded very poorly if I interrupted someone.

Interrupting is intended to reestablish connection. If it has the opposite effect culturally, then it's not the right tool. Focus on the principle: how you can work within the customs of the culture to reconnect. Is there a way of indirectly asking for what you need that they would understand?

Cross-cultural communication can be quite complex, especially since each of us often carries multiple layers of cultural conditioning. One simple way of thinking about it is that one always has three options. You can learn about and adapt to the other person's culture, they can learn about and adapt to yours, or together you can have a metalevel conversation about your cultural differences and work together. In this latter option, once you've acknowledged the different expectations, you might risk breaking a norm in a way that minimizes any offense. Begin with a gentle apology, "Forgive me . . ." or "I'm so sorry to interrupt . . ." and then venture your request.

Q: Listening is easy for me. I've been trying to speak up for myself more, but it's challenging. I feel as if I have to be forceful or sharp to speak. Do you have any suggestions for finding a balance?

We all have different conditioning; some find it easier to speak, some to listen, others find it easiest to be alone! It's great that you're noticing the pattern and working to expand your comfort zone so you can have as much flexibility as possible.

If we're not used to expressing ourselves, it can feel awkward or strident at first. If we haven't developed this capacity, it can take a lot of exertion to get to a baseline. I would encourage you to let things come to equilibrium on their own. Don't be too concerned with how it sounds coming out. If you're skilled at listening, you can clean up the mess if you express yourself in a way that's brusque.

In relationships where there's more trust, let the other person know this is something you're working on, which reduces anxiety and gives you a forum to practice. Over time, the more you speak up, the more your nervous system will learn to trust that you know how to advocate for yourself. Once that trust is established internally, the pressure and urgency to speak will begin to fade and your words will flow with more ease.

running the rapids

We don't rise to meet our expectations;
we fall to our level of training.
　　—BRUCE LEE

DIFFICULT, TENSE CONVERSATIONS are a normal part of life. Skillful communication doesn't necessarily prevent those situations. Rather, it helps us handle difficult conversations when they arise and try again when we blow it.

The difference between ordinary conversations and challenging ones is a bit like the difference between canoeing on open water and running rapids. Both involve paddling with balance, but the stakes are much higher and the skills more demanding in white water.

Think of a terrible argument you had with someone or a time when you tangled with a coworker. Intense emotions, personal blind spots, and mistaken assumptions can make high-stakes conversations unproductive and even explosive. The boat capsizes, your gear gets soaked, and you wash up on shore somewhere downstream. I once smashed a chair in my grandmother's living room, remember?

Fortunately, you've already learned the tools you need to handle white water. In this chapter I'll offer guidelines for how to prepare for a difficult conversation, practices to balance your nervous system, and some ideas for starting over when your words fall short of your intentions.

Navigating Tough Conversations

Preparing ahead of time for difficult conversations helps clarify what's important, reduces reactivity, and increases the likelihood that we will be able to engage in a way that is in line with our intentions. Paramount to this is our *internal* preparation, which includes:

- Nourishing yourself
- Investigating what's at stake
- Humanizing the other person

Nourishing Yourself

Nourishing yourself before a difficult conversation can help you feel clear, balanced, and well resourced. This means getting some empathy for any pain, anger, or upset you may feel. Empathy can reduce reactivity and create more space to hear the other person. Find someone you trust and be explicit about the kind of support you'd like. Ask them to listen and reflect what they hear matters to you. Later, if it helps, you can move on to analyzing, brainstorming, or getting feedback with your friend.

You can also use the self-empathy process in chapter 9 to sort through your emotions and identify your needs. (Sometimes this is the only option.) To find some space inside, try to connect with the more universal aspect of your needs. Can you sense them as complete and whole, as a natural part of your humanity, rather than as a something lacking or unfulfilled?

Investigating What's at Stake

Investigating what's at stake helps us recognize the most important aspects of a complicated or intense situation and can inform our choices about how to proceed. Pay attention to any blame or judgments that you hold. Avoid indulging or bypassing them. Instead, regard your judgments as valuable information about your heart. If you're high up on the ladder of inference, try to descend to more specific observations. Look deeper and ask, "What's holding this story together? What feelings and needs are expressing themselves as judgments?"

In this process of investigation, consider if there are other things at stake in the situation. Is your self-image involved, wanting to be seen in a certain way? What expectations, views, or beliefs do you have? Are you avoiding some feedback?

When canoeing, if one comes to an unfamiliar set of rapids the best practice is to pull ashore to scout the river and determine if it's safe. In challenging situations, consider if your goals are realistic. Do you have the capacity to have the conversation in the way you'd like? Does the other person? Is this the right time to have the conversation or even the right person with whom to talk? Are you asking someone to resolve something that they don't have the power to do?

To further determine how to approach things, investigate what parts of the conversation are relational and what parts are logistical. For example, my argument with my brother (when I smashed the chair) wasn't really about the logistics of sharing house chores. I had a relational desire to be seen, to receive empathy for how desperate and alone I felt with my emotions. Had I recognized this, I would have understood that my brother wasn't the right person to talk to at that time.

The knowledge gleaned from investigating the stakes can inform your approach. What do you want from the conversation? Understanding? Resolution? Are you entering with a range of ideas that might work for both people? What specific requests can you make to move forward?

Humanizing the Other Person

Humanizing the other person requires the humility and empathy to step outside of your own story and consider other perspectives. If you can put yourself in their shoes and imagine, even for a moment, what might be going on for them, it can have a profound effect on the conversation.[1] Whatever the situation, however confusing or harmful another's actions, there is some internal logic behind their choices. Use the empathy map from chapter 9 to explore their feelings and needs. Decide how you want to show up in this conversation and focus on that, rather than on proving a point or being right.

We want to be right, to feel vindicated, to win the argument. Try to look honestly at this. How often has being "right" ever helped to resolve relationships or problems? Would you rather win or find real resolution? Would you rather be right or be free?

Entering a difficult conversation, one can get totally hung up on being right and fail to see that this is a *strategy* to meet some deeper need. If the other person concedes that you are right, does that truly give you what you seek? Do you want empathy or acknowledgment for how their actions affected you? Do you long to know that they care? To find peace or healing? To affect a change in their behavior?

When you get clear on what you'd like, reflect on the conditions that would bring about that result. What intentions are most likely to support resolution? How can you create a quality of connection sufficient to disentangle this situation?

Be humble enough to consider in what ways, if any, you've contributed to the problem through action or omission. Nothing occurs in a vacuum; all relationships are cocreated. Can you be honest about that with yourself? Can you stretch your empathy further and try to see yourself and your actions through their eyes? Taking responsibility for your part frees your heart from defensiveness and invites the other person to reciprocate.

PRACTICE: Guidelines for Preparing

Explore as many of these suggestions as you find supportive.

> **NOURISH YOURSELF:** Seek the support of a trusted friend or take time for self-empathy. Explore your own feelings, needs, and values. Can you connect with the universal aspect of your needs to find some space inside?
>
> **INVESTIGATE:** Identify what's at stake for you:
> - Honor any judgments, blame, assumptions, or views you have. Translate them into observations, feelings, and needs.
> - Consider your own and the other person's capacity to have the conversation. Is this the right time, the right person?
> - What parts of the conversation are relational and what parts are logistical?
> - What requests do you have? Do you have creative solutions in mind?

HUMANIZE THE OTHER: Step outside of your story and consider alternative perspectives:

- Stretch your imagination to empathize with the other person.
- Consider your needs behind the desire to be right.
- What intentions will be most supportive to have this conversation?

Redirecting the River

Conflict can send a cascade of physiological effects through our body. Our breathing changes, stress hormones release, and (if we lack skills to meet this swell of energy) our cognitive function alters.

Every time we respond by blowing up, running away, or shutting down, we retrace and strengthen the neural networks for that behavior, like floodwaters carving a riverbed into a hillside. Inundated with stimuli, our sympathetic system prompts us to react with aggression, fear, or confusion, and we fall back on one of the four learned conflict behaviors (avoidance, confrontation, passivity, and/or passive aggression).

So how can we deal with the unhelpful physiological streams that we've fed within our nervous system? While it's not possible to control our life circumstances, we can make educated choices about how to navigate the rapids.

With mindful presence and skill, we can shift these patterns by carving *new* conduits into the hillside of our mind and body, creating different streams for that energy to follow. Progress is incremental, but every drop we redirect deepens the new riverbed, attracting more and more water to change the course of the river of consciousness.

If we don't remember to be mindful in difficult conversations, we're less likely to access our wisdom or good intentions, let alone any of the tools we've learned. And in tough situations, the main thing to be mindful of *is our nervous system.*

> **Principle:** Attending to our own reactivity, noticing the rise of activation and supporting the calm of deactivation, can help us make wiser choices about what to say and when.

Working with our nervous system to handle reactivity and redirect the river has three stages that flow naturally from one to the next, just like breathing in and breathing out:

- Recognizing activation
- Riding the waves
- Supporting deactivation

Recognizing Activation

Under ordinary circumstances, our body and mind naturally ebb and flow through activation and deactivation, arousal and settling, like waves rocking a boat. Breathing itself follows this rhythm. The elasticity of our nervous system, its resilience, is our ability to navigate this cycle with ease, tolerating the stress of sympathetic arousal, allowing the settling of parasympathetic deactivation, and returning to a baseline state of oriented awareness. This shows up as a relaxed alertness, an easy readiness with dynamic tone that can respond appropriately to changing circumstances.[2]

When something unusual occurs in the environment—positive or negative—we enter a temporary state known as *sympathetic activation* or *arousal*.[3] For example, say you see an old friend unexpectedly: everything animates, your face flushes, you breathe in deeply and perk up. Or, if you hear a loud sound: your body tenses for a moment—"Am I in danger?" Your head turns toward the sound, trying to determine its origin and meaning.

The degree of arousal—how fast the flood rages—depends on the intensity of the stimulation (actual or perceived). In a healthy nervous system, when the cause for stimulation passes (we meet the challenge; a threat vanishes; we lose interest), aspects of the *parasympathetic system* come back online to "calm the waters" in our mind and body. The system comes to rest as the cycle of activation completes, and we paddle along on open water.

During interpersonal conflicts, the sympathetic arousal can snowball. Danger signals get amplified, and—to use a very precise, technical term—we lose it. Our ability to access higher cognitive function in the prefrontal cortex declines and we're along for the ride, like losing our paddle in white water. We explode, flee, collapse, or check out. We may even enter a dissociative state as a form of self-protection. If the level of stimulation exceeds our capacity to respond, we freeze.

To redirect the river, we start by recognizing our nervous system activation patterns. With mindfulness we sense the changes of sympathetic arousal *in real time*. We get to know more intimately how activation feels both in the ordinary flow of life and in difficult situations. As we learn to catch its signals earlier we have more choices to handle it.

PRACTICE: Monitoring Activation

This activity builds on the chapter 5 practice, "Just say 'Oh!'"

As you move through your day, study what happens when your nervous system is activated. Whenever something of any significance occurs—you get some good news, you almost miss the train, someone cuts you off in traffic—notice the physiological effects in your body. Does your heart rate increase? Does your breathing change? Do you feel warmer? Try to maintain an attitude of curiosity and care rather than judgment. These are natural responses preparing you to meet a challenge or pursue a goal.

Extend this exploration to the interpersonal sphere. Pay attention to even small shifts in your nervous system when something stimulating occurs (positive or negative). Look for changes in breathing, heart rate, perspiration, muscle tone, jaw tension, or bodily sensation.

For advanced practice, see if you can observe these changes in others. Watch for shifts in posture, body language, color of skin, muscle tone, jaw tension, breathing, facial expression, tone of voice, pace, or volume.

Riding the Waves

Feeling activated is completely natural. It's ethically neutral and inherently benign. Mindfulness doesn't aim to suppress activation or achieve some imaginary neutral state. The goal is to become aware and adept at riding life's waves.

We each already know something about how to ride the waves and handle activation without reacting impulsively. Ever felt the inner agitation of wanting to say something but needing to wait for the right moment to interject? That's an experience of sympathetic arousal. Anytime you relate to that internal pressure wisely—taking a breath, shifting your weight, making a mental note—you're handling the activation. Doing it for even a split second can yield more choice about what to say and when.

In effect, awareness lends the ability to steer. It is through mindfulness that we can pause, track the reactivity in our body, and ride the wave rather than be capsized by it. Your ability to ride a wave of activation depends on your capacity to tolerate discomfort. In contemplative practice, every time you observe an itch, a knee or back pain, without immediately jerking, you are developing the inner balance to respond rather than react. If the wave is too big, step back, feel the energy in your body, and allow it to dissipate.

The paired practices of pausing and grounding are especially helpful in difficult conversations. Pausing—anything from a micropause to a full breath to a break in the conversation—creates the space to recognize activation. Then, grounding in the body provides an anchor to steady your attention instead of losing your center.

The mindfulness exercises in chapter 3 are excellent ways to develop these skills. Use whichever reference point is most available. The feeling of gravity can stabilize your awareness. The upright sense of the centerline may lend clarity and attentiveness, while the rhythm of breathing can soothe intensity. If the activation is strong, shift attention to the periphery of your body, feeling the sensations in touch points such as your hands or feet, or orient to sounds or physical space. These reference points widen awareness, which can provide much needed relief in challenging moments.

As you become more familiar with tracking activation in your body, you'll start to notice when you approach your tolerance threshold—maybe a quickening of the breath, a scattering of the mental process, or an intimation of rising energy. The key here is to learn how to slow down the conversation or pause it altogether *before* you hit that threshold.

In white-water canoeing, building skill slowly is essential: start small in class 1 rapids, taking time to learn. When the waters are dangerous or the rapids beyond your skill level, pull ashore, unload the gear, and portage to safer waters.

The guidelines for difficult conversations are the same. Whenever possible, do your best to take things slowly so your system can adjust.

This might mean breaking a difficult conversation into parts, having it via written correspondence, or asking someone else to be present. If the waters are too choppy—if the sympathetic arousal exceeds your capacity to handle it—the wisest response is to gracefully exit the conversation until you recover (see "Pausing a Conversation" in chapter 3).

PRACTICE: Riding the Waves of Activation

When you notice sympathetic arousal in conversation, practice subtly pausing and grounding to track the activation. Use whatever method(s) you've found most helpful and authentic to pause: a deep breath, a gesture, or a verbal request. Choose a reference point for grounding awareness in your body: gravity, the centerline, breath, touch points in your hands or feet. Experiment with widening your attention by orienting to sounds or the space around you.

Supporting Deactivation: Settling Downstream

Riding the rapids of activation means being with the whole process, the up and the down. Just as we learn to recognize and attend to the arousal, we can also train ourselves to notice, feel, and support any calming. This can occur at many points, in small ways, during and after a conversation. If we're skilled, we're sensing it all along, continually enhancing these naturally occurring intervals in our nervous system.

How do we notice and take advantage of deactivation amid churning waters? This requires getting skilled at choosing where to place our attention. Focusing on irritants—such as judgments, negative feelings, or displeasing aspects of another's words and actions—tends to fuel our reactivity, increasing nervous system activation. We can begin deactivating by attending to any calming, soothing, or simply *less irritating* aspects of experience. Developing our ability to notice how these feel in our body can bring our nervous system back into balance.

This is different than our normal way of being. We are accustomed to attending to whatever is most interesting, most intense, even if it's unpleasant. Like playing with a loose tooth, our mind is magnetically drawn to the point of greatest intensity.

Deactivation occurs both literally and figuratively as an outbreath. Any shift in the state of our nervous system is reflected in the breath's pace, depth, duration, or rhythm. We exhale. Muscle tension releases, our jaw slackens, our shoulders relax, our gaze softens, our breathing slows or deepens. We can train ourselves to notice these physiological signs. They're occurring continually in small ways all day long.

Activation is easy to spot; deactivation takes a more refined attention. It may not seem that interesting. It's subtle. It's what happens afterward, the outbreath, the cooldown. By deepening our sensitivity, we cultivate a taste for the soothing effects of the downward phase of the cycle.

This period, however brief, is the phase of healing, integration, and regeneration. To notice deactivation, we must become interested in the lull, a passing phase, or an "empty" moment. If we begin to inhabit these spaces, they calm our mind and body.

When we give mindful awareness to a feeling of ease or relaxation, it amplifies like a bell ringing, like the stroke of a bow resonating through the body of a cello. Taking small moments to feel the soothing quality of this deactivation nourishes us and strengthens resilience, in conversation and in life.

As we develop the art of attention and being mindful of our nervous system, we grow skilled at transforming ordinary moments, the spaces between things, into sources of rest and comfort. Sometimes we notice the deactivation first, and that gives way to a moment of quiet. Other times we notice the moment and the settling comes after. Still other times we sense our *need* for deactivation and intentionally create the space to settle with a word, gesture, or action. When the gaps are missing, we learn to create them.

In conversations, find the transitional space between exchanges or phrases, pauses or breaks in the flow of dialogue. Notice any settling when you complete a cycle of communication. In difficult conversations, even the smallest amount of agreement, acknowledgment, goodwill, or concession can provide a momentary raft in the flood of words and emotions. If those moments aren't apparent, *seek them out*. Shift your attention to sound or the space in the room, or use your creativity to insert a pause or take a break.

Shepherding a challenging dialogue to some resolution relies on our ability to find (or insert) these moments and to make the most of them. We can do this internally, with our own attention, and/or relationally, drawing out small successes by naming and appreciating them.

🔊 PRACTICE: Attending to Deactivation

Silent Practice

Find a quiet place, close your eyes, and take a few minutes to settle your mind and body. Allow your attention to gather with the sensations of breathing in and breathing out. As you breathe in, can you notice any increase in energy or vitality in your body? That's a subtle form of sympathetic activation. As you breathe out, can you notice any settling, calming, or soothing? That's deactivation.

Next, call to mind a slightly challenging conversation (past or future). Begin to feel the physiological effects of activation in your nervous system. Then put the issue aside, turning your attention back to a neutral reference point: gravity, the centerline, the breath, touch points in your hands or feet, sound, or space. As the arousal dissipates, pay close attention to any deactivation in your body: settling, loosening, calming, and any corollary changes in your breath.

Interpersonal Practice

During conversations, begin to look for and attend to any settling or ease you experience in the flow of dialogue. Try paying more attention to the outbreath. Look for natural pauses, breaks, or shifts. Feel any sensations of relaxation, release, ease, or settling in your body or breath.

As you practice with these stages—recognizing activation and riding the waves, noticing deactivation and allowing the churning waters to subside—you will learn to use them in other situations and in shorter periods of time. Simply notice what's happening: *the seeing itself creates the possibility for shifting the pattern.*

Over time, your body will begin to feel the potential for a new way of relating. You may experience a different order of being in tense situations, as new messages flow through your nervous system: "Ah, maybe I don't need to defend, attack, or try to disappear." Slowly your capacity to deal with more difficult situations will grow. You can learn to trust your ability to hear someone else without losing yourself and to have a voice without trying to control or overpower another.

Rehearsing

Another practical, effective way to prepare for a difficult conversation is to test things out with role-play. It can feel a little awkward if you've never done this before, but the potential benefits are great. Rehearsing a difficult conversation can teach you to stay balanced, yield insight, and support healing.

Use the role-play instructions below, concentrating on one or two tools. Being clear about what you're practicing helps focus your attention and enhances learning. To lead with presence and support deactivation, make a point to take a break ("in character" or not) whenever you notice yourself feeling reactive. This is a powerful way to build confidence and expand your nervous system's capacity for calming and grounding. To come from curiosity and care, reflect not only on *what* you say but also on *how* you say it. Recollect any helpful intentions you've identified, for example: being patient, building trust, or trying to collaborate.

PRACTICE: Rehearsing

To Practice on Your Own

Find a quiet place and take a few minutes to settle your mind and body. Imagine having the conversation with a *third person* whom you respect in the room: a mentor, an elder, even a historical or religious figure. How would it feel to have the conversation in their presence? How might you speak or act differently? If they were in your shoes, what might they say?

To Practice with Someone Else

Invite a friend or colleague to role-play with you. Describe the situation and one or two things about how the other person might respond. Choose the tools you want to practice. To focus your learning, limit the role-play to five or six minutes. If you get charged up, take breaks to let your nervous system settle.

Afterward, reflect on what you learned and get feedback from your friend. Ask for specific observations about what you did that helped. Did they trust you? Did they hear blame or criticism at any point? What ideas or suggestions might they have? Role-playing a second time can be a helpful way to integrate feedback.

The Real Conversation

Do your best to start things off on the right foot. If you have choice over where and when to talk, try to set supportive initial conditions: time, place, who's present. Consider how you can lay a foundation of curiosity and care prior to the conversation. For instance, a kind email or a few simple words can be a generous gesture that sets things in a good direction. Let the other person know that you're looking forward to talking and working together to figure things out.

How you open the conversation itself can be incredibly important. If you've initiated the dialogue, show respect for the other person by inquiring, "Is now still a good time?" This can create a sense of agreement and mutual respect from the start. Review the tools for framing (chapter 12). As much as possible, work to present things in a balanced way and name any shared goals or objectives.

Lead with presence. Pay particular attention to *pausing* and the *pace* of the conversation. Things tend to move quickly in heated dialogue; a lot of the work is about slowing down. The more you can find ways to naturally pause and deactivate, the easier it will be to stay clear, hear one another, and respond wisely. Taking time to reflect before you respond naturally downshifts the pace of a conversation. If you do it consistently, it can even create a rhythm of give-and-take that the other person picks up on and mimics, offering back their understanding for whatever you've shared.

Next, come from curiosity and care and try genuinely to understand. This will show up in your body language, your tone of voice, and other nonverbal communication that supports an atmosphere of goodwill and collaboration. When appropriate, state your intention explicitly: "I'd really like to understand where you're coming from . . ." or "I'm committed to figuring this out in a way that works for both of us." Such statements can shift the entire tone of a conversation. If you lose the capacity to listen, interrupt skillfully and ask if they can hear you for a bit. (If neither of you are able to listen, put the conversation on hold for a while.)

Focus on what matters and keep your attention flexible. Instead of belaboring the story of "what happened," listen for what matters to both of you. If you're hearing demands, internally translate them into requests and respond in a way that honors the other person's needs. When you can identify needs, you have more room to hear one another and think creatively about solutions.

As you weave these steps together, the fundamental orientation is to discern what matters most to each involved, to identify the needs and get them all out on the table, side by side. To do this requires being firmly rooted in a genuine intention to understand. Hold that angle of orientation in the conversation, applying some energy to counter the pull of less helpful, automatic reactions (protect, defend, judge, attack). Keep making that radical internal shift to curiosity and care. Demonstrating your care and commitment to collaboration usually helps the other person relax and engage more flexibly.

Finally, if the situation is complex, consider breaking it down into multiple conversations on different days. Your initial pass might just focus on empathy, trying to listen and hear the other person. Next time, share your side and endeavor to build mutual understanding. For the final pass, explore strategies for moving forward.

The Do-Over

Life is messy. In spite of our preparations, training, and best intentions, we all blow it from time to time. In the heat of the moment, an emotion or reaction gets the best of us. A wave of arousal rises, lifts us up, and we crash onto the rocks.

Where I grew up, we would play ball in the street on long summer days until daylight faded. Whenever there was a dispute about the game, if any kid called out "Do-over!" we'd stop arguing and redo the play. We can do something similar as adults.

A do-over is like pressing the reset button. We acknowledge where things went awry, restate our intentions, and ask the other person if they'd be gracious enough to let us try again. We can own our part for something as small as a single remark or as broad as an entire conversation. When we take responsibility for losing it, most people are happy to give us a second chance. It's rarely too late to ask for a do-over.

Depending on the situation, this may be as simple as making a request. Here are a few examples of how you might ask for a do-over during or after a conversation:

- "That didn't come out quite right. Can I try that again?"
- "I'm concerned some of the things I said aren't helping. Can we start over?"
- "Things didn't really go the way I was hoping when we talked. Could we rewind and try having the conversation again?"

A dear friend and fellow NVC trainer spoke with me recently about a challenging email she'd received. In exploring how she might respond, I suggested offering an empathic reflection. She laughed and said, "That's 'Empathy 101' but I didn't even think of it!"

When we're triggered, we're all beginners. In challenging situations, our most important and reliable skills are empathy and reflecting before we respond. These tools build trust, understanding, and connection. Be prepared to offer an empathic reflection more than once. This bears repeating: we might need to empathize three or four times before someone feels adequately understood around a single point. It can take great patience and fortitude to do this, but it can have dramatic effects. We balance empathy with a strong commitment to our own authenticity, shifting carefully between listening and expressing our side of things.

Principle: **When in conflict, if we aim to listen to the other person first it increases the chances that they will be willing to listen to us.**

I've mentioned my friend Sarah, whose mom passed away suddenly. During that same period, she had a difficult conversation with her brother. Having some flexibility in her life at that time, she had agreed to put personal projects on hold and move back to her hometown to look after their elderly father and sort through her mother's belongings. As so often happens in such times, tensions began to surface and trust began to erode between Sarah and her brother.

The conversation started off in a pretty rocky way. Sarah's feelings of helplessness and anger showed up as blame and reactivity. Having taken some of my classes, she recognized what was happening, apologized, and stated her desire to work together. She listened, reflecting his feelings and needs. At one point, when things got tense, she asked if he would give her a minute to breathe and handle some of her feelings, to which he agreed.

That pause transformed the conversation. She considered her own needs and spoke openly and vulnerably about the issue, sharing that she wanted to clear up any conflict as soon as possible because it was important to her that they be able to trust each other during this difficult period. Her sincerity touched him; he wanted the same thing. As they hashed out the details, Sarah summarized the conversation and their agreements with regard to future conversations, which they knew might be challenging. They ended by appreciating each other, their good qualities, and how they'd stuck with a difficult interaction and come through to the other side.

We don't need to be perfect, and it's rarely too late to recover from a misstep. If we can slow down, remember the principles, and come from our genuine good intentions, deep transformation and understanding are possible.

PRINCIPLES

Attending to our own reactivity by noticing the rise of activation and supporting the calm of deactivation can help us make wiser choices about what to say and when.

When in conflict, if we aim to listen to the other person first it increases the chances that they will be willing to listen to us.

KEY POINTS

Prepare for a difficult conversation by:

- Nourishing yourself with empathy or self-empathy
- Investigating what's at stake
- Humanizing the other person with empathy
- Rehearsing with a role-play

QUESTION & ANSWER

Q: How do I talk to people who have a very different communication style than I do? They speak quickly, more loudly, and don't have patience for pausing, expressing feelings, or processing.

Mastering these skills means finding the balance between authenticity and flexibility. The kind of situation you're describing includes an implicit request to relate more in their style. In fact, you may share many of the same needs: ease, flow, comfort, safety. The dance is about acknowledging your different preferences and finding a way to hear one another. Honor your own needs and be willing to let go and adjust.

Keep in mind that it's common to stumble or take longer to express ourselves when learning these tools. Just like learning a language, it can be hard to keep up with the pace of things until we're fluent. In the process, some will be more or less patient with us!

Q: How do you deal with situations where there is a power imbalance, such as if you're talking to a supervisor or someone with more power than you?

When we have less power than the other person, these tools become even more important. If we're unwilling to use violence to meet our needs (which I hope is the case), dialogue is an essential tool.[4] Our capacity to create meaningful human connection becomes our leverage.

How you approach the conversation depends on the situation. One avenue is to align with them by identifying any shared goals or purposes. Another useful angle can be to help them see how meeting your needs will contribute to them, directly or indirectly. The last option is to share your own vulnerability and appeal to the person's natural sense of care, compassion, or generosity. This may mean opening their eyes and heart to the human or moral cost of their current behavior or inspiring them to see the goodness and benefit of contributing in the way that you'd like.

Q: What about when the other person doesn't have these tools or when they just want to fight?

We cocreate our relationships; it takes two of us to dance. Regardless of whether or not the other person is familiar with these ideas and practices, *you* can shift the dialogue by how you relate. In martial arts, if you tense up or resist and your opponent is more skilled than you, they can easily take you down. Fighting back immediately puts you in the realm of struggle and power dominance—and right there you've already lost something important. You lose balance, your own equilibrium and responsiveness. But if your mind and body stay flexible and dynamic, you can redirect their energy and things can take a different course.

You can learn to respond to others without resisting or igniting more ire and to set limits and express yourself without tensing up or becoming rigid. When someone comes toward you with aggressive, blaming energy, if you respond with empathy, meeting their intensity in an authentic way, the game stops there. Try to see their behavior as a strategy to meet their needs. What do they want? If you can connect with that, you can start to defuse the situation.

conclusion
charting your course

Words that come from the heart will enter the heart. But words
that come from the tongue will not pass beyond the ears.
—ABŪ AL-NAJĪB SUHRAWARDĪ

WE'VE COVERED A lot of ground in these pages. It can seem like a lot,
and in many ways it is. Communication is rich and complex, and we've
explored many of its dimensions. The three steps to effective conversation
provide a framework that encapsulates all we've explored and hopefully
serves as a guide to say what you mean—to find your voice, speak your
truth, and listen deeply. As this particular conversation comes to a close,
I'd like to share a few reflections with you on how to integrate what you've
learned and where to go from here.

Turning the Ship

Life is not two-dimensional. As I mentioned when we first started, you can
no more learn to communicate solely from a book than you can learn to
swim from an instruction manual. Eventually you have to get wet.

Hopefully you've been experimenting with these tools all along,
putting them into practice whenever possible and seeing what works.
You've probably had some awkward moments or confusing exchanges
along the way. You may have even had one or two spectacular crashes!
Hopefully you've also had a few successes. When you're learning something new, it doesn't matter how many times you fall down. What matters
is whether or not you get back up.

I want to return to the image of turning a large ship at sea as a metaphor for shifting our communication habits. We each carry a massive amount of momentum that's been barreling ahead in one direction, speaking and relating in set ways for decades. It only takes two things to turn that ship and alter its course: adjust the rudder and hold the angle. For a ship leaving from London headed to New York, a mere two-degree change in its course at the outset of the journey will alter the destination by 195 nautical miles—putting that ship in Portsmouth, New Hampshire, or Chesapeake Bay, Virginia, depending on whether it was an increase or decrease in angle!

In that vein, I encourage you to take what you've learned from this book and hold fast to it. Identify what you've found most helpful and stick with it. Our brains learn through repetition. To make these tools second nature, to have them available at a moment's notice, we need to keep practicing, using them in small ways every day.

🔊 PRACTICE: Integration

Sit comfortably with your eyes closed and take some time to quiet your body and mind. If you like, let your awareness settle with the sensations of breathing in and breathing out.

Reflect on what you've absorbed over the course of reading this book. As you cast your mind back, over weeks or chapters, what stands out? What has been most useful for you? Allow your thoughts to roam freely as you consider these questions.

Finally, distill these reflections to their essence. What specific practices, tools, or principles would you like to integrate into your life?

Next Steps

There are many ways to continue your communication practice. You can review the principles and practices in this book, using them as an outline for further study and practice. Explore one practice each week, then review and move on to the next one.

As I mentioned at the beginning, having a dedicated practice buddy is a huge support. If there isn't someone in your life who shares your interest, check online forums, local groups, or classes to find an empathy buddy with whom you can speak regularly and practice these skills.

Finally, seek out community. Communication is by definition relational, and the more opportunities we have to practice it in real time, the more we learn. I teach courses online and in person here in the United States. While there are, at present, very few people teaching mindful communication in the ways that I have shared with you, there are many retreats, classes, and trainings in Nonviolent Communication happening all over the world. I highly encourage you to attend such programs, which share many of the same principles and practices in this book. (See the "Further Resources" section for more.)

Look Inside

In closing, I want to emphasize one point. If it's not already clear, *mindful communication is not about what we say*. It's not in the words. All of the tools—the technical pointers, tips, and principles—are designed to help you create more understanding in yourself and with those around you. If we get too hung up on the language, too narrowly focused on "saying it right," the magic of human connection gets lost.

To communicate well, to create understanding through awareness, begins and ends with what is inside you. Listen to others with genuine openness and humility. Really try to understand. To say what you mean, look inside. What is true for you? How do you actually feel, in this moment? What do you need? What matters? What is it you would like this person to understand or know about your experience? How would you like to invite them to join you in the interdependent dance of giving and receiving called life?

summary of principles

The Three Steps to Effective Conversation

1. Lead with presence.
2. Come from curiosity and care.
3. Focus on what matters.

The First Foundation: Presence

Effective communication requires presence.

- Given the complexity of communication, transformation occurs most readily through small shifts sustained over time.
- Presence lays the ground for connection.
- Lead with presence; begin conversation with awareness, return to and strive to maintain that awareness, and be honest with oneself about what's happening.
- The more aware we are, the more choice we have.
- Leading with presence includes mutuality, seeing the other person as an autonomous individual, and uncertainty, acknowledging and accepting the unknown, both of which create new possibilities in dialogue.

The Second Foundation: Intention

Intention determines direction.

- Our intentions, views, and experiences reinforce each other: views determine intentions, intentions shape experiences, and experiences confirm our views. Shifting our view therefore can change our intentions and our experience.
- Being aware of our habitual conflict styles allows us to transform

the underlying beliefs and emotions that hold them in place and to make different choices.

- The less blame and criticism, the easier it is for others to hear us.
- Everything we do, we do to meet a need.
- People are more likely to listen when they feel heard. To build understanding, reflect before you respond.

The Third Foundation: Attention

Attention shapes experience.

- The more we are able to differentiate between our strategies and needs, the more clarity and choice we have.
- The more we understand one another, the easier it is to find solutions that work for everyone. Therefore, establish as much mutual understanding as possible before problem solving.
- Being aware of our emotions supports our ability to choose consciously how we participate in a conversation.
- The more we take responsibility for our feelings, connecting them to our own needs rather than to others' actions, the easier it is for others to hear us.
- The more we hear others' feelings as a reflection of their needs, the easier it is to understand them without hearing blame, needing to agree, or feeling responsible for their emotions.
- Having empathy for ourselves increases our capacity to listen to others, whether or not they have the space to listen to us.
- Stating clearly what happened, without judgment or evaluation, makes it easier for someone to hear us and to work toward a solution.
- Translating judgments into observations, feelings, and needs can yield valuable information about what is and isn't working and provide clues for how to move forward.
- When giving feedback, be specific about what is and isn't working and why, which makes it easier to learn.
- The clearer we are about what we want and why, the more creative we can be about how to make it happen.
- Have ideas for strategies that meet as many needs as possible, which invites others to look for creative solutions.

- Stating how a conversation can contribute to both of us helps create buy-in and willingness.
- Whenever possible, check if the other person feels understood before moving on to a new topic or shifting the center of attention to your own experience.
- We have more clarity and power when we use fewer words with more sincerity. Speaking in short, succinct chunks makes it easier for others to understand us.
- Attending to our own reactivity, noticing the rise of activation and supporting the calm of deactivation, can help us make wiser choices about what to say and when.
- When in conflict, if we aim to listen to the other person first it increases the chances that they will be willing to listen to us.

useful communication phrases

Requests for Dialogue
- "Would you be willing to take some time to have a conversation with me about [topic]?"
- "Could we sit down together and look at what we both need to see if we can find a way to work this out?"

Offering Empathy
- "Let me see if I'm understanding. What I'm getting is . . . ?"
- "I want to make sure I'm getting it. It sounds like . . . ?"
- "Here's what I'm hearing . . . Is that right?"

Eliciting Information
- "Tell me more."
- "Anything else you'd like me to understand about this?"

Requests for Empathy
- "What would be most helpful for me is just to be heard. Would you be willing to listen for a bit and tell me what you're hearing?"
- "I just said a lot and I'm not sure it all came out the way I was intending. Could you tell me what you got from all that?"
- "What I just said is really important to me. Would you be willing to tell me what you're getting?"

Inserting a Pause
- "I'd like a moment to gather my thoughts."
- "I'm not sure. Let me think about that."
- "This sounds important. I'd like to give it some time."

- "I'd like some time to take that in. Can we pause here for a moment?"

Taking a Break: To Pause a Conversation

- "I'd really like to continue our conversation, and I'm not in the best frame of mind to do that right now. Can we take a break and come back to this . . . ?"
- "I'd really like to hear what you have to say, and I'm feeling a little overwhelmed, so I don't think I'll be able to listen well. Could we take a break and continue tomorrow?"
- "I'm committed to figuring this out together and don't quite have the space to think clearly now. Can we put this on hold until . . . ?"
- "I want to finish our conversation, and I don't think anything else I say right now will be useful. Could we take a break until . . ."
- "I'd really like to hear what you have to say, but the way you're saying it is making that very difficult. I wonder if you'd be willing to . . .
  . . . try explaining what's happening for you in a different way?"
  . . . take a break until we've both had a chance to reflect on this?"
  . . . let me have a moment to tell you what's going on for me?"

Interrupting

- "Let me make sure I'm still with you . . ."
- "I want to make sure I'm getting everything you said. Can we pause for a moment so I can make sure I'm following it all?"
- "I want to hear the rest of what you're saying, and I'm starting to lose track. Can I summarize what I'm hearing so far?"
- "I want you to continue, but I'm a bit confused. May I ask a question?"
- "I want to keep listening, and there's something I want to clarify. May I respond for a moment?"

Redirecting

- "I'm glad you mention that. Before we go there, I'd like to say one or two more things about . . ."
- "I appreciate you bringing that up. I want to discuss that in a minute, but first I'd like to touch on . . ."

- "Yes, that's important. Can we finish talking about this first, and come back to that in a moment?"

Hearing *No*

- "I'm curious to know, why not? Could you share more?"
- "What's leading you to say no? Do you have other ideas?"
- "Can we take some time to brainstorm ideas that could work for both of us?"
- "What would you need to know, or what could I do, to make it possible for you to say yes?"

Saying *No*

- "I'd like to say yes, and here's what's getting in the way of that right now."
- "I'm hearing how important this is to you, and I'm not seeing how I can make it work given that I also have a need for . . . Could we explore some other options that might work for you?"
- "I can't agree to that without a significant cost to myself in terms of . . . [other needs]. Would it work for you if we tried . . . instead?"

Requests for Do-Overs

- "That didn't come out quite right. Can I try that again?"
- "I feel like we got off to the wrong start. Could we start over?"
- "I'm concerned some of the things I said aren't helping. Would you be willing to let me try again?"
- "Things didn't really go the way I was hoping when we talked. Could we try having the conversation again?

notes

Introduction

1. Thich Nhat Hanh, *The Heart of the Buddha's Teaching: Transforming Suffering into Peace, Joy and Liberation* (New York: Harmony Books, 1998), 84.

2. Throughout the book I use the word *dialogue* on its own as a synonym for conversation and the phrases *true dialogue* or *real dialogue* to refer to the transformative kind of conversation indicated by Lochhead and others. When the atmosphere for such an encounter is not present, we can rely on an inner orientation to help foster such conditions. Author and NVC Trainer Miki Kashtan refers to this as "the discipline of dialogue," an orientation to collaboration that "at its heart, [is] a commitment to pursue the goal of an outcome that truly works for everyone even when others are only looking out for their own interest." See David Lochhead, *The Dialogical Imperative: A Christian Reflection on Interfaith Encounter* (Eugene, OR: Wipf and Stock, 1988), 51; Miki Kashtan, *Spinning Threads of Radical Aliveness: Transcending the Legacy of Separation in Our Individual Lives* (Oakland, CA: Fearless Heart Publications, 2014), 319.

3. Marshall B. Rosenberg, *Nonviolent Communication: A Language of Life* (Encinitas, CA: PuddleDancer Press, 1999).

4. Marshall B. Rosenberg, *Special Session on Social Change*, Switzerland, 2005.

5. See definition in glossary. For example, being a United States citizen affords one certain privileges in this country as well as in many areas in the world. Being white, or male, or educated, or able-bodied (and so on) each carry certain advantages in our current society. For more on this topic, see Peggy McIntosh, "White Privilege: Unpacking the Invisible Knapsack," National SEED Project, 1989. https://nationalseedproject.org/white-privilege-unpacking-the-invisible-knapsack. See also Miki Kasthan, "You're Not a Bad Person: How Facing Privilege Can Be Liberating," The Fearless Heart, November 26, 2016. http://thefearlessheart.org/youre-not-a-bad-person -how-facing-privilege-can-be-liberating. For an exploration of privilege and power within the context of Nonviolent Communication, see Roxy Manning and Janey Skinner, "NVC—Changing Consciousness,

Relationships & Systems," BayNVC, accessed April 12, 2018,
http://baynvc.org/nvc-changing-consciousness/.

Chapter 1: The Center of Our Lives

1. Human beings are social creatures that meet many needs interdependently.
    We evolved living in small bands, groups, and communities that engaged
    collaboratively to meet needs for shelter, food, and safety for the tribe. These
    origins express themselves in many ways. Within a human life, the need for
    social connection changes over time. It has been well established by
    researchers that people have a physiological need for connection (safe,
    healthy human touch and social engagement) beginning with birth and
    throughout the early years of life. The proper growth and development of the
    human brain and nervous system depend on continued contact and social
    engagement with healthy, well-regulated adults.

    As we grow, social connection becomes relevant for the development of
    empathy and emotional intelligence. During adolescence it manifests
    psychologically, in terms of identity formation and the development of ego
    strength, as well as biologically, for procreation. In adulthood, the need for
    social connection remains relevant in many of these ways (including
    spiritually, through the exploration of consciousness and subject-object
    duality) and simultaneously becomes a strategy to work together to meet
    other needs interdependently when desired or necessary.

2. As social creatures, we are keenly attuned to what our nervous systems are
    telling us about other people and our surroundings. Social engagement can
    calm or activate the nervous system, depending on the circumstances and
    each individual's internal state.

3. Key aspects of our communication are animated by the vagal system (a
    constellation of nerves including the vagus and trigeminal nerves). The inner
    ear filters out extraneous sounds and attunes to the human voice; facial
    muscles express emotion and other signals; the larynx controls vocal tone
    and helps articulate verbal communication. These form part of the human
    social engagement system, a third branch of the autonomic nervous system,
    distinct in its evolutionary trajectory as well as in its neural architecture.
    These ideas were proposed by Stephen Porges in his groundbreaking work
    on polyvagal theory. See Stephen W. Porges, *The Polyvagal Theory:
    Neurophysiological Foundations of Emotions, Attachment,
    Communication, and Self-Regulation* (New York: W. W. Norton, 2011).

4. Stephen W. Porges, "Neuroception: A Subconscious System for Detecting
    Threats and Safety," *Zero to Three* 24, no. 5 (May 2004): 19–24.

5. Traditional understandings of the autonomic nervous system identify two
    main branches: the sympathetic branch, responsible for basic physiological
    homeostasis and the fight-or-flight mechanism, and the parasympathetic
    branch, responsible for the rest-and-digest functions of the body.
    Sympathetic activation (or "arousal") marshals energy in the body for

action, regulates functions such as the heartbeat, and prepares us to meet a threat. The parasympathetic branch slows the flow of that energy, helping us to relax, unwind, and downshift from the arousal of sympathetic activation. (Porges' polyvagal theory introduced a third branch to the autonomic nervous system: social engagement, which is parasympathetic.)

Chapter 2: The Power of Mindfulness

1. Though many systems of meditation make distinctions between the terms *mindfulness*, *awareness*, and *presence*, for our purposes I will use these words synonymously. Each provides a slightly different connotation of the experience of being consciously aware.
2. I also noticed how our unconscious performance of gender roles—the man in charge, the woman who acquiesces—contributed to the situation.

Chapter 3: Relational Awareness

1. Speaking too slowly and calmly in a heated situation can be misattuned, leading the other person to interpret that we don't care, are trying to control the situation, or are judging them. Balance finding an easeful pace with engaging in an authentic way.
2. Orland Bishop, "Sawubona," *Global Oneness Project*, online video, 3:54, https://www.globalonenessproject.org/library/interviews/sawubona.
3. Martin Buber, *I and Thou* (London: Continuum, 1958), 17.

Chapter 4: The Blame Game

1. For more on this, see the work of Sharif Abdullah, who writes and teaches on social, cultural, and spiritual transformation. Sharif Abdullah, *Creating a World That Works for All* (San Francisco: Berrett-Koehler, 1999).
2. Competition and obedience to external authority are rooted in the economic power relations of a class-based society. For a more refined analysis of the socialization process and its intimate relationship with power, economics, and class, see Kashtan, *Spinning Threads of Radical Aliveness*.
3. The etymology of the word *conflict* suggests echoes of *conflagration*: *fligere*, "to strike" versus *flagrare*, "to burn, to blaze," though their roots differ (*bhlig-* versus *bhel-*, respectively).
4. It is essential to note the ways traditional relationship norms and varying degrees of access to resources and power play into situations of domestic abuse, so as not to simplify the "choice" to stay in a relationship to a personal one based on conflict conditioning.

Chapter 5: Where Are You Coming From?

1. Rosenberg, *Nonviolent Communication*, 1.
2. NVC encourages the practitioner to create connection *sufficient to*

accomplish the task at hand. In personal and intimate relationships, connection can be an end in and of itself. In other arenas, connection is in service of some shared goal. We aim to create enough understanding and genuine connection to accomplish that goal. Failure to recognize this can lead to frustrating experiences in which the practitioner's focus on connection is misattuned to their interlocutor. For example, if I ask for a glass of water, I'm not wanting empathy for my thirst!

3. Daryl Davis, *Accidental Courtesy: Daryl Davis, Race and America*, directed by Matt Ornstein (Los Angeles: Sound & Vision, 2015), https://accidental courtesy.com.

4. Dialogue and nonviolent resistance share the creation of the Beloved Community as their goal. Dialogue with those in power is the first request; nonviolent resistance creates pressure toward dialogue, "pushing the powerful into a moral corner" in order to change the way systems function. For more, see Kashtan, *Spinning Threads of Radical Aliveness*, 319.

5. Carl Safina, *Beyond Words: What Animals Think and Feel* (New York: Picador, 2015), 13.

6. Terry Dobson, "A Soft Answer," Eastern Healing Arts, accessed January 4, 2018, http://easternhealingarts.com/Articles/softanswer.html.

Chapter 6: Don't Let the Call Drop

1. Mark Nepo, *The Exquisite Risk: Daring to Live an Authentic Life* (New York: Three Rivers Press, 2005), 5.

2. Carl R. Rogers, "Distinguished Contributors to Counseling Film Series," American Personnel and Guidance Association, accessed April 4, 2018, https://www.youtube.com/watch?v=iMi7uY83z-U.

3. For an inspiring exploration of the premise that empathy is an innate part of being human, see Jeremy Rifkin, *The Empathic Civilization: The Race to Global Consciousness in a World in Crisis* (New York: Jeremy P. Tarcher/Penguin, 2009).

4. Kashtan, *Spinning Threads of Radical Aliveness*, 98.

5. See the work of Sherry Turkle, such as *Alone Together: Why We Expect More from Technology and Less from Each Other* (New York: Basic Books, 2017).

6. Kashtan further notes the tragic dilemma in modern society around the need for empathy and the conditions that block access to it. She writes, "Empathy presupposes the ability to transcend the self and reach out to another. Since it calls for a temporary suspension of our own needs, it is not likely to emerge as a widely available ability in a society replete with rampant capitalism, immediate gratification through consumerism, and hyper-autonomy, mixed with violence and a general lack of generosity. In this kind of context most of us have an incentive to harden our hearts to be able to survive. It is a context which makes the gift of empathy both

desperately needed and sorely lacking." Kashtan, *Spinning Threads of Radical Aliveness*, 98.

7. Thomas Gordon, *Leadership Effectiveness Training: L.E.T.* (New York: Perigee, 2001).

8. *Maya Angelou: And Still I Rise*, directed by Bob Hercules, Rita Coburn Whack (Arlington, VA: American Masters Pictures, 2016), http://maya angeloufilm.com.

9. Richard Davidson, Paul Ekman, Daniel Goleman, and others delineate "compassionate empathy" or "empathic concern" as the third kind of empathy, which involves a different set of brain circuits from cognitive or emotional empathy.

10. Ta-Nehisi Coates, *Between the World and Me* (New York: Spiegel & Grau, 2015), 10.

11. Recent research demonstrates the connection between mindfulness and empathy. See Richard J. Davidson and Daniel Goleman, *Altered Traits: Science Reveals How Meditation Changes Your Mind, Brain, and Body* (New York: Avery, 2017).

12. Okieriete Onaodowan, "To Walk a Mile in My Shoes, You Must First Take Off Your Own," TEDxPaloAlto, accessed February 4, 2018, https://www .tedxpaloalto.com/talks.

Chapter 7: Getting Down to What Matters

1. In the fields of mediation and conflict resolution, a similar distinction is made between *positions* (strategies) and *interests* or *concerns* (the needs at play).

2. To say that all needs are universal is a complex terrain philosophically. Are some needs—such as authenticity—more culturally specific? Some theorists, including Ken Wilber, have proposed a development model in which various needs become salient at different stages of development. The perspective I am presenting here, which is at the heart of Rosenberg's method, is a pragmatic one: needs are *more* universal than strategies, and looking to the underlying motivations of our actions connects us with one another.

3. Chilean economist and social theorist Manfred Max-Neef identifies nine basic categories of needs: subsistence, protection (safety), affection, understanding, participation, leisure, creation, identity, and freedom. See Manfred A. Max-Neef, *Human Scale Development: Conception, Application and Further Reflections* (New York and London: The Apex Press, 1991).

4. Kweku Mandela, "My Grandfather Taught Me Forgiveness," Huff Post (blog), March 19, 2014 (3:38 p.m.), https://www.huffingtonpost.com/kweku -mandela/my-grandfather-taught-me-_b_4994928.html.

5. Miki Kashtan makes an elegant distinction using the terms *self-sufficiency*, the myth that we can survive independently without anything from outside, and *self-reliance*, the ability to mobilize our inner resources to face a challenge.

6. Gender is fluid, and the reality of our individual conditioning around these roles varies widely.

7. Adapted from an exercise originally created by Inbal Kashtan and Miki Kashtan.

8. I am speaking here primarily of relational and higher-level needs, and certainly not about acquiescing to social systems that hinder or prevent meeting more basic needs.

9. For more on this, see the work of NVC trainer Robert Gonzales, who differentiates between "deficiency" and "fullness" consciousness of needs. We can be aware of a need as a lack, something unfulfilled within us, or as a fullness, a universal quality that is complete in itself as an aspect of our humanity.

10. For more on this, see Miki Kashtan, "Wanting Fully Without Attachment," *Tikkun 25*, no. 1 (January/February 2010): 39, http://www.tikkun.org /article.php/jan10_wanting.

11. Adapted from an exercise originally created by Inbal Kashtan and Miki Kashtan.

Chapter 8: Emotional Agility

1. To read more about my choice to ordain as an anagarika, see http://www .OrenJaySofer.com/blog/finding-the-middle-way.

2. Some psychological systems draw distinctions between primary affect (bodily, not necessarily conscious), feelings (conscious), and emotions (more socially constructed and including stories).

3. The nuances of classical Western philosophy in this area are complex, and the modern notion of emotion does not map neatly onto earlier concepts. The early Greeks (Plato in particular) had a system of thought in which reason, will, and desire worked together, with reason as the guiding principle. The Stoics suggested that "passions" on their own were dangerous and needed to be structured, organized, and understood by reason. These ideas were reinterpreted by early Christians and the church fathers (second and third century A.D.), who cast the passions as manifestations of Satan and evil forces, which in turn have informed the modern view of emotions as being dangerous and irrational. Personal communication, Rabbi Jack Bemporad, December 4, 2017. For more, see Jan Plamper, *The History of Emotions* (Oxford: Oxford University Press, 2012); Peter Goldie, ed., *The Oxford Handbook of Philosophy of Emotion* (Oxford: Oxford University Press, 2012); Anthony Damasio, *Descartes' Error: Emotion, Reason, and the Human Brain* (New York: Penguin, 1994); and Kashtan, *Spinning Threads of Radical Aliveness*, 87–89.

4. "Emotions can be explained as specialized states, shaped by natural selection, that increase fitness in specific situations. The physiological, psychological, and behavioral characteristics of a specific emotion can be analyzed as possible design features that increase the ability to cope with the

threats and opportunities present in the corresponding situation." See Randolph M. Ness, "Evolutionary Explanations of Emotions," *Human Nature* 1, no.3 (1990): 261–289.

5. Paul Eckman suggests that emotions evolved as a way for humans to solve dangerous problems quickly, without reliance on the relatively slower process of thinking. See *Emotions Revealed* (New York: Holt 2003). Antonio Damasio has published research illustrating the central role of emotions in decision making and social cognition. See *Self Comes to Mind: Constructing the Conscious Brain* (New York: Vintage, 2012).

6. Psychologist Rollo May offers another analogy: "Instead of one's feelings being limited like notes in a bugle call, the mature person becomes able to differentiate feelings into as many nuances, strong and passionate experiences, or delicate and sensitive ones, as in the different passages of music in a symphony." Rollo May, *Man's Search for Himself* (New York: W. W. Norton, 1981), 74.

7. Research (and experience) shows that when we can consciously feel the initial swell of emotion we are more able to stay balanced. A lot of the positive social benefits of mindfulness (emotion regulation, executive control) derive from this ability to sense our own emotions. For more, see Zindel V. Segal, J. Mark G. Williams, and John D. Teasdale, *Mindfulness Based Cognitive Therapy for Depression* (New York: Guilford Press, 2012).

8. In addition to the somatic component, emotion regulation can include other strategies such as altering thoughts or behavior to better cope with negative emotions.

9. This relationship between thoughts and emotions is the basis of much cognitive therapy.

10. Activating the prefrontal cortex and disrupting activity in the amygdala. See J. David Creswell, Baldwin M. Way, Naomi I. Eisenberg, and Matthew D. Lieberman, "Neural Correlates of Dispositional Mindfulness during Affect Labeling," *Psychosomatic Medicine* 69, no. 6 (July/August 2007): 560–65.

11. Fred Rogers, "Fred Rogers testifies before the Senate Subcommittee on Communication" online video, 6:50, May 1, 1969, https://www.youtube .com/watch?v=fKy7ljRr0AA.

Chapter 9: Enhancing Empathy and Inner Resilience

1. For additional resources and practices on savoring the good, see Rick Hanson, *Hardwiring Happiness: The New Brain Science of Contentment, Calm, and Confidence* (New York: Harmony Books, 2013).

2. Psychological scales have been developed to measure the degree to which we feel empathy. See: https://greatergood.berkeley.edu/quizzes/take_quiz/empathy and https://psychology-tools.com/empathy-quotient.

3. Recent research indicates that empathic care and empathic distress are linked to different regions of the brain. See Yoni K. Ashar, Jessica R. Andrews-Hanna, Sona Dimidjian, and Tor D. Wager, "Empathic Care and

Distress: Predictive Brain Markers and Dissociable Brain Systems," *Neuron* 96, no. 6 (June 2017): 1263–73, doi.org/10.1016/j.neuron.2017.05.014.

4. The analogy of riverbanks for self-regulation, the somatic exercises that follow, and the principles that underlie them come from Somatic Experiencing. See, for example, Peter A. Levine, *Waking the Tiger: Healing Trauma* (Berkeley: North Atlantic Books, 1997).

5. Carl R. Rogers, *A Way of Being* (Boston: Houghton Mifflin Company, 1995), 12.

Chapter 10: How to Raise an Issue without Starting a Fight

1. Bahiya Sutta, Udana 1.10 in John D. Ireland, trans., *The Udāna & the Itivuttaka* (Kandy, Sri Lanka: Buddhist Publication Society, 1997), 19.

2. Tittha Sutta, Udana 6.4 in Ireland, *The Udāna & the Itivuttaka*, 86.

3. See note 5 of the introduction, page 257.

4. For more on the Ladder of Inference, see Peter M. Senge, *The Fifth Discipline Fieldbook: Strategies and Tools for Building a Learning Organization* (New York: Crown Business, 1994).

5. See John M. Gottman, *Seven Principles for Making Marriage Work: A Practical Guide from the Country's Foremost Relationship Expert* (New York: Three Rivers Press, 1999).

6. Martin Luther King, Jr., "An Address by the Reverend Dr. Martin Luther King, Jr.," (speech, Cornell College, Mount Vernon, IA, October 15, 1962), http://news.cornellcollege.edu/dr-martin-luther-kings-visit-to-cornell-college.

7. For an example of devising collaborative solutions without agreement on observations or moral beliefs, see the case study on Minnesota Child Custody Dialogue group: https://baynvc.org/minnesota-dialogues.

Chapter 11: If You Want Something, Ask for It

1. Researchers have noted the ability of children as young as one year old to "comfort others in distress, participate in household tasks, and help adults by bringing or pointing to out-of-reach objects." See Margarita Svetlova, Sara R. Nichols, and Celia A. Brownell, "Toddlers' Prosocial Behavior: From Instrumental to Empathic to Altruistic Helping," *Child Development* 81, no. 6 (November-December 2010): 1814–27, www.ncbi.nlm.nih.gov/pmc/articles/PMC3088085.

Chapter 12: The Flow of Dialogue

1. For those with NVC training, this structure will be familiar as Rosenberg's "giraffe dance."

2. There are no absolute rules for conversation. While listening first and offering empathy is generally useful, conversation is a living process, requiring us to adapt and change with shifting circumstances. Sometimes we

listen, sometimes we speak, sometimes we stay silent. The skill of self-empathy gives us more options.

3. The root of the word *logos* (as in *dialogue*) is *leg-*, "to collect, gather." Hence the idiom "to gather one's thoughts" before speaking.

Chapter 13: Running the Rapids

1. The genuineness of our intention to understand means that this empathy is radically different from trying to manipulate or think *for* the other person in an attempt to get what we want.

2. Effectively handling a stressor strengthens resilience in the nervous system, a little like exercising a muscle. See Kelly McGonigal, *The Upside of Stress: Why Stress Is Good for You, and How to Get Good at It* (New York: Avery, 2015).

3. When this activation is strong enough and associated with something negative, many colloquially refer to it as feeling *triggered*, a term that originally referred to the stimulation of traumatic memories.

4. At the level of societal change, nonviolent resistance becomes an equally important tool to pressure those in power to engage in dialogue.

glossary

Activation: The stimulation of energy in the body to carry out an action in response to a desired goal or perceived threat in the environment; sympathetic arousal, including engagement of the fight-or-flight mechanisms.

Affect labeling: The cognitive process of naming emotions.

Anchor: A reference point to which we return to strengthen mindful presence.

Center of attention: The party on whom attention is focused in a conversation in any given moment; the one who "has the floor."

Centerline: The midline of the torso, halfway between front and back, in the middle of the left and right sides of the body.

Choice point: A moment of awareness in which we decide whether to speak or listen.

Chunking: Speaking one piece of content at a time, in small, manageable parts.

Communication: A process of interaction or exchange creating understanding.

Connection: *See* social connection.

Connection request: A question intended to confirm that message sent was message received, foster mutual understanding, and water the seeds of trust and goodwill. Connection requests also are used to determine if there is sufficient trust and understanding to move toward exploring solutions.

Deactivation: The settling of energy in the body in response to completing an action, meeting a need, or resolving a perceived threat; parasympathetic settling, or releasing of sympathetic arousal.

Emotional contagion: A phenomenon of having one person's emotions stimulate similar emotions in others.

Emotions: Multifaceted, affective experiences, felt in the body.

Empathic distress: An emotional state characterized by the inability to tolerate the perceived pain of another.

Empathy: The capacity to understand or feel what another person is experiencing from their point of view.

Empathy spectrum: The range of access to feeling empathy in human beings.

Feelings: *See* emotions.

Flooding: Repeating ourselves, trying to say everything all at once, or sharing more information than the other person can process.

Framing: Summarizing an issue or area of discussion in a broad and neutral way, often in terms of any shared needs, goals, or values.

Intention: The motivation or inner quality of heart that drives our words and actions.

LGBTQI: Lesbian, gay, bisexual, transgender, queer (or questioning), and intersex.

Logistical conversation: The aspects of a conversation that attempt to solve a problem concretely, including any agreements made.

Mindfulness: Being aware of what's happening in the present moment in a balanced and nonreactive way. *See also* presence.

Needs: Core values that motivate our actions. They're what matter most, the fundamental, root reasons for why we want what we want.

Observation: A concrete, specific, and neutral statement of an event, of what we see or hear in our environment, distinct from evaluation or interpretation.

Orienting: Connecting to one's environment through the senses.

Presence: Embodied awareness of our direct sensory, mental, and emotional experience. *See also* mindfulness.

Privilege: Special rights or advantages available to a particular person or group of people based on a certain attribute, status, or membership in that group. Privilege grants preferential treatment and/or enables access to resources due to legal and/ or social norms, and it exists independently of any particular action or inaction by those who possess it. It often exists independently of any awareness on the part of the privileged individual or group of the presence of any disparity, the benefits to the privileged party, or the costs to others. (See note 5 of the introduction, page 257.)

Protective use of force: The conscious, intentional, and temporary use of force to create safety, employed out of care, without malice or ill will.

Redirecting: Gently guiding a conversation back to a chosen phase or topic.

Reflection: A restatement of or inquiry about what's been said to confirm understanding.

Relational conversation: The aspects of a conversation focused on the quality of connection, emotions, or how parties are relating.

Request: A question about one's willingness to perform a specific action to meet needs. Requests are strategies and are distinct from demands.

Social connection: The need for and experience of safe, healthy human contact and enjoyable social engagement. (This need changes in its manifestation throughout a human life, and in its relative significance on physiological, emotional, biological, psychological, and spiritual levels. For more, see note 1 of chapter 1, page 258).

Solution request: A question proposing a concrete strategy or suggesting an agreement to attend to needs; a question offering an idea about how to move forward in a situation.

Splintering: Digressing in a conversation by introducing new pieces of content before the current topic is complete.

Strategy: An attempt to meet needs tied to a specific person, place, action, time, or object.

Touch points: Areas of strong sensation in the body such as the hands, feet, lips, or tongue.

Tracking: Following specific elements of process or threads of content in a conversation.

View: A particular perspective on, way of looking at or understanding something; it can be consciously chosen or unconsciously held.

further resources

Mindful Communication Resources

For training and personalized coaching in Mindful Communication, visit: www.OrenJaySofer.com.

For the guided audio exercises in this book and additional practices, visit: www.OrenJaySofer.com/book-audio.

Recommended Reading

Goldstein, Joseph. *The Experience of Insight: A Simple and Direct Guide to Buddhist Meditation.* Boston: Shambhala Publications, 1987.

———. *One Dharma: The Emerging Western Buddhism.* San Francisco: HarperOne, 2003.

Hanson, Rick. *Hardwiring Happiness: The New Brain Science of Contentment, Calm, and Confidence.* New York: Harmony, 2016.

Kashtan, Miki. *Reweaving our Human Fabric: Working Together to Create a Nonviolent Future.* Oakland, CA: Fearless Heart Publications, 2015.

———. *Spinning Threads of Radical Aliveness: Transcending the Legacy of Separation in our Individual Lives.* Oakland, CA: Fearless Heart Publications, 2014.

Kornfield, Jack. *A Path with Heart: A Guide through the Perils and Promises of Spiritual Life.* New York: Bantam, 1993.

Kramer, Gregory. *Insight Dialogue: The Interpersonal Path to Freedom.* Boston: Shambhala Publications, 2007.

Levine, Peter A. *Waking the Tiger.* Berkeley: North Atlantic Books, 1997.

Rosenberg, Marshall B. *Nonviolent Communication: A Language of Life.* Encinitas, CA: Puddledancer Press, 2015.

———. *Practical Spirituality: Reflections on the Spiritual Basis of Nonviolent Communication.* Encinitas, CA: Puddledancer Press, 2005.

Rothberg, Donald. *The Engaged Spiritual Life: A Buddhist Approach to Transforming Ourselves and the World.* Boston: Beacon Press, 2006.

Sucitto, Ajahn. *Parami: Ways to Cross Life's Floods.* Hertfordshire, UK: Amaravati, 2012.

———. *Turning the Wheel of the Truth: Commentary on the Buddha's First Teaching.* Boston: Shambhala Publications, 2010.

Meditation Retreat Centers & Training

Participating in a silent meditation retreat is a powerful way to deepen self-understanding, build mindfulness, and strengthen the foundation of presence. I highly recommend the following centers and their programs.

Barre Center for Buddhist Studies: www.bcbsdharma.org
Cloud Mountain Retreat Center: www.cloudmountain.org
Gaia House: www.gaiahouse.co.uk
Insight Meditation Society: www.dharma.org
Insight Retreat Center: www.insightretreatcenter.org
Next Step Dharma: www.nextstepdharma.org
Spirit Rock Meditation Center: www.spiritrock.org

Community Meditation Centers

Buddhist Insight Network: www.buddhistinsightnetwork.org
Cambridge Insight Meditation Center: www.cambridgeinsight.org
Common Ground Meditation Center: www.commongroundmeditation.org
Insight Meditation Center: www.insightmeditationcenter.org
Insight Meditation Community of Berkeley: www.insightberkeley.org
East Bay Meditation Center: www.eastbaymeditation.org
Mission Dharma: www.missiondharma.org
New York Insight Meditation Center: www.nyimc.org
San Francisco Insight: www.sfinsight.org
Seattle Insight Meditation Society: www.seattleinsight.org

Nonviolent Communication Training

Bay Area Nonviolent Communication: www.baynvc.org
Center for Nonviolent Communication: www.cnvc.org
Miki Kashtan: www.thefearlessheart.org
NVC Academy: www.nvctraining.com

index of practices by topic

The following index includes all practices from the book. You can use this for easy reference to find a specific practice or exercise you'd like to review. Practices with this symbol ◀⟩ contain companion guided audio exercise that can be found online at www.OrenJaySofer.com/book-audio.

attention, 5
  caring and, 79
  in identifying needs, 111, 120, 133
  and intention, alignment of, 207
  inward and outward focuses of, 17
  presence and, 16
  shifting, 34, 158, 209, 212
  training, 21, 109–10, 224, 225,
    237–39
authenticity, 245
  capacity for, 122
  committing to, 188–89, 243
  in connection requests, 197, 207
  discerning, 68
  in empathy, 166, 167, 246
  in expression, 45, 107, 123, 170, 184
  in giving feedback, 183
  needs and, 130–32, 150
  in reflection, 97, 153
autonomy, 67, 70, 106, 117, 121, 148,
    191, 221
awareness, 15, 25, 92, 236
  balancing, 52–53
  of breath, 19
  in conversations, 31, 35
  embodied, 53
  empathy and, 166
  in formal meditation, 158
  as foundation of communication, 16
  internal and external, shifting
    between, 51–52
  living with, 24
  maintaining, 26, 27, 38
  natural, 25
  in process tracking, 218
  relational, 42, 50–53, 54
  strengthening, 37–38
  of unmet needs, 124
  use of term, 26, 259n1
  See also self-awareness

blame, 187, 244
  as default intention, 71
  as default pattern, 95, 128
  as hindrance to being heard, 130
  meeting with balance, 89
  noticing, 230
  of ourselves, 68, 72, 118
  reducing, 75, 87
  requests and, 201
  transforming patterns of, 133, 151
  as unmet needs expressed, 121, 122
blame game, 61, 63, 70, 147–51,
    154–56, 172, 180
body
  awareness of, 35
  emotions in, 137, 140, 143, 155,
    262n2
  felt sense of, 119–20
  innate intelligence of, 163
  signs of default patterns in, 81
  See also embodiment; grounding
body language, 20, 57, 93, 94, 138,
    195, 241–42
breath, 22, 135
  activation and, 234, 236
  in cultivating presence, 28, 32, 33–34,
    39
  emotions and, 31, 146
  nervous system and, 19, 32, 48, 238
  pausing and, 45, 47, 48
  signs of default patterns and, 81
  speech and, 18–19

calming, 8, 31–32, 49, 146, 233,
    237–39, 240, 244
care, 13, 109, 209, 225
  about loss of empathy, 101
  building capacity for, 77–79, 82
  in daily life, 80
  in difficult conversations, 241–42
  embodying, 86–87
  engaging in conflict with, 67
  as foundation for mindful communi-
    cation, 5, 57, 87
  and honesty, balancing, 227
  in identifying needs, 119
  importance of, 75–76

and intentions of others, 88
in listening, 95
meeting pain with, 36
natural sense of, 246
need for, 114
in requests, 202
staying connected to, 85
children, 59, 62–63, 191–92, 264n1
chunking, 222–24, 225
clarity, 14, 132, 186
from being succinct, 222, 225
in competitive confrontation, 67
from differentiating between
strategies and needs, 120, 121, 132
in difficult conversations, 186, 216
grounding and, 34, 236
in mindfulness, 26, 32
need for, 131, 152, 188
from translating judgments, 182, 185
vulnerability and, 123
cognitive empathy, 102–3, 106, 161,
164, 168
collaboration, 71, 78, 133
connection in, 195
creating conditions for, 209
mutual understanding in, 76, 128
reflection in, 98, 106
support for, 109–10, 126, 191, 198
trust in, 217
vulnerability in, 122
communication, 2, 5, 183–84
challenges of, 94
"communication roadblocks," 101
completing cycles of, 94–98, 106,
195, 221–22, 224, 238
cross-cultural, 227
defining, 15–16
field of, 7
flexibility in, 110
listening as core of, 92
as multidimensional and holistic, 20,
22
patterns of, 13, 14, 15, 20, 21
presence, role of in, 25

shifting habits of, 21, 22, 248–49
stylistic differences in, 245
three systems of, 4–5
See also mindful communication;
nonverbal communication
community, 2, 40, 113, 117, 118,
144–45, 249
compassion, 3, 132
cultivating, 88
and empathy, differences between,
169
as invitation into presence, 37
as natural impulse, 76, 100, 246
need for, 67, 127, 134, 206
seeing needs and, 121
staying connected to, 73–74, 135
toward oppressors, 148
for unmet needs, 124
compassion fatigue. See empathic
distress
competitive confrontation, 66–67, 71,
233
conditioning, 8, 18, 20, 21, 22, 125,
133, 208, 227
confidence, 9, 23, 143, 207, 240
conflict, 61, 78
etymology of term, 64, 259n3
habitual styles of, 64–70, 71, 233
identifying needs and, 126–28, 130,
132
listening during, 93, 94–95
observations during, 187–88
physiological effects of, 233
sense of identity and, 19
slowing down in, 49, 259n1
sympathetic arousal in, 234–35
views of, 63
See also difficult conversations
conflict avoidance, 65–66, 67, 68, 69,
71, 233
confrontation. See competitive
confrontation
connection. See social connection
connection requests, 195–97, 200, 207

consciousness, 14, 73, 178, 179, 189,
  233, 258n1
conversations
  arc of, 209
  awareness in, 17, 38
  conscious choices in, 43
  as dynamic, 225
  ease in, 207
  emotional awareness during, 145, 154
  emotional expression during, 152
  focusing on needs in, 127
  foundation for effective, 5, 109, 209,
    211, 247
  giving and receiving in, 204–5
  intention, cultivating during, 80
  lack of absolute rules for, 219, 264n2
  mindfulness in, 32, 54
  navigating emotions in, 136
  pace in, 48–49, 54, 226, 241, 259n1
  presence in, 25, 26, 35
  relational and logistical, 215–16, 217,
    226, 231
  requests in, 190, 205–6, 206–7
  taking an extended break in, 47–48
  as training ground for presence, 42,
    54
  transitional space in, 238–39
  See also difficult conversations
creativity, 78
  in difficult conversations, 238
  empathy and, 104
  intention and, 75
  loss of, 63, 67, 70
  need for, 77, 113
  needs and strategies in, 198
  from transforming patterns, 122, 133
  from trust, 217
criticism, 16, 37, 61, 72, 75–76, 87,
  241, 252
curiosity, 109, 128, 209, 225
  about loss of empathy, 101
  building capacity for, 77–79, 81, 82
  in daily life, 80
  in difficult conversations, 241–42

embodying, 86–87
  as foundation for mindful communi-
    cation, 5, 57, 87
  in identifying needs, 119
  importance of, 75–76
  and intentions of others, 88
  in listening, 95
  in meeting "no," 202, 203
  staying connected to, 85

daily life, 3
  curiosity and care in, 80
  emotions in, 156–57
  empathy in, 102–3
  mindful communication in, 6, 7, 32,
    35–36
  mindfulness in, 32
  See also modern life
deactivation, 19, 233, 234, 237–39,
  240, 241, 244
defensiveness
  in conflict, 61
  as default pattern, 71–72, 95
  freedom from, 232
  triggering, 174
  as unmet needs expressed, 121
  views and, 63
  weeding out, 75
demands, 191, 193, 194, 198–99, 202,
  207, 242
depression, 105, 123, 139, 203
dialogue, 257n2, 260n4
  connecting through, 93
  empathy in, 100, 104
  entering flow of, 224–25
  handling intensity in, 51
  internal, 22
  listening in, 91
  mutuality in, 50
  needs in, 126–30
  self-empathy in, 160
  shifting, 89
  skill in, 158
  space and balance in, 82

staying connected with, 86–87, 109–10
humility, 168–69, 176, 205, 231, 232, 249

identity, 19, 22, 166–67
individualism, 116, 117–18, 191
intelligence, 37, 163, 170. *See also* emotional intelligence
intention, 5, 21, 71
  accessing, 233
  to be present, 35–36, 39
  choosing, 57, 73
  to connect, 48, 107
  defining, 60
  in difficult conversations, 242
  importance of, 75
  in internal preparation, 230
  in listening, 93–94, 98
  in Nonviolent Communication, 8
  of others, assumptions about, 149–50, 156
  pausing and, 45
  readjusting, 46
  recollecting, 240
  reconnecting with, 184, 202
  in requests, 198–99, 201, 207
  shifting, skill in, 83–84, 85, 88
  view as determining, 63–64, 70
  wholesome, 186
intention to understand
  assumptions and, 85
  curiosity and care in, 78–79, 87
  in empathic listening, 105–7, 129
  empathy and, 99, 265n1
  feelings of others, 151
  mindfulness and, 79–80, 88, 118–19
  power of, 75–78
  staying connected to, 219
  trusting, 225
  valuing needs and, 128
interconnectedness/interdependence, 117, 118, 132, 191, 199

interpretation, 172–74, 178, 179–80, 216
interrupting, 219–20, 221, 223, 224, 226–27
intimacy, 78
  connection and, 17, 25
  loss of, 67
  need for, 116, 151
  passivity as obstacle to, 69
  presence and, 38
  through conflict, 73
intuition, 69–70, 104, 111, 130, 197, 206
investigation
  of assumptions, 40
  of default patterns, 72
  of default strategies, 65
  of emotions, 143, 148
  of expectations, 84
  in internal preparation, 230–31, 232, 245
  mindfulness and, 27
  of perception, 177
  of vulnerability, 55

joy, 2, 9
  appreciative (*mudita*), 159
  of giving and receiving, 192, 199, 205
  inner resource of, 166, 168
  in mindfulness, 38
  as natural impulse, 76
  tone of, 143, 144
judgment, 64, 138
  awareness of, 177, 230
  inner narrative of, 16, 74
  lack of, 163, 171
  language expressing, 149
  observation and, 172, 173
  reactive, 109, 237
  transforming patterns of, 133, 160
  translating negative, 151, 180–82, 185, 187, 232
  unmet needs as, 121–22

of others, responding to, 204, 206
overriding one's own, 203–4
personal and universal, 124–26, 133
positive and negative statements of,
  130
requests and, 191, 193, 194
seeing through lens of, 120–21, 133
shared, 213, 214, 215, 227
and strategies, differentiating
  between, 112, 120–21, 132, 246,
  261n1
transforming relationship to, 134–35
translating judgments into, 180, 181,
  182
universality of, 77–78, 87, 88,
  111–12, 119, 230, 232, 261n2
valuing both one's own and others',
  126–30
ways of discussing, 130–32
nervous system, 17, 18, 22, 117, 141
autonomic, 19, 258n3, 258n5
balancing, 36, 42, 72, 229
breath and, 19, 32, 48, 238
mindfulness of, 46, 235, 236, 238
patterns in, 70
presence and, 26
retraining, 207, 212, 228, 239–40
settling, 44
shifting patterns of, 233–34
social engagement and, 41
See also activation; deactivation
no, hearing and saying, 202–4, 206
nonverbal communication, 22, 57, 75,
  76, 87, 197, 241–42
nonviolence, 199–200
Nonviolent Communication (NVC),
  3–4, 7, 76
author's experiences with, 59–60,
  196–97
giraffe dance, 264n1
intention of, 8, 73
model, 74, 133, 138, 170, 200–201,
  259n2
needs, view of in, 112, 114, 261n2

observation form of, 174
studying, 249

observations, 109–10, 133, 224
awkward feelings about, 186–87
of internal experience, 178
and interpretations, distinguishing,
  172–74, 182
neutral, 188–89
pointers on making, 174, 185–86
purposes of, 170–71, 173
recognizing multiple perspectives in,
  175–76
requests and, 194
in tracking, 215
translating judgments into, 180, 181,
  182

pain, 188
being open to others', 88, 163, 166,
  168
chronic, 190
compassion and, 169
empathy for, 122, 123, 158, 161, 164,
  230
expressing, 138, 151–52
healing with presence, 36–37, 39
as hindrance to empathy, 100–102,
  160
from losing presence, 28–29
mindfulness of, 43, 80, 236
of not being heard, 184–85
of unmet need, 124, 135
passive aggression, 69–70, 71,
  233
patience, 113, 116, 208
with communication styles, 245
curiosity and, 78
in empathic reflection, 243
in learning to identify needs, 119
limits of, 219
in requests, 202
self-empathy and, 160
in speaking up, 184

patience (*continued*)
in tracking, 215
in working with emotions, 144

pausing, 20, 23, 25, 54, 162, 202, 223
challenges of, 46–47
creating and signaling, 47–48
during difficult conversations, 236, 237, 241, 244
noticing, 48
purpose of, 45–46
tracking and, 224
perceptions, 2, 151
attention to, 147, 154
of differences, 61–63
investigating, 177
mindfulness of, 178
observation and, 173
of others, 206
presence, 5, 17, 21, 207
benefits of, 25, 39
challenges of, 17–18, 22, 42
at choice points, 43
communicating through, 38
connecting and disconnecting to, 27–29
defining, 16
dynamic flexibility through, 45
empathic field of, 166, 167
feeling overwhelmed by, 39–40
four methods for cultivating, 32–35
as grounding, 31
for healing, 36–37
increasing capacity for, 27, 29, 39
leading with, 11, 26, 30, 31, 38, 49, 50, 53, 54, 82, 87, 95, 109, 209, 240
listening with, 92, 93–94
as natural state, 29, 30
offering, 205
pausing and, 45
practicing and experiencing, differences between, 54
recognizing another's, 49–50

returning to, 26, 36, 46–47, 81, 82, 84, 212, 224
in speaking and listening, differences in, 22–23
three areas of practicing, 35
in tracking, 223–24
uncertainty in, 53
use of term, 26, 259n1
variety of ways of, 39
See also mindfulness
problem solving, 105, 127, 195, 197, 205, 216–17, 263n5

reactivity, 244
emotion regulation and, 144
fueling, 237
managing, 39, 233–34, 244
noticing, 80, 82, 236
observation and, 173
presence and, 31–32, 53
protection from, 188
reducing, 230
reconciliation, 86, 153
redirecting, 221–22, 224, 226
reflection
empathic, 97, 104, 106, 129, 221, 243 (*see also under* listening)
from others, 155, 195–96, 197, 200, 207
verbal, 94–98, 99, 105, 131–32
rehearsing, 240–41, 245
relational conversation, 15, 215–16, 217, 226, 231
relationships, 118, 226
changing dynamics of, 89
cocreating, 232, 246
conflating observation and evaluation in, 173
conflict avoidance in, 66
emotions in, 139
feedback in, 183, 185
mutuality in, 49
negativity bias in, 178
presence in, 17–18

vulnerability in, 122
relaxation, 29, 234, 238
  in conversation, 7, 44, 48–49, 209, 225
  need for, 40–41, 112, 120
  nervous system during, 19, 258–59n5
  pausing for, 45
  in requests, 199
  in speaking up, 184
requests, 110, 150, 190, 224
  clarity in, 192–93
  considering others' needs in, 191
  and demands, difference between, 202
  providing context for, 200
  skill in, 205–8
  three qualities in formulating, 193–94
  in tracking process, 217
resilience, 135, 238
  empathy and, 99, 103, 202
  inner, 114, 158–59, 160, 164, 168, 178
  of nervous system, 234, 265n2
  presence as doorway to, 36–37
  strengthening, 72, 238, 265n2
role-playing, 240–41, 245
Rosenberg, Marshall B., 3, 4, 8, 15, 61, 73–74, 113
  on feelings, 149
  on four key aspects of experience, 109–10
  on habit and nature, 187
  on making requests, 198–99
  on needs, 132
  on protective use of force, 85–86
  two questions of, 84–85, 88, 202
  on violence, 121
  See also Nonviolent Communication (NVC)
rushing, 28–29

safety
  in competitive confrontation, 67
  conflict avoidance and, 66
  evolutionary drives for, 18, 22

  lack of, in disconnecting with presence, 28, 40–41
  need for, 43, 68, 77
  orienting and, 30
self-awareness, 1, 11, 26, 103, 223
self-centeredness, 92, 206
self-compassion, 72, 160, 208
self-criticism (inner critic), 72, 160
self-empathy, 160–61
  blame and, 72
  in difficult situations, 88, 230, 232
  inner resource of, 166, 168
  nourishing with, 245
  purpose of, 167, 264–65n2
  in requests, 202
self-expression, 170–71, 177, 184–85, 222–24
self-protection, 15, 71–72, 161, 235
self-reliance, 114, 261n5
self-sacrifice, 113, 117
self-sufficiency, 116–18, 191, 261n5
shame, 120, 139, 145, 191, 203
silence, 20, 91, 92, 99, 138, 167, 208
social change, 2–3, 8, 14n, 191
social connection, 15, 17, 258nn1–3
  attempts that backfire, 107
  from balancing awareness, 52
  conflict avoidance and, 66
  deep presence in, 17
  devaluing need for, 118
  differences in, 73
  enriching, 183
  expectations and, 59–60
  identifying others' needs and, 126, 130
  increasing, 53
  interrupting and, 227
  language leading to, 174
  magic of, 249
  maintaining, 93–94, 106, 204
  need for, 67, 68, 69, 77, 116, 160
  nervous system and, 41
  presence as ground for, 25, 38
  reflection and, 98

social connection (*continued*)
  sufficient to meet needs, 74, 259n2
  without agreement, 164–65, 166, 168
socialization, 65, 100, 259n2
  differences and, 100
  emotions in, 139, 141
  influences of, 61, 259n2
  in making requests, 207
  of needs, views of, 116, 117
solution requests, 195, 198–200
somatic empathy, 103, 106, 161, 164, 168
Somatic Experiencing, 4, 5, 15, 264n4
spaciousness, 51, 120, 144, 208
speaking up, 184–85, 190, 207, 227–28, 247
splintering, 220–22, 226
strategies, 15, 205
  being right as, 232
  in conflict, 126, 128, 134
  and needs, differentiating between, 112, 120–21, 132, 246, 261nn1–2
  observation as, 188
  of others, responding to, 204
  requests and, 191, 193, 198
  saying "no" as, 203
stress, 28, 36–37, 65, 160, 173, 233, 234
succinctness, 222–24, 225
suffering, 2, 76, 160, 164. *See also* pain
sympathetic arousal, 31–32, 234–35, 236, 237, 265n3

taking a break, 39–40, 47–49, 162, 168, 194, 222–23, 240–41, 250, 255. *See also* chunking, pausing
thoughts
  and emotions, distinguishing, 137, 144–45, 149–51, 155, 263n9
  feedback loops of, 141
  gathering, 223, 265n3
  in mindfulness practice, 34

observation and, 173
signs of default patterns in, 82
tracking, 219
touch points, 32, 34, 39, 236
tracking, 226
  center of attention, 218–20, 225, 264n2
  content, 220–22, 224
  process, 215–17
trauma, 4, 123, 155, 265n3
trust, 128, 133
  building, 216–17, 218
  in connection requests, 195, 197
  from empathic listening, 129
  empathy and, 163
  eroding, 70
  in intention to understand, 225
  lack of, working with, 88
  in ourselves, 44
  in relationships, 226–27
  vulnerability and, 122

understanding. *See* intention to understand

values, 111, 112n, 148, 187. *See also* needs
verbal reflection. *See under* reflection
views
  filtering of, 178–79
  in framing, 214
  intention and, 63–64, 70, 77
  shifting, 71
violence, 74, 103, 113, 121, 191, 245, 260n6
voice, 20, 22
  finding one's own, 9, 184–85, 247
  sense of identity and, 19
  tone, 57, 93, 138, 235, 241–42
vulnerability, 22
  in competitive confrontation, 67
  in difficult conversations, 244
  discernment in sharing, 122

about the author

OREN JAY SOFER teaches meditation and Nonviolent Communication in both Buddhist and secular contexts. He first became interested in contemplative practice in high school, went on to complete a degree in comparative religion from Columbia University, and later spent two and a half years living as an *anagarika* (Buddhist renunciate) in the Ajahn Chah Thai Forest lineage. Today, his teaching combines classical Buddhist training with the accessible language of secular mindfulness.

Oren is a member of the Spirit Rock Teacher's Council, a Certified Trainer of Nonviolent Communication, and a Somatic Experiencing Practitioner for healing trauma. He also has served as the senior program developer at Mindful Schools, is the founder of Next Step Dharma (nextstep dharma.org), and is cofounder of Mindful Healthcare (mindfulhealthcare .net).

PHOTO BY SHEILA MEZES